THE T Hatton, Erin Elizabeth, 1974-

The temp economy

THE TEMP ECONOMY

From Kelly Girls to Permatemps in Postwar America

Erin Hatton

Foreword by Nelson Lichtenstein

TEMPLE UNIVERSITY PRESS
Philadelphia

TEMPLE UNIVERSITY PRESS
Philadelphia, Pennsylvania 19122
www.temple.edu/tempress

Library of Congress Cataloging-in-Publication Data

Hatton, Erin Elizabeth, 1974–
    The temp economy : from Kelly girls to permatemps in postwar America / Erin Hatton;
foreword by Nelson Lichtenstein.
        p. cm.
    Includes bibliographical references and index.
    ISBN 978-1-4399-0080-2 (cloth : alk. paper) — ISBN 978-1-4399-0081-9 (pbk. : alk.
paper) — ISBN 978-1-4399-0082-6 (e-book)   1. Temporary employment—United States.
2. United States—Economic policy—21st century.
I. Title.
    HD5854.2.U6H38 2010
    331.25'7290973—dc22   2010019343

∞ The paper used in this publication meets the requirements of the
American National Standard for Information Sciences—Permanence
of Paper for Printed Library Materials, ANSI Z39.48-1992

Printed in the United States of America

042611-P

CONTENTS

FOREWORD

Nelson Lichtenstein

E rin Hatton's exploration of the temp industry is a most revealing probe into the transformation of work and obligation in modern America. Her book is important because it uncovers the shifting ideological and cultural tropes deployed to degrade New Deal–era labor standards and also because it explores, in a wide variety of firms and industries, how this new category of worker became highly functional to capital in an era of economic instability and globalization. But the rise of temping was hardly a naturalistic process, a product of some abstract "demand" for contingent labor. Rather, it was advanced, constructed, and legitimized by innovations in the legal environment, in managerial practice, and in regulatory policy.

Of course, readers should not think that the temp industry, composed of well-known firms such as Manpower, Olsten, and Kelly Services, is some kind of strange encrustation attached to the main body of a more stable and humane labor relations regime. These firms employ at least three million workers; of even greater import, much of the strategy they have developed is now being deployed in virtually every kind of workplace, including retail stores, high-tech offices, distribution centers, and even many institutions of higher education. It is not just that third-party employment is rife, but that even when a worker gets her paycheck directly from the firm where she works, the employment relationship has a highly contingent and debased character. The transformation in the very meaning and nature of work has been institutionalized in many sectors of the economy, but perhaps nowhere with greater impact and élan than in retail, where Wal-Mart, the nation's largest company, built a new employment model by purposely churning its workforce, even as its executives celebrated a corporate culture that analogized the firm to a family or a congregation. For most Wal-Mart "associates," an awkward shift, frustrated expectations, and conflict with their manager leads to dismissal or a huffy good-bye within a year or two of being hired. Turnover therefore averages between 40 and 50 percent overall, and it is far higher for those newly hired.[1] This employment pattern replicates that which the temp agencies seek to perpetuate and now constitutes a new normality for tens of millions.

But as Hatton demonstrates, this kind of chronic job insecurity actually constitutes a radical break from the managerial practice and state social policy that was the norm, or at least the ideal, during most of the twentieth century. When the great mass-production factories and assembly lines were built a century ago, turnover seemed the subversive handmaiden to inefficiency and social unrest. "Just as quicksand cannot be kneaded in the hands into a solid lump," wrote one personnel executive in 1916, "so also will it be difficult to take hold of an ever-changing mass of employees and transform it into a homogeneous, intelligent, contented body."[2] World War I and the era of labor radicalism that followed seemed to confirm that judgment. High labor turnover was economically inefficient and socially dangerous. An entire profession (that of personnel management) and an entire corporate outlook (welfare capitalism) were designed to promote a linkage between workers and the companies for which they worked. In the 1920s, "progressive" firms such as General Electric, Metropolitan Life, Kodak, and National Cash Register all invested heavily in what would later be called corporate "human relations."[3]

The Great Depression proved that the provision of job security was beyond the capacity of any individual company. We remember the Social Security Act of 1935 for the pension system it put on the books, but that law was also designed to stabilize employment, and workers' income, by establishing a national system of unemployment insurance and by putting in place a corporate tax system designed to encourage managers to provide steady employment and avoid layoffs. At that time, cyclical employment in manufacturing seemed the great problem: Retail trade, the hospitality industry, and office work remained uncovered by the law or unaffected by it.

But today such service and retail work stands at the core of the economy, with a workforce larger than that of manufacturing, mining, and construction. Here the work culture and the managerial ethos stand in opposition to much of the labor legislation put in place during the mid-twentieth century. The forty-hour workweek, which was codified in the 1930s and made a social norm in the 1950s, no longer exists. Hourly employees at most retail stores and restaurants work an unpredictable workweek that varies with the season. Meanwhile, a huge proportion of all American workers—perhaps 30 percent—are now defined as employees "exempt" from the U.S. wage and hour laws. Professionals, consultants, subcontractors, and the self-employed are no longer covered by overtime pay, unemployment compensation, or the expectation of steady employment. Add to this a corporate culture that celebrates the long workdays characteristic of high tech, finance, law, and health care, and one gets a virtual evisceration of the eight-hour day and the forty-hour week for tens of millions of working Americans.

Hatton concludes her book with an assessment of how courts, laws, and unions have either constrained the growth of temporary work during the last few years or made it somewhat more palatable. I was struck by the near banality of the new rules and regulations: They were commonsense reforms that, among other things, made the existing employer responsible for the health, safety, and equitable wages of those who first hired in via a temp agency. But they all required both social vision and political will to put in place. Fortunately, Hatton's perceptive and thorough research provides us with many of the historical and sociological tools necessary to reconstruct the work life of millions of Americans on a far more secure and humane basis.

PREFACE

Why the temp industry? I first became interested in this topic during my years in graduate school at the University of Wisconsin–Madison. In the 1990s, the state of Wisconsin was an early leader of the "work first" approach to welfare policy. From the beginning, the temp industry played a key role in the state's new Welfare to Work program. In fact, in the first year of the program temp agencies were the largest provider of jobs to former welfare recipients.[1] And when welfare reform went national in 1996, President Clinton invited Mitchell Fromstein, CEO of leading temp agency Manpower, Inc., along with a handful of other corporate executives to the White House to talk about how their businesses could help find jobs for people on welfare.[2] This single moment seemed to capture the essence of the temp industry at the end of the twentieth century: It was a cultural colossus at the center of hot-button cultural, political, and economic debates. And it was presented as if it were all so normal. How had this come to pass?

From previous research, I knew that the modern temp industry had begun in the years after World War II. What I did not know was how this relatively young industry had grown to such impressive proportions, both in size and scope. Not only were temp agencies sending out millions of workers a day; the temp industry had also become a kind of gauge for the economy as a whole: Many economists would point to declines in temporary employment as an early sign of recession, and to rising numbers of temps as an indication of economic recovery.[3] How was it, I wondered, that the temp industry had taken on this kind of structural role in the U.S. labor market?

Meanwhile, in popular culture, temping had come to epitomize the worst of the "new economy." A slew of movies, novels, and magazines dramatized the downsides of being a temp: low pay, monotonous "dumbed-down" work, and unrelenting job insecurity with little chance of escape. Why had temping become a cultural symbol of what had gone wrong with the American economy? At the same time, perhaps not coincidentally, workers, activists, and journalists had begun launching very public challenges to the temp industry, most famously Microsoft's "perma-temps" who sued the computer giant for the same benefits that regular employees received. Why, I wondered, had the temp industry become such an important arena for political and social conflict?

The underlying question that I kept returning to was this: How had the temp industry become an institutionalized player in the primary labor market, rather than remaining on the margins as contingent work had historically done? Although sociologists and historians had not yet asked this question, it seemed to be generally accepted that the temp industry had grown in direct proportion to business demand. According to this logic, when employers hit hard times they naturally turned to the temp industry as part of a broader effort to cut costs. Yet I was unsatisfied by this assumption. How did employers even know about the temp industry in the first place, and what did they think they were getting by using temps? How had temping become legitimate work—not just for secretaries, but also for doctors, accountants, and engineers? And why had the temp industry become a cultural scapegoat for America's economic woes?

Researching these questions led me beyond the story of the temp industry into broader narratives about the transformation of work in America. The degradation of work in the last decades of the twentieth century is well-traveled territory. The temp industry's role in that story, however, is not. I hope that readers will find it as compelling (and surprising) as I do.

ACKNOWLEDGMENTS

A great many people helped make this book possible. First, my graduate advisors Erik Olin Wright and Jamie Peck gave me expert advice, unfailing support, warmth, and charm from the beginnings of this project to its very end. Chip Hunter nearly always went above and beyond the call of duty on my behalf. Jane Collins took on this project with an already full plate; her care and advice were essential. Thanks, too, to Laura Dresser and Joel Rogers at COWS for helping me carve a path through graduate school that was both instructive and rewarding—a path that eventually led me to this book.

While writing this book, I sought the advice of many people along the way, often through half-formed questions in slightly panicked e-mails. Thanks to the many folks on the receiving end of such messages: Jamie Peck, Sanford Jacoby, George Gonos, Nik Theodore, Thomas O'Connor, Nan Enstaad, Laura Dresser, and Edward Lenz (and more, I'm sure). Many thanks to Lisa Fine for her invaluable comments on the completed manuscript, as well as to Yoke-Sum Wong for her interest and support of my work.

I am lucky to have been at the University at Buffalo while revising this project. My colleagues have been wonderfully supportive—giving me much-needed opportunities to both discuss and escape my book.

Special thanks in this department to Mary Nell Trautner. I also owe many thanks to my department chair, Bob Granfield, who has repeatedly gone out on a limb for me. In addition, I have been very fortunate to benefit from a UB gem: the Baldy Center for Law and Social Policy. Among the many opportunities the Baldy Center offers UB faculty are workshops for manuscripts-in-progress. My heartfelt thanks to Rebecca French and the Baldy Center for enthusiastically sponsoring one of these workshops for this book. The best outcome of this event was the opportunity to work with Vicki Smith and Julie Kmec, who graciously traveled across the country to take part in it. Their astute commentary on the manuscript was both broad and deep; their kindness was palpable. Also, a round of applause for my UB colleague-friends who participated in the day-long workshop: Carl Nightingale, Martha McCluskey, Susan Cahn, David Herzberg, Dianne Avery, Gwynn Thomas, Mary Nell Trautner, Robert Adelman, Kristen Schultz Lee, and Sarah Robert. They took considerable time away from their own work to read and comment on mine. Without a doubt, everyone who participated in the workshop made this a better book.

I reserve my deepest thanks for my family. My mother-in-law Vickie Herzberg read the entire manuscript in its early stages, offering me incredible advice, love, and support. Both she and my father-in-law Don Herzberg sat through readings of my work, offering tips and encouragement. Meanwhile, Rachele, Lynda, Bob, and all the outlaws never stopped cheering me on from the sidelines. My parents, Annette Hatton and John Hatton, were always just a phone call away when I needed to cry, complain, or crow. And my boys—Rex, Leo, and Felix—gave me joy and laughter throughout. Then there's David, my beloved editor-at-large. I couldn't have done it without you.

THE TEMP ECONOMY

INTRODUCTION

The Temp Economy

I t is almost a cliché to talk about the decline in Americans' work lives over the last decades of the twentieth century. Time and again, newspaper headlines have lamented what the *New York Times* called the "downsizing of America":[1] wage freezes and massive layoffs; closed factories and jobs moved abroad; permanent employees replaced by contingent workers. Wages stagnated and access to benefits declined. The possibility of lifetime employment was replaced with the likelihood of chronic job insecurity and episodes of unemployment. Career ladders collapsed, with more and more workers finding themselves stuck at the bottom.

The temp industry has become a classic symbol of this degradation of work. Temping is the quintessential "bad" job: On average, temps earn lower wages and receive fewer benefits; and they have less job security, fewer chances for upward mobility, and lower morale than those with full-time, year-round employment.[2] What's more, by increasing the flexibility of the labor supply, the temp industry contributes to downward pressure on wages, decreased employment security, and limited upward mobility for all workers, not just temps.[3]

By the early twenty-first century, the U.S. temp industry had become a behemoth, sending out some three million temps a day and reaching an astonishing 90 percent of employers each year.[4] This expanding army of temporary workers, and the extraordinary growth of the industry that profits from them, has led to laments about the "temping of America" and the "age of the disposable worker."[5] Although on the surface these pop-culture pronouncements seem overdrawn—after all, temps make up less than 3 percent of the U.S. labor force—there may be more than a kernel of truth in them. In fact, this book argues that the temp industry has been much more than just a symbol of the degradation of work. It has been an active player in the drama. First, the temp industry's business is literally to sell degraded work: The temp industry provides American employers with convenient, reliable tools to turn "good" jobs into "bad" ones (and bad jobs into worse ones). But the temp industry has also operated on another, equally important level—in the cultural arena, where battles over "common sense" about work and workers take place. The temp industry's high-profile marketing campaigns have had a powerful impact on this cultural battlefield, helping establish a new morality of business that did more than sanction the use of temps; it also legitimized a variety of management practices that contributed to the overall decline in Americans' work lives.

These cultural changes in the second half of the twentieth century were indeed remarkable. By the turn of the twenty-first century, even as some corporate executives continued to extol the value of their employees, it became widely acceptable to talk about workers—*all* workers, from the highly skilled to the day laborer—as costly sources of rigidity in an economy that required flexibility. As Berkeley economist Brad DeLong observed in 2009, companies "used to think that their most important asset was skilled workers. . . . Now, by contrast, it looks as though firms think that their workers are much more disposable—that it's their brands or their machines or their procedures and organizations that are key assets. They still want to keep their workers happy in general, they just don't care as much about these particular workers."[6] Or, as management guru Peter Drucker said more bluntly in 2002, "Employers no longer chant the old mantra 'People are our greatest asset.' Instead, they claim 'People are our greatest liability.'"[7]

One example of this cultural shift came in the early 2000s with the emergence of a new catchphrase among corporate executives: "the 7 percent rule." According to this "rule," if a company announced major layoffs, its stock price would jump 7 percent. Although studies proved this to be false (in fact, stock prices often fell with reports of layoffs), business owners continued to expect that cutting people, much like getting rid of old, expensive machinery, would boost profits.[8] It seems that some workers had even come to accept this new attitude: "If I were a business owner and I was not making a profit," one recently unemployed worker told the *New York Times* in 2001, "I would lay people off too."[9]

Of course, not all employers described their workers as costly liabilities, nor did all employers treat them as such. Nonetheless, by the end of the twentieth century it had become sound business sense to cut workers in order to boost the bottom line. Perhaps the most famous example of this was "Chainsaw" Al Dunlap, who gained fame and notoriety in the 1990s by "saving" ailing companies such as Scott Paper and Sunbeam. He did so, in large part, by aggressively cutting thousands of employees. During his eighteen-month stint at Scott Paper, for example, Dunlap eliminated one-third of the company's workforce, some eleven thousand employees.[10] And in his first year at Sunbeam, the "celebrity downsizer" axed 50 percent of the company's workers, reportedly the largest share of any workforce ever laid off; then a year and a half later he laid off another 40 percent of the remaining workers.[11] Although by the end of the decade Dunlap had fallen from grace amidst accusations of fraud, throughout most of the 1990s he was hailed as a corporate star.[12] His 1996 memoir, *Mean Business: How I Save Bad Companies and Make Good Companies Great*, was a national best-seller and his business dealings were regularly front-page news.[13]

Dunlap's hard-hitting management style was perhaps extreme, but he was very much part of a broader cultural milieu in which it was acceptable—even advisable—to treat workers as profit-busting liabilities. Not coincidentally, as we will see, this was the same kind of logic that the temp industry had been pushing for decades. And by the end of the twentieth century, the temp industry was flourishing right alongside Dunlap and the era's many other corporate raiders. In fact, at that time the temp industry was one of the fastest-growing sectors of the economy.[14] On bookstore shelves alongside Dunlap's memoir sat titles such as *The Temp Survival Guide: How to Prosper as an Economic Nomad of the Nineties*, offering workers advice for "survival in the post-employment age."[15]

While much about this business climate was new, the view of workers as liabilities was not. It was just the latest iteration of a long-standing management philosophy that I call the liability model of work. This philosophy dates back to the very beginning of management theory in the 1800s. Its underlying assumption is a zero-sum relationship between workers and profits. Any dollar spent on employees—in terms of wages, benefits, training, and so on—directly subtracts from the bottom line. Labor costs should thus be kept to a minimum: Employees should be paid the lowest possible market wage; jobs should be routinized and deskilled so that workers can be easily (and cheaply) replaced; unions should be avoided; permanent employees should be replaced with more disposable contingent workers; and production should be relocated or outsourced to take advantage of lower wages and labor standards. Today, policy scholars often refer to these as "low road" business practices.[16] The liability model of work, I argue, is the theory behind such practices.

Although the view of workers as liabilities has probably always dominated management circles in terms of prevalence and practice, it has never wholly monopolized management thought. Rather, it has repeatedly collided with a very different business philosophy that I call the asset model of work. This management approach rejects the assumption of a zero-sum relationship between workers and profits, instead proposing that the two can build on each other.[17] Historically, there have been two distinct strands of the asset model. Both are important, so I will take a moment with each in turn.

The first strand is the Human Relations approach—a management philosophy that views workers as key generators of profits because of their company-specific expertise and loyalty. The bottom line is still central, but tending to employee welfare is considered profitable because it boosts workers' commitment, motivation, and productivity. Of course, not all employers who claim to follow this philosophy and call their workers "assets" actually treat them as such. For many, such language has been a barely concealed tactic to avoid unionization—trading real benefits for the occasional employee luncheon or "employee of the month" nomination. But in some cases, employers have genuinely embraced the asset model by making a real investment in workers in the form of good wages and benefits, skills training and the chance to move up, opportunities for input and innovation, generous leave policies and other perks, strong labor relations, and more. Policy scholars often refer to these as "high road" practices.[18] The asset model is the theory behind such practices.

The second strand of the asset model is a labor union philosophy. Instead of relying on the enlightened generosity of employers, this more radical approach relies on union power and labor law to force employers to safeguard workers' welfare. And instead of seeing workers' well-being as good for the bottom line, this union approach seeks to expand the meaning of the "bottom line" to include worker welfare. A company's success, according to this union philosophy, must be measured not only by its profits but also by the success of its workers. Perhaps the best example of this union approach came in the years after World War II when, after nearly two decades of struggle, organized labor managed to institutionalize the asset model for a substantial number of workers in the unionized industrial sector. The resulting contract, famously known as the Treaty of Detroit, has become an iconic symbol of union triumph, economic prosperity, and greater equality. The treaty's reach was far from universal, but, at the time, many hoped that it would serve as a platform to build on—to expand the meaning of a good job by increasing wages, benefits, and job security, while also making such jobs available to greater numbers of workers.[19] And indeed many postwar employers—both union and nonunion—soon adopted key tenets of the Treaty of Detroit, such as annual cost-of-living adjustments and pension benefits.[20]

In fact, in the post–World War II era, the Human Relations and the labor union strands of the asset model converged: Organized labor had institutionalized asset model jobs for a growing number of workers and, at the same time, management circles were generally inclined to believe that tending to workers' welfare was profitable. The result was a strong and growing core of "good" jobs, as well as a powerful collective understanding of what a "good job" was.[21] The cultural strength of the asset model at that time had real consequences for workers: It limited employers' ability to treat them as costly liabilities, even if they were not protected by union power. Of course, it did not prevent employers from engaging in aggressive labor practices—red-baiting, work speed-up, and union busting, to name a few. But even those employers who fully believed that workers were liabilities did not adopt Al Dunlap's openly hard-line approach—not because it was literally unavailable to them, but because it was culturally unavailable.

All this had changed by the end of the twentieth century. Not only had it become culturally acceptable for employers to see workers as nothing more than expensive liabilities; they were often expected to do so, even by some of their own workers.[22] This shift was so profound that corporate executives had come to expect rewards for cutting employees—in the form of increasing stock values or, for Al Dunlap and others like him, fame and fortune. As a consequence, the 1990s witnessed an extraordinary trend: Company after company announced major layoffs, even while reporting record-breaking profits. In the postwar era, this might have provoked an outcry over the betrayal of workers, but by the end of the century it was hailed as smart business sense.

What accounts for this sea change in cultural attitudes toward work and workers? Most explanations point to what economists Bennett Harrison and Barry Bluestone called "the Great U-Turn."[23] In the late 1960s and 1970s, massive structural changes—such as deindustrialization, globalization, and deep economic recessions—heightened competition and put a vise grip on corporate profits. It was this harsh economic climate, the argument goes, that imposed a new reality on American businesses. They had to become "lean and mean" in order to compete.

As Harrison, Bluestone, and other scholars have pointed out, however, the lean and mean route—downsizing, outsourcing, slashing wages, and attacking unions—was not the only way to survive difficult economic circumstances.[24] Yet this was the path that most employers chose. Why? How did employers come to believe that these low-road strategies were the best route out of economic hardship? How did they even learn what it meant to be "lean and mean"? Where did they get their information and how did they put it into practice? And, most perplexing of all: Why did this new conventional wisdom, born out of economic calamity, continue to gain strength even after economic prosperity returned?

Answering these questions leads us to the messy terrain of culture, where labor market players make claims about what is—and is not—"sound business sense." These claims can be found in the pages of popular magazines and books, newspapers and trade journals, on television and radio shows, and in court and congressional hearings. It is in these arenas that CEOs and union organizers, legislators and workers, compete to define the "truth" about work. And it is in these arenas that new ideas about work become established, with profound consequences for American workers. Structural forces set the context for such battles, but they do not determine the outcome.

This book argues that the temp industry became a significant force in these cultural battles over work in the second half of the twentieth century. Starting in the years after World War II, long before it was regarded as a major economic player, the temp industry launched a series of remarkably successful campaigns that helped undermine the cultural strength of the asset model and legitimize the view of workers as liabilities. First, in the 1950s, early industry leaders cast temp work as "women's work" in order to justify an entirely new category of "respectable" (white, middle-class) but marginal work. In doing so, temp leaders were capitalizing on the deep cultural ambivalence about white, middle-class women working. The result was a new and growing sector of the economy that stood in stark contrast to the then-prevalent asset model of work. Whereas increasing numbers of employers in the postwar era were offering workers health insurance and other benefits, temp agencies were not. Arguing that temps were only housewives working for "pin money," temp executives successfully created a sector of the economy that was effectively beyond the reach of a range of worker protections—health benefits, unemployment insurance, and (in the future) antidiscrimination laws—and that would later be resistant to union organizing efforts.

Having gained entrée into the labor market by constructing temp work as women's work, temp leaders then moved from the margins into the primary sector of the economy. In the late 1960s and 1970s, they dropped the Kelly Girl image and sold a new product: a revitalized and fully updated liability model of work. In the temp industry's version of the model, human labor was analogous to machine work—only the product of the labor had any value, while workers themselves were expendable. Through massive advertising campaigns, temp executives sold this model of work to business executives who were already troubled by tough economic times. Their efforts helped forge a new "common sense" about how to manage labor and profits, and contributed to a major shift in American cultural beliefs about work. By the 1990s, the temp industry and its liability model of work were thriving (although, as we will see in Chapter 4, organized resistance to the temp industry had also begun to emerge).

How did temp executives exert influence over such broad and dynamic social practices? In part, it was because they wielded a loud and persuasive bullhorn. Industry leaders published books, advertisements, articles, newspaper columns, newsletters, legal guides, pamphlets, and billboards. They produced radio and TV commercials, held seminars, and spoke at conferences. They conducted national employment surveys and served as expert witnesses in government hearings. They launched literacy campaigns and volunteered to clean up city parks. They sponsored stock car races, held typing contests, created board games—and much more. The targets of this remarkable campaign were both expansive and widely diverse: white, middle-class housewives and their husbands in the 1950s and 1960s, and workers of all stripes thereafter; union leaders in the 1950s and 1960s; business owners in the 1960s and beyond; government officials in the 1980s and 1990s; and the public at large throughout.

To say that this campaign was influential is not to say that temp executives created or controlled such a broad social transformation. Far-reaching and fundamental changes such as these are produced by a range of actors and forces. The temp industry was not the only, or even the most powerful, actor seeking to undermine the cultural strength of the postwar asset model. Nonetheless, it was a persistent, creative, and effective part of a broader coalition working to revitalize the notion of workers as liabilities. Its unique contribution, I argue, was in modernizing the liability model of work and then delivering it in an easy-to-use package to thousands of businesses. This alone did not transform the meaning of work, but it was a crucial element of this change.

It is important to be clear that macroeconomic forces still matter, even in a story driven by the purposeful actions of people. Context always matters. Most importantly, the economic squeeze of the 1970s pushed employers to make difficult decisions about how to survive and compete in the new global economy. And it was at that time that temp industry employment suddenly skyrocketed. Seemingly overnight the industry went from a cluster of small but thriving businesses to become an important economic institution. This historical coincidence has led many observers to assume that the industry's success was simply a case of being in the right place at the right time: When employers needed flexibility, the temp industry was there to provide it.[25] Industry executives themselves encouraged this interpretation of events. For example, in 1994, Samuel Sacco, then executive vice president of the National Association of Temporary Services, claimed that "for the temporary help/staffing services company, the client companies are the primary drivers.

They drive the industry by demanding flexibility in their company's operations."[26] And a year earlier, Mitchell Fromstein, then president of Manpower, declared in characteristically colorful language: "We are not exploiting people. We are not setting the fees. The market is. We are matching people with demands. What would our workers be doing without us? Unemployment lines? Welfare? Suicide?"[27]

However, such attempts to attribute the success of the temp industry and its model of work to market forces overlook important questions about how and why these changes took place. For instance, how did employers come to interpret new economic pressures as a staffing problem? And why did they turn to the temp industry to solve it? Assuming that it was the inevitable outcome of economic change means ignoring a substantial historical record of the temp industry actively creating and shaping employer demand. The notion of workers as liabilities—as a "costly burden" or an "expensive headache"—did not come from economic downturns. It came, at least in part, from the temp industry's countless campaigns to "educate" employers. Temp executives told business owners again and again that the only way to survive downturns was to cut workers; even when times were good, they argued, employers should cut workers to boost profits. In short, workers were costly liabilities.

This campaign to revitalize the liability model of work, along with the provision of temps to implement it, made the temp industry much more than a passive beneficiary of economic change. It was an active player in transforming the meaning of work. Industry leaders were not just in the right place at the right time: They gave employers directions (and, perhaps, transportation) to the "right place," and when employers arrived, they were there waiting.

The temp industry's ideas about work and workers would have had little impact if it had simply implemented them in its own business offices. But the temp industry's survival—and its ability to expand—depended on selling its version of the liability model to other businesses. As Lisa Adler has noted, the success of the temp industry fundamentally depended on "its ability to transform the labor processes of *other* industries."[28] Industry executives, in other words, had to persuade employers that their model of work was a "normal way . . . to do business."[29] This process of persuasion is the subject of this book.

Such campaigns have a long pedigree. From the earliest days of mass consumerism, American companies have created a "need" for products where none existed. The classic example is Listerine's invention of a whole new disease—"halitosis"— in the 1920s to convince the American public that bad breath was a serious problem that required mouthwash.[30] In the same way, the temp industry created a market for its liability model of work. Temp leaders invented their own disease. They called it "overstaffing." The root of the problem, they maintained, was workers who "drain[ed] away profits in salaries, benefits, and overhead." The "cure," of course, was temps. Such notions about the "problem of overstaffing" grew along with the industry, reaching an apex during the corporate downsizing crazes of the 1980s and 1990s. Temp industry campaigns thus penetrated not only the economy but also the economy of ideas. The liability model they sold became such common sense that, by the turn of the twenty-first century, it seemed reasonable to expect the value of a company to rise when its employees were fired.

The story of the temp industry thus offers important insight into broader issues in the contemporary U.S. economy. At the start of the twenty-first century, American workers are struggling with a variety of problems: the outsourcing of jobs to developing countries, corporate re-structuring, and a large-scale attack on worker organization. Although debate continues over how these trends have affected productivity, there is little question that workers have suffered as a consequence. In fact, Pierre Bourdieu has argued that insecurity—or *précarité*—has become the source of many social problems.[31] The story of the temp industry offers a unique window into the mechanics of these problems, revealing them as products of human effort rather than simply built-in features of the new economy.

But the temp industry's story is not simply a way to study economic problems; it is also a laboratory for solving them. Knowing how a problem was constructed is the first step in understanding how to fix it. The story of the temp industry reveals that economic "realities" are created by economic actors. Thus, the concluding chapters of this book look to new actors who are trying to build a different economic reality, one that retains the flexibility of the temp industry while eliminating its exploitation. It synthesizes their diverse strategies to begin sketching an asset model of work updated for the twenty-first century. It re-imagines the "workplace" as a site with substantial legal, cultural, and economic significance that counters the growing problems of volatility, insecurity, and vulnerability that affect not only temps but all workers in America today.

To tell this story it is necessary to define some key concepts. First and most importantly, what exactly is the temp industry? In the broadest sense, it belongs to a growing category of employment known as "contingent work." This phrase was coined by Audrey Freedman in the mid-1980s and generally refers to any employment relationship that departs from the standard of full-time, full-year, fixed-schedule, single-employer work. By definition, then, "contingent" or "nonstandard" work includes not only temporary employment but also part-time, day labor, and on-call work, as well as contract-company employment, independent contracting, and other self-employment.[32]

The kind of contingent labor known as "temp work" is defined not by its temporary nature (indeed, many temps work for years at a single job) but by what is called its "triangular employment relationship."[33] In this work arrangement, the temp agency acts as the legal employer of temps and contracts out its workers to various businesses.[34] For their part, workers sign up with one, or several, agencies and are sent out to jobs at a variety of businesses. They might work at a particular job for just one day, or they might work there for a year or more. Although workers are "hired" by the temp agency, they do not receive a paycheck unless they are sent out on assignment.

Temp agencies typically charge businesses about twice the workers' hourly wages. This means that employers sometimes pay more in wages for temps than for regular employees, but their total labor costs still remain lower because they avoid expenses such as recruiting, interviewing, screening, and training new workers. More importantly, employers do not have to provide temps with health benefits, pension plans, or vacation time. Nor do they have to pay workers' compensation or unemployment insurance taxes, which can rise significantly with each claim for benefits. And, finally, employers can dismiss temporary workers with little threat of legal action—and then call them back if needed.[35]

How do temp agencies make a profit if all of these costly expenses are shifted to them? One explanation is simply economies of scale.

Because temp agencies recruit, interview, train, and manage the administrative paperwork for thousands of workers, the actual cost per employee is relatively low. Unlike most other companies, this administrative work is not peripheral to temp agencies' business; it *is* their business. A second way temp companies make a profit is through their expertise in avoiding some of these expenses, particularly workers' compensation and unemployment claims. Drawing on their extensive legal resources, industry leaders have aggressively disputed such claims in the courts and have had remarkable success.[36] They have also sought to avoid worker protection costs by influencing the making of employment law itself. For instance, industry executives lobbied for—and won in at least seventeen states—laws that deny temps' claims for unemployment insurance if they fail to contact the temp agency before applying for benefits.[37] This means that temps can be required to accept any job (at any pay) before qualifying for unemployment compensation, making it far more difficult for them to be considered "unemployed." In those seventeen states, at least, the temp industry has become a key broker of citizenship rights.

Because it seems to embody many of the adverse changes in the U.S. economy, the temp industry has been a central topic of concern for labor market scholars. Although few have attended to the cultural story I tell here, there is extensive literature that my work builds on. In general, scholars have examined three aspects of the industry: its pervasiveness in the American economy and, increasingly, the global economy; its impact on labor market mechanisms; and the experiences of temp workers themselves.

Much of the research on the temp industry has documented its pervasive reach in the American economy—and with good reason. As many scholars have observed, the industry has grown dramatically since the late 1940s when the first modern temp agencies were founded. By the start of the twenty-first century, the temp industry had become an economic powerhouse, sending out millions of workers a day.[38] And recent studies suggest that, instead of using temps to fill in for absent employees or to meet short-term spikes in demand, employers are increasingly using temps as part of a long-term strategy to permanently "temp out" specific jobs or job categories.[39] Although temps are popularly associated with clerical work, numerous studies have shown that the industry has long outgrown its pink-collar days, penetrating virtually every sector of the economy.[40] Not only has the industry expanded across sectors, researchers have noted, but it has also grown vertically with the proliferation of upper-echelon corporate temp agencies and low-end day labor agencies.[41] In addition, scholars have charted the industry's geographical development, from its mid-twentieth-century midwestern origins to its global reach by the turn of the twenty-first century.[42]

A second area of research has examined the temp industry's impact on the fundamental workings of the economy. For instance, Katz and Krueger found that temp employment accounted for half of the reduction in unemployment in the boom years of the 1990s, indicating that the industry has taken on what Jamie Peck and Nik Theodore have called a "quasi-structural" role in the U.S. economy.[43] What's more, according to Peck and Theodore, the temp industry has exerted downward pressure on labor standards for all workers in terms of wages, job security, and advancement, as well as diminished employment growth throughout the economy.[44] Other researchers have added to this picture by arguing that the temp industry exacerbates labor market discrimination and inequality.[45] Looking at the history of the industry, George Gonos has described how temp industry leaders' long-term and ultimately successful legal battle to become the official employer of temps has changed the very nature of the employment relationship. According to Gonos, the traditional employer-employee relationship—the basis for workers' social protection and material well-being since the New Deal—was effectively "severed" by the institutionalization of the temp industry's triangular employment relationship between worker, agency, and employer.[46] Finally, Lisa Adler and Leah Vosko have used gender as a lens of analysis in examining the temp industry and its impact on employment restructuring. Adler found that the temp industry's success came from its ability to take advantage of traditional gender narratives of women, including women as workers, homemakers, and sexual objects.[47] And according to Vosko, the spread of temporary employment relationships once associated only with women's work has contributed to the "feminization" of employment throughout the economy.[48]

A third brand of research has examined temporary workers themselves. Many studies have shown that temps are disproportionately young, female, nonwhite, immigrant, and less educated than their permanent counterparts.[49] And in terms of wages, benefits, job security, upward mobility, and morale, temping is almost always associated with worse characteristics than full-time, year-round work, even when controlling for differences between workers.[50] Yet a number of researchers have pointed out that temporary work may offer a rewarding entrée into the labor force for some, particularly former welfare recipients and other at-risk workers.[51] Other studies have analyzed the motivations for working in temp jobs. Scholars have found that a variety of "push" and "pull" factors—or choices and constraints—lead workers into temporary employment. While some have argued that independence and flexibility "pull" people into temp work, many others have found more mixed results in weighing these factors.[52]

A central premise animating the best of this well-developed literature is that the temp industry has been an agent of change rather than a passive bystander. In this vein, scholars have examined the temp industry's role in actively shaping three different spheres: the market, law, and culture. For example, Jamie Peck, Nik Theodore, and Cynthia Ofstead have examined the industry's market-making efforts by showing how temp leaders' decisions shaped the industry's development against the backdrop of larger structural forces.[53] The location of a temp agency—in inner-city immigrant neighborhoods, for example—influences not only the resulting population of temps but also the job opportunities that are available (or not) to workers.[54] George Gonos has analyzed the temp industry's role in the legal sphere by demonstrating that the expansion (indeed, the very existence) of the temp industry depended on its aggressive legal battle to be recognized as the de jure employer of temps.[55]

The temp industry's role in shaping American culture, however, has been much less examined. In their book *The Good Temp*, Vicki Smith and Esther Neuwirth took a first step in this cultural arena by examining temp leaders' efforts to shape the industry's reputation through the creation of a new product—what Smith and Neuwirth call "the good temp."[56] The cultural scope of *The Temp Economy* is at once broader and deeper, analyzing the temp industry's long-term campaign to define conventional wisdom about work in the worlds of business, politics, and law. Temp industry efforts to legitimize the notion of workers as liabilities, I argue, not only facilitated the growing use of temps but also laid the groundwork for a host of broader changes in the workplace, including corporate downsizing, outsourcing, and the comprehensive attack on organized labor—ultimately making "permanent" employment look a lot more like temp work. In a self-reinforcing cycle, these changes strengthened the temp industry's institutional status and the legitimacy of its liability model of work.

To tell this story, I analyzed two broad categories of data: cultural artifacts that the temp industry produced to sell its model of work from the late 1940s to the early 2000s, and a wide array of cultural responses to the temp industry from other labor market actors. For the first category, I examined some fifteen hundred temp industry documents—articles, newspaper columns, books, and much more—in both business and popular media, as well as more than one thousand temp industry advertisements. For the second category, I analyzed tens of thousands of government papers and court documents from virtually every level of the American legal system, as well as magazines and books written by temps, popular and scholarly coverage of anti-temp activism, and union challenges to the industry. (See the Appendix for a more detailed description of these data.)

This is a substantial body of data, and it tells a remarkable story. But no study could cover every aspect of such a long and complex tale. This book is not about the experience of being a temp, for example, nor does it offer a quantitative analysis of the temp industry. And although I focus on temp industry leaders' campaign to modernize and market the liability model of work, I do not intend to suggest that they were the only set of actors in this drama. Workers, union leaders, business owners, politicians, and many others took part in these battles over the meaning of work, pushing for or against the growing strength of the liability model in the last decades of the twentieth century.

Yet looking closely at one of these labor market actors—the leaders of the burgeoning temp industry—is a valuable task. Beyond telling a largely unknown story about the temp industry, it also drives home two important but often ignored aspects of the American economy. First, it reminds us that the meaning and experience of work are shaped by people, not faceless economic forces. While people's actions are influenced by macroeconomic structures, they are not determined by them. Second, and related, it reminds us that the meaning of work is created by people and can also be changed by people. Even though the liability model of work has found renewed strength and acceptance at the start of the twenty-first century, its permanence is not a foregone conclusion. This has important ramifications for the many activists struggling to protect American workers from its often devastating impact. For this reason, the Conclusion of this book looks to workplace activists as a source for a new model of work—a revised asset model that would reverse many of the problems underlying the "temp economy."

At the broadest level, *The Temp Economy* can be divided into two parts. The first part examines the temp industry's role in cultural battles over the meaning of work, and the second looks at the impact of those battles on the meaning and experience of work. The chapters are arranged in chronological order, each focusing on an important moment in the development of the temp industry.

Chapter 1 illustrates how temp leaders successfully gained entrée into a postwar labor market characterized by widespread support for the asset model of work. This was no easy task. Given the considerable power of unions and the popular association of temp agencies with abusive employment agents, early industry leaders faced an uphill battle in establishing temp work as a legitimate sector of the economy. To avoid these obstacles, industry executives strategically sold temp work as women's work—suitable for white, middle-class housewives with a little extra time on their hands—even though the industry employed substantial numbers of men. Temp leaders thus entered the postwar cultural debate about women and work, often in surprising ways. For example, even as they challenged the myth of domesticity by depicting work as the cure for "housewifeitis," they reinforced gender inequalities by emphasizing the secondary nature of temp jobs—and temporary workers ("extra work for extra women"). This strategy was remarkably successful. The "Kelly Girl"—dress, heels, white gloves, and all—became a popular icon, and, more importantly, the temp industry gained widespread cultural legitimacy.

Chapter 2 looks at how temp executives of the late 1960s and 1970s sought to build on their success by expanding into new populations and sectors, including traditionally male "breadwinning" employment. In order to do so, however, they needed to revamp their model of work; the Kelly Girl strategy would no longer serve. In its place, temp leaders constructed the no-holds-barred "semi-permanent employee," an updated liability model of work in which permanent workers were nothing but a "costly headache." Indeed, it was little more than a modern-day version of the nineteenth-century "Babbage principle," which held that employers should replace skilled workers with unskilled labor wherever possible. If anything, however, the temp industry's version went further, calling for no commitment to workers whatsoever: All workers, skilled or unskilled—including corporate executives—could be replaced by temps. Even though this model of work was not new, it was a dramatic break from prevailing theories of personnel management, which held that worker commitment and innovation were necessary to preserve productivity and profits. Despite the presence of these competing theories, however, the temp industry's campaign was strikingly successful: Temp employment skyrocketed in the 1970s and continued apace in the decades that followed. More importantly, by the mid-1980s the cultural battle had largely been won. Many employers openly declared their workers to be profit-limiting liabilities, not the profit-boosting assets they had claimed just a few years earlier.

With such major battles seemingly won, Chapter 3 turns away from industry efforts to sell ideas about work and focuses instead on the consequences of those efforts. Just as temp executives of the 1970s helped revitalize the idea of workers as liabilities, temp leaders of the 1980s helped companies put this ideology into practice on an unprecedented scale. In the 1980s, a new generation of corporate executives unapologetically laid off thousands of workers, cut training programs, and outsourced jobs. American businesses, they proclaimed, had to be "leaner and meaner" in order to compete in the newly globalized economy. Lean and mean companies still needed workers, however, and they found those workers in temps. The temp industry thus played a fundamental role in the wave of corporate restructuring that swept the business world in the 1980s. Not only did more companies use greater numbers of temps; they used them to create a permanently two-tiered workforce: one group of workers that could expect decent wages, benefits, and training, and another that could not. The expansion of the temp industry thus affected not only temps but virtually all workers, who experienced greater job insecurity, fewer advancement opportunities, and lower wages as a result.

At the start of the 1990s, it looked as though this seemingly limitless expansion of the temp industry would continue unchecked. Manpower replaced General Motors as the largest employer in the United States, and the temp industry continued to grow and gain power like never before. Perhaps it was because of the industry's new cultural and political clout that organized opposition began to emerge on a variety of levels. In the 1990s, temps, community activists, union leaders, and government officials sought to protect workers' interests by promoting permanent jobs and improving temporary ones. Chapter 4 examines their campaigns.

Resistance efforts challenged the temp industry in two important ways. First, they questioned the temp industry's long-standing assertion that the employer–employee relationship was defined by remuneration— that is, by whoever issued a worker's paycheck. They sought to revise the meaning of employment to include issues of place, time, control, and autonomy. In this expanded definition of work, employers could retain flexibility by using temps, but they would not be able to exploit temporary workers by treating them as second-class, full-time employees. Second, some activists argued that temping need not be a "bad" job. By improving temps' wages, benefits, and working conditions, as well as by confining temping to truly *temporary* jobs, they sought to mitigate many of the traditional downsides of temporary employment.

Temp industry executives were successful in fending off most of these challenges, in part because of the growing power of both the industry and the liability model of work. In addition, resistance efforts themselves were isolated and piecemeal. Unable to fully dethrone the notion of workers as liabilities, they could only chip away at some of the industry's more extreme abuses. Yet their efforts were an important first step. Taken together, they can be thought of as creating a blueprint for a new model of work— one that takes the best aspects of the temp industry and adds to them the meaningful acceptance of workers as people. Although such a blueprint is far from displacing the liability model of work, it can be seen as a move toward a new understanding of workers as assets. In the Conclusion, I build on these resistance efforts to propose a new model of work—a revised asset model for the twenty-first century—that seeks to keep the flexibility of the temp industry while eliminating its exploitation.

1 | THE MAKING OF THE KELLY GIRL

"I rent women."

—JOHN BRANDT, EXECUTIVE VICE PRESIDENT
OF KELLY GIRL SERVICE, 1958[1]

A group of suburban, white, middle-class housewives gathered in a local hotel, not to exchange pie recipes or tips for home furnishings, but to talk about the drudgery of housework and the benefits of working for wages. They watched a film that praised working outside the home as a way for housewives such as themselves to experience exciting opportunities and a new sense of self-fulfillment. A "consciousness-raising" group during feminism's "second wave"? No. The year was 1961, two years before the publication of *The Feminine Mystique*, Betty Friedan's best-selling book that is often credited with reviving middle-class feminism. Rather, this was a meeting held by the Kelly Girl Service to recruit white, middle-class housewives for temporary work. "The next time you get fed up with the household routine," the man in the film urged, "join the Kelly Girl Service."[2]

This Kelly Girl meeting was not an isolated event. It was part of a massive public relations campaign designed by the leaders of a "new" industry: temporary help.[3] In the 1950s and 1960s, millions of Americans were exposed to this industry through a barrage of advertisements in a wide range of media, including magazines (from *Business Week* to *Good Housekeeping*), newspapers, seminars, brochures, books, radio and television shows, and even songs, films, and board games produced by temp industry leaders. Take Elmer Winter, for example. Cofounder and president of the temp agency Manpower, Inc., Winter wrote a newspaper column syndicated in 150 newspapers across the country, numerous journal and magazine articles, and at least six books during the postwar era alone. In 1960, his company purchased an entire printing company just to produce its advertising materials. Manpower executives used it quite heavily, distributing over seven million pieces of promotional literature every year.[4]

In their campaigns, industry leaders sold temporary work as "women's work," and white, middle-class housewives were both the target and the product of their sales pitch.[5] The image of temp work that industry leaders marketed was best illustrated by the famous "Kelly Girl," who was feminine, young, white, and middle-class. With this image, industry leaders drew on the long-term cultural association of "respectable" women (that is, white, middle-class women) with office work.[6] Yet temp executives of the 1950s and 1960s repackaged this image as their own, flooding popular media outlets with pictures of young, white, middle-class women as temps. These images gained powerful cultural currency, even spawning women's career fashions and fabric prints. As the *New York Times* noted in 1962, Kelly Girl "has joined with 17 leading department stores throughout the country and Henry Rosenfeld, Inc., manufacturer of popular-price misses' dresses, to design and market special Kelly Girl fashions."[7]

The campaigns were quite a success. Although the modern temp industry had really only begun in the late 1940s, by the end of the postwar era it had become an established sector of the economy. The handful of small midwestern agencies that had launched the industry had grown dramatically, opening new offices throughout the United States and abroad. At the same time, many new temp agencies had opened their doors—so much so that by the late 1960s some fifteen hundred temp agencies had flooded the market, bringing in $330 million a year.[8]

But this kind of success was not at all certain when temp agencies first opened their doors in the years after World War II. At that time, industry leaders faced the possibility of substantial opposition on two fronts. First, most people assumed that the temp industry was simply an extension of a more familiar—and roundly condemned—kind of business: the private employment industry, which was notorious for its abuses of workers. Industry leaders knew that this popular assumption could lead to major resistance from the many opponents of the private employment industry—the social activists and policymakers who had successfully shut it down earlier in the century. The second potential threat came from labor unions. At that time, organized labor was near the peak of its power. Unions represented more than 30 percent of the workforce, and their impact on employment relations was even greater. The worker protections that they had fought so hard to achieve—worker's compensation, pensions, health benefits, and more—had been adopted by many nonunionized employers as well. But temp leaders were creating a new category of work (and workers) that would be exempt from such protections—a fact that could lead to potentially ruinous opposition from organized labor.

The temp industry succeeded in circumventing these obstacles through what I call the Kelly Girl strategy. They cast temp work as women's work, suitable for white, middle-class housewives with a little extra time on their hands. This strategy allowed the temp industry to avoid opposition on both fronts. In the first case, their portrait of temporary work as white and middle-class distanced the industry from the notorious private employment industry, which had been widely associated with immigrants and nonwhite workers.[9] And, in the second case, the Kelly Girl strategy would forestall resistance from labor leaders who had long been primarily concerned with male industrial workers, often actively excluding women from their rank and file.[10] But temp agencies did not employ solely women. Nearly all of them employed men as well, and the leading temp agencies—Manpower in particular—employed substantial numbers of them. Yet this fact was almost entirely obscured by the feminized image of temporary work that industry leaders created.

Casting temp work as women's work also had other, unintended consequences for the temp industry. Creating and marketing a new category of women's work led temp leaders into the postwar cultural debate about women and work, often in surprising and contradictory ways. For example, even as they challenged the domestic ideal by depicting work as the cure for "housewifeitis" (well before Betty Friedan's "problem with no name"), temp leaders also reinforced gender stereotypes. Drawing on the long-term marginalization of women workers as "mere seekers of 'pin money,' "[11] temp executives repeatedly emphasized the secondary nature of both temp jobs and temporary workers ("extra work for extra women").[12]

In this apparent contradiction, temp industry leaders were not alone, although they were unusually emphatic and outspoken. Airlines, for example, joined with the popular media to advertise flight attendants' glamour and spunk, even while continuing to highlight their essential domesticity. "The archetypal stewardess," historian Kathleen Barry has observed, "was enjoying the chance to travel briefly while training for the ultimate female 'profession' of homemaking."[13] In a similar vein, the archetypal temporary worker was already a successful homemaker, looking for a little extra money to supplement her husband's income without disrupting her duties at home. (And for those "girls" who were not married, temp industry leaders pointed out, temping "offers an added benefit. . . . They have a chance to 'case the field' and work in as many offices as they wish in order to expose their charms to potential husbands.")[14]

Although the Kelly Girl strategy was developed to help the temp industry break into the postwar labor market, its significance extends beyond the 1950s. By defining temporary work as women's work, industry leaders did more than just add a new occupation to the expanding pink-collar sector. They took the idea of women's work and used it to justify an entirely new category of "respectable" (white, middle-class) but marginal work. With this strategy, industry leaders established a new sector of the economy that would not only prove beyond the reach of a range of worker protections—including health benefits, unemployment insurance, antidiscrimination laws—but also remain resistant to union organizing efforts. Flight attendants, for example, went on to become successful union organizers demanding greater respect, better wages, and increased job security for women workers.[15] Temps, however, have remained on the margins—from the Kelly Girls of the 1950s to the millions of temporary workers today.

The implications of this cannot be underestimated. By creating a new stratum of second-class "respectable" work, the temp industry established a beachhead for launching broader campaigns against the worker obligations that had, after decades of bitter conflict, come to be associated with the concept of "work" in core areas of the American economy. And it was these campaigns—launched by not just temp industry leaders, but also employers, business associations, and political leaders—that helped undermine the cultural strength of the asset model in the years after World War II and empower a new version of the liability model by the end of the twentieth century. The origins of this remarkable shift can be traced—at least in part—to the gendered strategies of early temp industry leaders.

This chapter begins with a brief outline of the development of the temp industry in the postwar era and continues by examining the two major threats to the industry's survival: its popular association with private employment agencies and the power of organized labor. The chapter goes on to show how industry leaders used the Kelly Girl strategy to turn these obstacles into opportunity and launched a new way of organizing work.

The Emergence of the Temp Industry

The early years of the temp industry were, by and large, a story of tremendous success. Despite popular perception that the industry flourished only as businesses "demanded" greater flexibility in the 1970s and 1980s, the temp industry actually came into its own far earlier.[16] From their humble beginnings in the late 1940s, industry leaders had already established temp work as a major business by the end of the next decade.[17] By 1961, fully 53 percent of businesses in the United States had used temp industry services, and throughout the 1960s industry leaders reported remarkable growth in profit and scale.[18] In 1963, for example, there were about 1,000 temp agencies employing some 400,000 workers a year and bringing in $160 million in sales.[19] By 1970, the industry employed 185,000 workers a day with around $2 billion in annual sales.[20]

Although reliable data on the postwar temp industry are difficult to obtain (the Bureau of Labor Statistics did not begin collecting annual industry data until 1982), early reports indicate that its growth was driven by the two largest temporary help agencies: Kelly Girl Service and Manpower, Inc. In 1947, William Russell Kelly founded Russell Kelly Office Service with three employees, twelve customers, and $848 in sales. In 1955, the company opened its first branch office in Louisville,

Kentucky, and by the end of the year it had thirty-five offices across the United States. By 1957, company sales had reached $6,751,441. In 1962, with 148 branches and $24 million in sales, the company went public.[21] By 1965, Kelly Girl was operating 169 offices and reported $37.5 million in sales, a 22 percent increase over the previous year.[22]

Founded in 1948, Manpower, Inc., was run as a sideline by two Milwaukee lawyers, Aaron Scheinfeld and Elmer Winter, for the first seven years of its existence. By 1956, however, Scheinfeld and Winter had turned their full attention to the rapidly growing company; with 91 branches in 65 cities across the United States and ten offices abroad, Manpower had emerged as the leader of the young industry, employing some four thousand workers a day.[23] In 1957, Manpower's sales volume was around $12 million, nearly twice that of Kelly Girl, its closest competitor. In 1962, along with Kelly, Manpower went public with 270 offices across four continents and over $40 million in sales.[24] By 1965, Manpower was operating a total of 355 offices in the United States and 23 countries abroad, and reported $86 million in sales (not including another $43 million in branch sales and franchise fees), a 16 percent increase from the previous year.[25] By 1967, the young temp agency had grown so much that it employed more workers than long-standing corporate giants such as Standard Oil of New Jersey and the U.S. Steel Corporation.[26]

Although Manpower and Kelly dominated the temp industry in the postwar years, there were a handful of other early industry leaders. Workman Service (later renamed Workman Girl) was reportedly the first modern temp agency, founded in Chicago in the late 1920s. Workman Service was apparently alone in the field until the 1940s when a number of other temp agencies were started around the Midwest. Labor Pool, founded in Chicago in 1946, became the first modern temp agency to focus exclusively on industrial work. A year later—the same year that Kelly was founded in Detroit—Employers Overload was established in Minneapolis. And in 1948, at the same time that Manpower was founded, Western Employers Service (later Western Girl) became the first West Coast temp agency. These were not the only temp companies at the time. Low barriers to entry meant that many agencies opened (and closed) their doors on a regular basis, although most of them did not follow the expansive growth trajectory that characterized Manpower and Kelly. Nonetheless, these countless smaller temp companies accounted for a significant portion of the industry. In 1960, *Fortune* magazine noted that although the top five temp agencies—Manpower, Kelly, Employers Overload, Western Girl, and Workman—took in some $67 million in sales, "an unknown number of similar firms operating on a local level may pick up as much as $50 million more."[27]

By the end of the postwar era, the temp industry was no longer just a cluster of successful but relatively small businesses. It had emerged as a well-established sector of the economy. In 1967, Manpower's Elmer Winter proclaimed that "temporary help—once the poor relation of the employment agency business—has become a mature, fast-growing industry in its own right."[28] He was right. Early evidence of this came in 1966 with the formation of the industry's first professional association, the Institute for Temporary Services (ITS).[29] At the same time, the industry had begun to develop internationally. Not only were temp agencies such as Manpower rapidly expanding abroad; there was also a new push to organize the industry on an international scale. In 1966, temp leaders in Europe organized the First World Congress of Temporary Services in Paris. William Olsten, president of Olsten Temporary Services, represented the U.S. temp industry at the conference. As Olsten explained, the purpose of the meeting was "to formalize the international confederation, elect officers, establish a code of ethics, and confirm the temporary service industry's importance as a socio-economic force in the countries in which it functions."[30]

Not surprisingly, the burgeoning temp industry had begun to attract attention in the business world. In 1965, for example, a trade analyst for *Barron's* noted that the young temp industry had already "blanketed the country."[31] That same year, another industry analyst proclaimed that, "as a cost cutting technique for management, 'renting people' is definitely here to stay."[32]

This was a remarkable statement in 1965. Businesses at that time were far from struggling. In fact, at that time America was in the middle of one of the longest economic expansions in history. Corporate profits were setting record highs and the stock market was booming. And businesses were not the only ones thriving. Workers, too, were benefiting from the nation's prosperity: Poverty was declining, unemployment was down, and wages were growing.[33] As economists Bennett Harrison and Barry Bluestone pointed out, the spirit of prosperity that pervaded those years was aptly portrayed by David Halberstam's description of the debut of the Ford Mustang:

> It came out in 1964, at what would prove to be the highwater mark of the American century, when the country was rich, the dollar strong, and inflation low. . . . The economy was expanding. Though many of the forces that would afflict American industry were already beginning to form, they were not yet visible, and the domestic economy had never seemed so strong. . . . There was enough for everyone; the country was enjoying unparalleled prosperity, and the pie was bigger than ever. The pie would turn out to have its limits after all, but at the halcyon moment, the future seemed unbounded.[34]

Yet even during those "halcyon" days, employers were "renting" people in order to cut costs. This is significant not only because businesses were reaping the benefits of record-breaking economic expansion, but also because the very survival of the temp industry had been uncertain just a few years earlier.

Padrones and the Private Employment Industry

When the modern temp industry emerged after World War II, its founders asserted that theirs was a "new" industry. Most observers at the time, however, did not agree. Government officials, union leaders, and social activists widely believed that temp companies were simply newer versions of the long-established—and highly disreputable—private employment agencies. The ignominy of the private employment industry can be traced to the public outrage over so-called padrones earlier in the century. In the early decades of the twentieth century, padrones, who were often immigrants themselves, provided new immigrants with jobs and supplied companies with cheap labor. Accused of luring workers to America to take bogus jobs, charging exorbitant fees, and ruthlessly exploiting unknowing immigrants, padrones aroused the ire of novelists such as Horatio Alger and social reformers such as Grace Abbott in Chicago.[35]

By the 1930s padrones had largely disappeared, but they had been replaced by employment agents, who were widely accused of padrone-like abuses such as sending workers to "phony" jobs, charging excessive fees, and physically abusing workers.[36] These employment agents were said to take advantage of not only recent immigrants, but also black southerners—especially female domestic servants—who, at the time, were migrating in large numbers to northern cities in search of work. Iowa's commissioner of labor declared employment agents to be the most "despicable, double-dyed villains that ever lived."[37] The Ohio commissioner of labor agreed, charging that the purpose of private employment agents was "to fleece the jobless."[38]

By the 1950s virtually every state had imposed extensive regulations on the private employment industry. These laws usually required employment agents to register, obtain a state license, and post bond; they capped fees charged to workers; they prohibited fee sharing between agents and employers; and they banned the practice of sending "scabs" to replace union workers on strike. Some states even required employment agents to have lived in an area for a minimum time period, to provide references from "reputable citizens of the community," and to obtain the state's permission before moving in order to prevent them from collecting fees and leaving without providing workers with jobs.[39]

When the modern temp companies were founded in the late 1940s, many observers and regulators considered them to be private employment agencies.[40] In 1955, for example, the Supreme Court of Nebraska described Manpower, Inc., as "obviously" an employment agency and ruled, as a result, that it must comply with state licensing laws.[41] One year later, the Florida Industrial Commission argued before the Florida Supreme Court that Manpower was just another private employment agency prone to the many "evils" of that industry.[42]

Manpower and other early temp agencies strongly resisted such classification in order to avoid the thicket of regulations surrounding the private employment industry. The crux of the matter, they argued, was their claim to employer status.[43] Temp industry leaders maintained that employment agents were simply labor market intermediaries; they connected people in need of work with employers in need of labor. Workers found jobs through employment agents but were not employed by them. By contrast, they claimed, temp agencies did not link workers to employers but were employers in their own right, contracting out their specialized labor to firms. They proposed a different parallel: A temp agency was like a painting company whose employees worked under the direction of the homeowner, or an accounting firm whose employees provided bookkeeping services for its customers.[44] In each case, employees provided services to a variety of businesses but were not employed by them. Another key distinction they pointed out was that temp agencies did not charge fees to workers as employment agents did. The "mark-up"—the difference between what temp agencies charged firms and paid to workers—was not, they claimed, a "fee."[45]

In 1956 the Florida Supreme Court agreed with temp industry leaders. Manpower, the court ruled, was not an intermediary but the employer of its temporary workers. The judges found that Manpower "retains control over its employees, and can substitute one employee for another in any particular job. It deducts the withholding tax from the employee's salary, pays the social security tax, carries unemployment and workmen's compensation on each employee, and has its employees bonded."[46] This did not end the controversy, however. Only a year earlier, for example, the Nebraska Supreme Court had reached the opposite conclusion. As sociologist George Gonos has shown, these cases were only a small part of the long and costly legal battle that industry leaders fought for their companies to be considered official employers of temporary workers, and thus to be distinguished from the temp industry's disreputable ancestor, the private employment industry.[47]

These legal battles were crucial to the survival of the early temp industry, but they do not tell the whole story. There was another combat zone, so to speak: culture. In the pages of newspapers, magazines, books, and more, early temp industry leaders launched a cultural campaign that would reify their legal claims and, more importantly, legitimize temping as a "new" sector of the economy.

Unions in the Postwar Era

Before turning to this campaign, however, we must turn to the second major obstacle that temp leaders faced: labor unions. In the mid-1950s, when the first temp agencies were just taking off, unions were at the peak of their power, representing some 35 percent of the labor force.[48] Unions were natural opponents of the temp industry, as their strength would be severely undermined by the emergence of a sector that relieved employers of hard-won worker protections, including pensions, health benefits, and other elements of the newly expanding social safety net.[49]

Not surprisingly, union leaders resisted the incursion of temporary work into their strongholds in the largely male industrial sector.[50] For example, in the early 1960s District 727 of the International Association of Machinists filed a grievance against the Lockheed Aircraft Company, demanding that the company stop using temps in an effort to erode the union's bargaining unit. Meanwhile, Local 887 of the United Auto Workers filed a similar grievance against North American Aviation, charging that the company was using temps to avoid paying the higher wage rates and benefits of permanent employees. "It's a black market that is fattening itself on the aerospace industry," said union leader Thomas McNett. "[This] makes it incumbent on this union to do all in its power to wipe out the job black market."[51]

Although nearly all of labor's opposition to the temp industry was in the industrial sector, there were a few exceptions. In the early 1960s, for example, union officials at the Office Employees International Union (OEIU) repeatedly voiced their complaints about the rapidly expanding temp industry. As described in a 1962 OEIU pamphlet, union leaders objected to the rise of temp work because it "not only tend[s] to eliminate permanent employment for office and clerical workers, but provides a regular kickback of daily wages to the companies providing the services. Worse still, the OEIU has found in its experience that the Manpower agencies are perfectly willing to provide scabs in companies against whom we are conducting strikes."[52]

These kinds of union objections to the temp industry were surprisingly rare in the postwar era, however.[53] This was, in part, because temp executives made substantial efforts to placate labor leaders, especially in the industrial sector. For example, it was common practice for temp executives to sign contracts affirming that temporary workers would not cross picket lines or replace strikers.[54] In fact, this would become a key tenet of the industry's newly minted code of ethics in the mid-1960s.[55] Manpower went a step further, promising to get union officials' approval before sending temps into a unionized workplace. As Manpower's Elmer Winter proclaimed in the trade journal *Steel* in 1961, "We have always maintained good relations with the unions. In every plant where a union is involved, we clear the use of Manpower with the union. If it objects, we pull out."[56] Although the pamphlet from the OEIU suggests that this promise was not always upheld, it is likely that Manpower showed greater deference to the more powerful industrial unions than it did to the significantly weaker unions in the white- and pink-collar sectors. In point of fact, Manpower and other temp agencies rarely had to contend with white- or pink-collar unions, because most private-sector office workers stayed out of the labor movement until the 1970s.[57]

Treading carefully around powerful labor unions helped early temp industry leaders sidestep serious resistance in the years after World War II. But their most important strategy was much less direct, and ultimately much more powerful. Drawing on the long-standing assumption that women's work was of little interest to postwar unions, temp executives launched a far-reaching cultural campaign that cast temporary work as the domain of white, middle-class women.[58] In so doing, they created a new kind of women's work, and an influential new kind of marginal employment.

The Making of the Kelly Girl

Early temp industry leaders strategically utilized images of gender, race, and class to construct the archetypal temp worker. Best seen in the image of the Kelly Girl, which remains a cultural icon some half a century later, this strategy publicly cast temp work as the sphere of white, middle-class women. Like portrayals of Rosie the Riveter during World War II, these images showed white, middle-class women as both workers and feminine. Unlike Rosie the Riveter, however, they showed women working for glamour, self-fulfillment, and independence, rather than patriotic service to their country. Yet both images portrayed women as temporary workers: Rosie was working only until her soldier came home from the war; Kelly was working only until her kids came home from school.

Kelly Girls were not alone, of course. Flight attendants, for example, were also advertised as "glamour girls" working for fun, adventure, and, ultimately, husbands.[59] The ranks of temps, however—unlike the ranks of flight attendants—included significant numbers of men, despite the

Kelly Girl image. Why, then, did industry leaders package temp work as "women's work"? The Kelly Girl strategy achieved several crucial goals. First, constructing temp work as women's work reduced any perceived threat that the industry might pose to "breadwinning" male jobs and the unions that represented them. In fact, industry leaders were quite explicit about this: "The temporary service industry poses no threat to labor," declared the president of Olsten Temporary Services, "but instead supplements the labor force with housewives and mothers—women who might never have returned to work but for the emergence of this much needed industry."[60] Second, the Kelly Girl strategy allowed temp leaders to distance their industry from padrones and private employment agents. The "respectability" of their white, middle-class "ladies" was intended to show just how far removed temping was from padrones and their nonwhite, foreign-born workers.[61]

The Kelly Girl strategy also allowed the temp industry to take advantage of the charged and contradictory gender politics of the postwar era. Even as white, middle-class women entered the labor force in the 1950s in greater numbers than ever before, cultural pressure for them to conform to "traditional" ideals was formidable.[62] Temp industry leaders capitalized on this disjuncture by urging women to work while at the same time promising that their jobs would not compete with the domestic sphere. In short, they argued that temp work was the perfect "compromise" for middle-class women in the postwar era.[63] Industry executives maintained that housewives could work in temporary jobs and still keep up with their domestic duties. This contention addressed the ambivalence some middle-class women felt about the competing roles of housewives and wage earners, while it opened doors for others who could not work because of policies that excluded married or pregnant women from employment.[64] At the same time, temp leaders were responding to—and taking advantage of—many women's interest in financial independence, skill acquisition, and self-fulfillment through work.

As the examples that follow demonstrate, the images of gender, race, and class constructed by temp industry leaders were complicated and often incongruous. For instance, even as they opened up new ways of thinking about white, middle-class women as viable workers—and about domestic life as unsatisfying—these images reinforced the belief that women were housewives first and workers second. And, perhaps more importantly, even as they introduced new categories of "respectable" (white, middle-class) work, these images strengthened and institutional-ized the divide between "breadwinning" (male) employment and second-ary (female) jobs. Indeed, the most notable outcome of their efforts was a new kind of work that was at once "respectable" and marginal.

The most basic element of the Kelly Girl strategy was to take on ex-plicitly feminine names: Kelly Girl Service, Western Girl Service, Workman Girl Service, American Girl Service, White Collar Girl Ser-vice, Right Girls, and more. Although Manpower was a notable excep-tion, company leaders adopted a highly "feminine" public image as well. Beginning in 1961, they called their temps White Glove Girls, and they went on to lead the industry in constructing and publicizing this white, middle-class, feminine portrait of temp work.[65] (Indeed, it was Man-power that developed and distributed a board game called "White Glove Girl." The object of the game was to earn money for family vacations, home remodeling, new clothes, and the like. Once this had been accom-plished, the players had to return home again—the first to do so was the winner. These themes of women working for "extras" while preserving their domesticity dominated the temp industry's postwar campaign.)

The fact that agencies took on feminized names did not mean that they employed women exclusively, however. Although many began by hiring mostly women, by the early 1960s almost every temp agency em-ployed significant numbers of men as well. In fact, by that time, both Western Girl and Kelly Girl had established male industrial and techni-cal divisions—called Western Men and Labor Aides, respectively—and nearly half of Manpower's workers were men.[66]

Because the companies started out employing women workers, their feminized names might be seen as an honest (if out-of-date) reflection of their employee base rather than a conscious strategy. However, evi-dence indicates otherwise. When the first temp agencies were founded, all had gender-neutral names. It was only in the late 1950s that temp executives—seemingly en masse—took on female-specific company ti-tles. For instance, the first modern temp agency, founded by Sam Work-man in 1929, was Workman Diversified Enterprise, Inc., later simplified to Workman Service. In the late 1950s, however, Workman changed the company's name to Workman Girls. Similarly, in 1957, William Russell Kelly changed his company's name from Russell Kelly Office Service to Kelly Girl Service. And a year later, W. Robert Stover changed his agency's name from Western Employers Service to Western Girl Service.[67]

Yet feminizing the industry's image went far beyond simply adding the word *girl* to agency names. In their phenomenal public relations campaign, temp leaders emphasized again and again that theirs was an industry exclusively for women. This theme was captured perfectly in a 1962 speech by Kelly Girl vice president Terrence Adderley before the New York Society of Analysts. "We can think of 60,000 reasons why our 60,000 female employees want to work on a temporary basis," Adderley declared, "but we cannot think of one good reason why a man, other than a student or a man between jobs, would *want* to work as a temporary employee."[68] Yet it was that very same year—1962—that Kelly executives were adding industrial and technical divisions designed to employ men.

Temp industry leaders were relentless in their efforts to paint a feminine portrait of temporary work. Starting in the mid-1950s, thousands of pictures of Kelly Girls, White Glove Girls, Western Girl's Cowgirls, American Girls, and more dotted the pages of popular magazines and newspapers, including *Newsweek, Business Week, U.S. News and World Report, Good Housekeeping, Fortune,* and the *New York Times.* In a single year—1961—Manpower executives spent $1 million to ensure that their White Glove Girls appeared in the Sunday papers of every major metropolitan area in the country. Manpower also created a range of promotional materials that encouraged women to become one of their white-gloved temps, including posters ("Be a girl in the white gloves") and an official how-to instruction manual ("Girl in the White Gloves Handbook"). Meanwhile, company leaders mailed countless advertisements directly to business owners with taglines such as "This pair of white gloves will be important to your business" or "Office help going on vacation? Call for the girl in the white gloves."[69]

The image these campaigns presented was of a white, middle-class, and patently "feminine" workforce. A full-length picture of Kelly Girl in 1960, for example, showed a stylish young white woman wearing white gloves, high heels, and jewelry, along with a hat and purse adorned with the Kelly Girl logo.[70] Manpower's White Glove Girl was quite similar.

As shown in the *New York Times* in 1962, she was a well-coifed Sandra Dee look-alike, wearing a dress, high heels, and, of course, white gloves.[71] Early in this campaign, Manpower's advertisements were a "feminine" hot pink, contrasting sharply with magazines' black-and-white color scheme. Typically, the ads pictured the head, shoulders, and—most prominently—the white gloves of Judy Newton, the same Sandra Dee–like model who became the public face of Manpower in the 1960s. "For the very best temporary office help," the captions commonly read, "call Manpower for 'The Girl in the White Gloves.'"[72]

The carefully crafted femininity of such images turned these White Glove Girls and Kelly Girls into—as the advertising magazine *Printer's Ink* put it in 1962—"respectable sex symbols."[73] Indeed, company leaders explicitly promoted the sex appeal of their women workers. In a highly publicized public service project called the "Kelly Beautification Program," for example, the temp agency sent Kelly Girls to plant flowers in New York City's public parks. However, as an article in *Time* magazine quipped, "Some clients might feel piqued that the 'temporaries' do not always look like the pert young things Kelly has been sending to plant gladioli and publicity in city parks."[74]

Temp industry leaders advertised male temp work as well, but minimally. Such ads represented less than 3 percent of their promotional effort.[75] But, for the most part, these advertisements did not portray images of men; instead, they showed pictures of tools and, in some cases, even women. A 1965 ad for Kelly Girl's industrial division Labor Aides, for example, featured a very large loading hook: "If you have boxcars to unload, bales to lift, stock to move, or anything else that needs unskilled or semi-skilled help, Labor-Aides temporary workers will save you money."[76] Kelly leaders produced a number of variations on this theme, with depictions of sledgehammers, loading dollies, and a variety of other industrial tools.

Manpower also publicized male temp work, but instead of depicting masculine tools, company leaders depicted images of White Glove Girls faced with "unladylike" jobs. One such advertisement in the *New York Times* pictured a white, middle-class woman wearing a dress, high heels, and the white gloves that had become the company's iconic symbol. She held one gloved hand on her hip, the other to her chest, and exclaimed: "Me unload lumber? Heavens no! I'm Manpower's

Kelly Girl, 1960
Source: *Chicago Daily Tribune,*
22 June 1960, p. C6

Manpower's "Girl in the White
Gloves," 1963 Source: *U.S. News and
World Report,* 20 May 1963, p. 88

'Girl in the White Gloves' and my job is helping you temporarily with office work." But the text below the image assured business owners that Manpower did have men to handle "unladylike" jobs, including unloading and loading, stacking and sorting lumber, and cleaning— "you name it."[77]

It is important to note what temp industry leaders were *not* portraying—men and nonwhites. Doing so would, on the one hand, highlight their encroachment into jobs claimed by powerful industrial

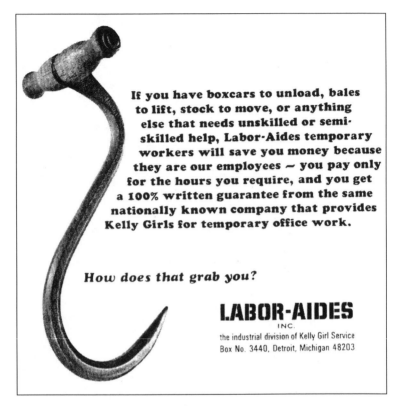

If you have boxcars to unload, bales to lift, stock to move, or anything else that needs unskilled or semi-skilled help, Labor-Aides temporary workers will save you money because they are our employees — you pay only for the hours you require, and you get a 100% written guarantee from the same nationally known company that provides Kelly Girls for temporary office work.

How does that grab you?

LABOR-AIDES
INC.
the industrial division of Kelly Girl Service
Box No. 3440, Detroit, Michigan 48203

Ad for "Labor Aides" from Kelly Girl Services, 1965
Source: *Newsweek,* 19 July 1965, p. 4

unions and, on the other hand, muddle their carefully constructed distinction from the disreputable private employment industry, which had targeted immigrants and racial minorities. There were a few exceptions to this rule, however. In 1964, for example, Manpower ran an advertisement in *Newsweek* that portrayed a white, working-class man holding a pair of work gloves. "Need temporary help? Call for 'the reliables' from Manpower!"[78] Images such as this, however, were extremely rare—appearing in less than 1 percent of industry ads—and were nearly overrun by Kelly Girls, White Glove Girls, American Girls, Workman Girls, Right Girls, and countless other feminized pictures of temp work.[79]

In addition to portraying the archetypal temp worker as female, temp industry leaders were careful to portray her as "respectable"—that is, white and middle-class. This was most clearly evidenced in the white gloves that were nearly ubiquitous in (and largely unique to) temp industry advertisements. Needless to say, the "class" and "femininity" conveyed by the white gloves was no accident. In his 1968 book *Your Future as a Temporary Office Worker*, Manpower's Elmer Winter described the company's strategy: "We chose white gloves as a symbol . . . because they seem to represent everything that is feminine, neat, and proper. They symbolize quality and efficiency."[80]

Temp industry leaders further emphasized the class distinction of their female workforce by highlighting their "skills," "know-how," and "special training."[81] These were not recent immigrants or black migrants looking for a break through private employment agents; they were "specially certified" (white, middle-class) workers.[82] A 1960 Kelly ad in the *Chicago Daily Tribune*, for example, described "the exacting Kelly Girl testing procedure that assures you the right girl for the right job."[83] In fact, Kelly promoted its workers' skills so thoroughly that it guaranteed customer satisfaction. A 1963 advertisement in *U.S. News and World Report* asked business owners: "Rushed at year end? Insist on the girl with the guarantee! She knows all about inventories. Figures and figuring are old hat to her. You know she's qualified by the 100% guarantee she hands you in writing." To emphasize this point, the ad included a miniature copy of the "Kelly Girl Guarantee."[84]

Manpower, too, highlighted its women workers' "special skills," "savvy," and "accuracy and productivity."[85] In 1964, the company launched a $1.5 million campaign to promote the "special training" of its White Glove Girls.[86] Advertisements in this campaign commonly showed a White Glove Girl holding a "Certificate of Training" with her white gloves. The headline of one such advertisement read, "SPECIAL TRAINING makes *the difference* between Manpower White Glove Girls [and] other temporary office workers."[87] Another ad boasted that Manpower's White Glove Girls were trained "in the special skills of temporary office work by a training course that took Manpower a year's study to prepare. Four manuals, 25 chapters, so advanced that leading firms and schools are asking to use them."[88] Advertisements such as these appeared in more than twelve million direct mailings to business owners, as well as in popular magazines and local newspapers across the country.[89]

Industry leaders' emphasis on the "special skills" of their women workers differed markedly from the few ads featuring male temps, whose skills were either not mentioned or who were vaguely referred to as "unskilled or semi-skilled." A 1964 Manpower advertisement for industrial work, for example, simply described male temps by their job titles: "Unloaders, warehousemen, shipping help, clean-up crew, laborers and machine operators are all a part of Manpower's service. Our men are called '*The Reliables*'—and they're just that! They show up on time—come to you fully bonded and insured—work hard as long as you need them."[90] The unskilled nature of the jobs seemed to speak for itself, and the primary "skill" these workers were said to bring was punctuality. This emphasis on male workers' lack of skill, particularly in comparison with the glowing descriptions of female temps' "know-how," is not surprising, however, given the industry's need to avoid union opposition. Advertising skilled male workers would have encroached on union territory and likely provoked antagonism from labor leaders.

Temp executives also emphasized the class distinction of their female workforce with frequent reminders that these women did not have to work. Capitalizing on cultural assumptions that white, middle-class women were financially supported by their parents or husbands, industry leaders repeatedly cast temps as "proper" (white, middle-class) housewives, dabbling in temp work in their spare time to help pay for a few luxuries. In 1958, for example, the executive vice president of Kelly Girl described what he called the "typical Kelly Girl": "She doesn't want full-time work, but she's bored with strictly keeping house. Or maybe she just wants to take a job until she pays for a davenport or a new fur coat."[91] Elmer Winter of Manpower agreed, right down to the fur coat. In describing the perks of work for women, Winter asked: "As for real luxury items, why not? That space over the fireplace has been crying for a good painting. Why not invest in one? How about that winter vacation, or that fur coat you've always felt you didn't have any right to ask for, which will not only keep you warm but do something to your morale?"[92]

The implication that these women did not need to work was captured perfectly by the title of a 1956 article in *Good Housekeeping*: "Extra

Money for Extra Work for Extra Women." The article, essentially an advertisement for Manpower (it even concluded with the company's contact information), opened with the following question: "Do you occasionally have a few free hours you'd like to put to work to earn some extra spending money?" After describing the benefits of temping, as well as Manpower's size and services, the anonymous author advised, "If you have extra time you would like to turn into extra money, you may want to investigate the services of a temporary help business."[93]

Describing temp work—and temp workers—as "extra" was common in industry leaders' marketing campaigns. Temps were secondary workers who would not undermine the authority of male breadwinners, nor would they trespass into union territory. In short, they would not threaten the newfound cultural legitimacy of the temp industry. The secondary status of temps was highlighted in Manpower's 1957 self-published history, *Manpower, Inc.* "The opportunities afforded by Manpower for a woman who need not earn all of her living expenses are excellent," the book advised. "It is ideal for a married woman with responsibilities that do not permit her absence from the home every day of the week."[94] A few years later, in the women's magazine *McCall's*, Elmer Winter of Manpower echoed this message. Winter declared that temporary workers were "women who have no illusions about embarking on a grandiose career. . . . They consider [work] simply as something nice, something extra. It is not their primary motivation."[95] Kelly executive Norman Jackson also promoted this view of temps. In a 1967 article in *Forbes* magazine, Jackson conceded, "It's true that temporary workers don't get pensions or six-week vacations." But, he maintained, "You also have to take cognizance of the people who want these jobs. By and large, they are married women on the young side, who want the extra money to supplement their husbands' incomes, or they're older women whose children have married and gone away."[96] Industry leaders even went so far as to suggest that temping was not "work" at all but more like a pastime. In 1961, for example, a Kelly Girl advertisement in the *New York Times* blared, "HOW TO MAKE Lots of Money WITHOUT WORKING." Although the text of the ad conceded that the only way to do so was to win the lottery, marry a millionaire, or inherit a fortune, the ad proclaimed temp work to be "the next best thing."[97]

Industry leaders repeatedly described temps as marginal workers. They were secondary earners who wanted to remain so, content to work for a little extra money without ambition for a "grandiose career." This claim was not unique to the temp industry, of course. The flight attendants of the era, for instance, were also said to work for glamour and excitement rather than for a fulfilling career or as a way to support their families.[98] But, as we will see in the following chapters, temp executives were not simply selling a new category of pink-collar employment. They were launching a new way of organizing work that would help revitalize and spread the liability model to all workers, not just those on the margins.

What's more, the portrayal of temp workers and their wages as "extra" stood in stark contrast to the reality of most temps at the time. In an early 1960s study, economist Mack Moore found that the vast majority of women who sought temporary jobs did so out of real economic need. Nearly three-fourths of women cited "To earn money" as the most important reason for working, while less than 15 percent said they worked for "relief from the boredom of housework." And these women were not working to pay for fur coats, as suggested by temp industry executives. They temped to pay household bills and to save for their children's education. "To have extra miscellaneous items from time to time" was listed half as many times as the need to meet daily living expenses.[99] This is not surprising given that in the postwar era women had only limited ability to support themselves and their families. They had little access to mortgages, credit cards, or other kinds of loans because their earnings were widely assumed to be temporary or part of a man's "family income." And key stepping stones to the middle class—the GI Bill and union membership—were generally closed to them.[100]

Temp industry leaders thus crafted a strategic response to the obstacles presented by the disreputable private employment industry and union power: They exploited a sector of the labor force whose employment opportunities had been restricted by both cultural norms and discriminatory employer practices. As a result, temp work became women's work. Yet even as they affirmed the secondary nature of temp work (and temps), industry executives went to great lengths to emphasize the "respectability" of temping. The archetypal temp—the famed Kelly Girl—was white and middle-class, for she did not need to work, and she was highly skilled. The use of this image was not coincidental, nor was it merely a reflection of the industry's primary workforce. And although the image was developed in the temp industry's self-interest, it was also influenced by women's interests.

Temporary Work as the "Modern Compromise": "What more could a woman want?"[101]

Well before Betty Friedan and other second-wave feminists used the language of self-actualization to encourage middle-class housewives to pursue careers, temp executives offered similar advice. They urged women to seek independence, equality, and even self-fulfillment through employment outside the home. Temp leaders thus unexpectedly took part in the long-term cultural debate about women and work. In the postwar era, this debate was once again coming to the fore, as more women than ever before were working outside the home, particularly married women with young children.[102] Gender traditionalists responded to these trends with a conservative backlash: There was a widespread push to contain the "threat" of women workers by describing them as a problem that needed to be resolved, and there were renewed campaigns to strengthen a domestic ideal that romanticized housewives and stay-at-home mothers.[103] Industry leaders capitalized on this tension between the reality of women working and the cultural pressure against it by offering temporary work as the perfect "compromise": Women would gain self-fulfillment through work without dethroning the domestic ideal.[104]

The temp industry was not the only employer in the expanding pink-collar sector to encourage housewives to seek work outside the home. But few others used the proto-Friedanian language of "self-actualization" to do so. Hospitals, for instance, urged nurses who had left the workforce to return out of "obligation" to ease the severe nursing shortage.[105] Temp agencies, by contrast, openly encouraged married women and even young mothers to work—not out of obligation, but to fulfill their own personal desires. For example, in an early brochure, the leaders of Kelly Girl waxed poetic: "In every woman's heart there's a yearning . . . to meet new people . . . to go to new places . . . to earn her own money . . . to do new things." As described in *Fortune* magazine, the brochure pictured a "smartly clad young woman entering a lavender automobile, trying on a new hat, and chatting over cocktails in an elegant restaurant that looks like the Four Seasons."[106] Temp work, Kelly leaders seemed to be saying, offered (white, middle-class) women self-fulfillment (answering that "yearning" for something more), independence (their "own" money), and even glamour and excitement (new people, places, and things).

Manpower also used the language of self-actualization to sell temp work to women. For example, a 1965 ad in the *Chicago Tribune* depicted a fashionable woman with a floppy, wide-brimmed hat over one eye and a gloved finger at her lips. "Ssshhhh!" she seemed to be saying, as though telling a secret. The text below announced:

SHE LEADS A DOUBLE LIFE . . . AND LOVES IT! She's a temporary office worker when she chooses . . . and a homemaker all the time. She's a Manpower White Glove Girl, and she loves her double life, because it gives her a refreshing change, because she earns good money, because it makes her happy. She works when she wants to . . . and meets new people all the time . . . enjoys life more. Could you lead a double life? . . . You could if you call Manpower for an appointment, or stop in for an interview. Do it today . . . have a double life to enjoy![107]

Although Manpower leaders gave lip service to traditionalist concerns about women working (a "worker when she chooses . . . and a homemaker all the time"), their real emphasis was on the sense of fulfillment, autonomy, and glamour that wage work offered. Moreover, the sexual intrigue of the "double life" in the advertisement should not be overlooked. All the same, Manpower was no radical feminist force. Such ads may have enticed women with seemingly dangerous rebellion—into the world of work, and perhaps more—but they also promised to return them home again, safe and sound, where domesticity reigned supreme.

Nonetheless, for the postwar era, temp leaders were unusually forthright about the benefits of wage work for women. This was the central theme of Elmer Winter's remarkable 1961 book, *A Woman's Guide to Earning a Good Living*. The Manpower president began his book by promising to "talk to you frankly about every phase of women-in-employment."[108] And he did. Covering topics such as skills training, working mothers, searching for a job, and starting one's own business, *A Woman's Guide* was, on the whole, a celebration of working women. For instance, Winter argued that working outside the home gave women a new sense of independence and self-respect. At work, he explained, "you are no longer merely the daughter, the wife, the mother, but an independent being, greeted by the elevator operator, your fellow workers, the boss and the waitresses in the company cafeteria."[109] Winter also previewed other key concerns of second-wave feminists, such as the importance of shared domestic duties. "At the supper table," Winter wrote, "it's a pleasant relief to be able to tell stories of something that happened somewhere else to you instead of sitting quietly while your husband talks about his office day."[110] And this kind of equal footing at the dinner table, Winter claimed, would give women more equality in all aspects of domestic life. "If both wife and husband arrive home in the evening tired from their jobs, the likelihood is that they will share the domestic chores. . . . The stigma of housework's being only for the sissies or the henpecked went out with the iceman. Both partners work; both take pride in their home. It's a partnership all the way through."[111]

In contrast to the exciting world of work, Winter described the life of a housewife as "depressing" and a "drudgery." "It takes a most unusual woman not to get fed up with the day-in, day-out round of domesticity, despite all the mechanical aids," he wrote. "Even the latest model in deep freezes or washer-dryers is not the most stimulating of company as a steady diet. Almost every woman of my acquaintance has confessed to me that there are many times in her domestic rounds when she suffers from 'housewifeitis.' "[112] Working for wages, Winter promised, would give women the cure for this "disease."[113] "Why is it," he asked, "that every woman with a job she enjoys gives forth such an aura of inner fulfillment? So often among our friends, my wife and I have seen the 'befores' and 'afters': before, neurotic, complaining, restless; after, serene and with a renewed sense of living."[114]

Other temp leaders sold work as the route to self-fulfillment as well. In their 1963 book *Work Smartly*, Kelly Girl executives (and brothers) William Russell Kelly and Richard Kelly wrote: "Many women have the feeling that household work after a time loses importance both to their families and to themselves. These mothers can no longer get emotional satisfaction from housework. . . . Many women seek temporary jobs as a means of self-expression."[115]

Temp executives were selling self-fulfillment to women much as a door-to-door salesman would have sold them a new oven cleaner. But they were not alone. As the middle class expanded in the postwar era, automobiles, modern appliances, and even prescription tranquilizers such as Miltown were being sold—to middle-class women in particular—as an essential part of a new lifestyle based on convenience and psychological self-fulfillment.[116] Selling happiness to housewives through consumer goods was the product of two major cultural developments of the 1950s and 1960s. First, women and their consumption of household items had been placed at the front lines of the Cold War by politicians such as Richard Nixon in his famous "kitchen debate" with Soviet premier Nikita Khrushchev in 1959.[117] Second, rhetoric about the need for self-fulfillment had begun to dominate pop psychology in the 1960s, culminating in the emergence of the popular "Human Potential Movement" with its emphasis on realizing one's potential.[118] Temp industry leaders were just a few of the many to capitalize on this cultural convergence of gender, consumerism, and psychology.

Furthermore, Elmer Winter and other temp executives were not the only ones discussing the downsides of domestic life, even in this culturally conservative era that championed housewives and stay-at-home mothers. As historian Joanne Meyerowitz has observed, even before feminist critiques of domesticity entered popular discourse, national media frequently portrayed domesticity as exhausting and isolating.[119] But temp executives did more than just describe the downsides of domesticity. By promoting work as the cure for "housewifeitis," Elmer Winter and other industry leaders joined (at least in part) an ongoing dialogue among elite white feminists dating back to Charlotte Perkins Gilman in the 1890s—one that would soon be reignited by Betty Friedan and the second-wave feminists later in the decade.

Yet, as noted before, Elmer Winter and other industry leaders were not exactly feminists. Winter, for example, was a lawyer and a businessman. Although he was not divorced from politics (he would later become quite active in the affairs of Israel), Winter did not espouse feminism. He may have supported (some) women's desires for independence, equality, and fulfillment through wage work, but his writings repeatedly emphasized the primacy of women's service to their husbands and families. Thus, at the same time as he quoted Simone de Beauvoir and Virginia Woolf, he also declared that "it is downright wrong for any married woman to allow her own personal ambition (whatever her motivations) to upset the equilibrium of those to whose welfare she should be dedicated."[120] The Kelly brothers agreed: "A wise woman is always a wife and mother first."[121]

In encouraging women to seek self-fulfillment in work without dethroning domesticity, then, temp industry leaders went only so far as their own interests led them and no further. This rhetoric—like that of airlines at the time, which encouraged women to work for glamour while also imposing strict age limits and marriage bars—both exacerbated and capitalized on cultural ambivalence about women working in the postwar era. Indeed, such cultural ambivalence provided a perfect opportunity for temp industry leaders, who were able to promote temp work as an ideal solution—a "modern compromise" that allowed women to have it all, both work and domesticity. This argument was captured perfectly in a 1960 article in *Chatelaine*, a popular women's magazine in Canada, which quoted an executive from the Canadian temp agency Office Overload:

> The modern compromise for the married woman is part-time temporary work: working hours tailored to suit her particular responsibilities, the bonus interest of varied offices and industries to work in, and that extra kick, a few more dollars in the family purse! What more could a woman want? Wilbur can have the measles without the whole fragile structure of the mother's working life toppling around her. . . . This compromise satisfies some forty-thousand women across Canada who work on such a basis for the company I represent.[122]

With temporary work, in other words, women would gain all the benefits of wage work without dethroning domesticity. As a 1965 Manpower advertisement in the *Chicago Tribune* assured, housewives' family duties need not suffer because of temp work. The headline read, "ME WORK? I'd love to but . . ."

Try the "temporary office-work" way of working. No "buts" about it. You'll enjoy it, and you'll still have time to be a good wife and mother. You set your own work schedule when you're a Manpower White Glove Girl. Work near home whenever possible. Get paid highest rates. And, as a White Glove Girl, you're recognized as the very best in temporary office help.[123]

As the above quotations suggest, industry leaders promised women workers flexibility that would allow them to walk the tightrope between the desire to work and cultural pressure against doing so. Office Overload promised that women could tailor their work hours and still be able to take care of their sick children; Manpower offered them the chance to work near home, set their own schedules, and still have time to be a good wife and mother. In a similar vein, Western Girl promised women "dream jobs" with all the flexibility they could desire: "Hitch your wagon to Western Girl where those 'dream' jobs are waiting now! Dream of working the hours you choose . . . dream of working as long or as little as you wish . . . dream of selecting firms, assignments and fields you prefer . . . at HIGH temporary rates! Who has more of the 'Dream' temporary jobs? WESTERN GIRL."[124]

For some women (or their husbands), such promises of flexibility may have made it easier to swim against the conservative tide and work outside the home. But this did not mean that temporary work actually offered the flexibility its boosters promised. In his 1963 study of the temp industry, Mack Moore found that women applying for temporary jobs needed to be available to work full days every day of the week; those available for less time were simply not called for jobs. "A very common advertising appeal used by [temp agencies]," Moore noted, "is 'work at your own convenience.' A more appropriate appeal might be: 'Work at *our* convenience, refuse work at *your* convenience.' "[125] In other words, if women wanted to work, it would be entirely at the convenience of the temp agency. The only "flexibility" that temping offered was the ability to turn down work—and even that was somewhat illusory, since doing so could diminish the chances of getting future job offers.

If temping did not provide much in the way of real flexibility, it did offer many women a way to navigate the cultural tensions surrounding work outside the home. As limited as this empowerment may have been in feminist terms, the Kelly Girl strategy still proved a remarkable success, although more for the temp industry itself than for women workers. By the end of the postwar era, the industry had grown dramatically. With origins as an industry that aroused doubt and suspicion, it had become accepted by businesses and workers as a legitimate sector of the economy. Kelly Girls were used to gain publicity for New York City parks and to sell new fashion designs. And Manpower employed more workers than quintessential American companies such as Standard Oil and U.S. Steel.[126]

The story of the temp industry's significance could have ended with temping as a small but thriving sector of contingent work for marginalized workers. But as the next chapter will explain, industry leaders of the 1970s sought to expand beyond the walls of secretaries' offices and into factories, hospitals, science labs, and even corporate boardrooms. And, thanks to their Kelly Girl strategy, the obstacles that would have prevented them from such expansion had been significantly weakened. Temp agencies were no longer associated with exploitative private employment agents; indeed, padrones and the private employment industry had become distant memories. And soon union power, too, would fade as an obstacle to the temp industry. By the 1970s, temp leaders were well situated to move beyond the Kelly Girl and create not only a new image of temp work but a new model of employment for all workers.

2 | THE INVENTION OF THE SEMI-PERMANENT EMPLOYEE

In an early 1970s advertisement, Olsten Temporary Help Services announced a new invention: "the semi-permanent employee." Guglielmo Marconi invented the wireless telegraph, the ad said; Thomas Edison invented the phonograph; and Alexander Bell invented the telephone. "Now," company leaders proclaimed, "Olsten invents The Semi-Permanent Employee. The *Semi-Permanent*, a new kind of temporary employee . . . not for days or even weeks, but for two- and three-month periods to help your business grow more profitably."[1]

This new "invention," Olsten told readers of the *Personnel Journal*, would boost profits by shrinking the payroll (to "a slim, trim personnel budget, not one which chokes profitability"), by smoothing the ebb and flow of the business cycle ("you needn't carry 'dead wood' for months when business is slow"), and by cutting training costs (employers would get "trained personnel without having to engage in expensive and unprofitable retraining").[2]

Olsten was not alone. Around the same time, Kelly Services (formerly Kelly Girl Services) published an advertisement announcing their own invention, the "Never-Never Girl," who:

Never takes a vacation or holiday. Never asks for a raise. Never costs you a dime for slack time. (When the workload drops, you drop her.) Never has a cold, slipped disc or loose tooth. (Not on your time anyway!) Never costs you for unemployment taxes and social security payments. (None of the paperwork, either!) Never costs you for fringe benefits. (They add up to 30% of every payroll dollar.) Never fails to please. (If our Kelly Girl employee doesn't work out, you don't pay.)[3]

With these inventions—and others like them from Manpower, Western Services, Staff Builders, Task Force, and more—temp executives of the late 1960s and early 1970s turned their attention away from selling "extra women" to do "extra work." They were now selling much more: a revised liability model of work in which employers would gain all the benefits of a long-term, productive workforce without any of the downsides. By using semi-permanents and Never-Never Girls, industry leaders proclaimed, business owners would no longer lose sleep over the rising cost of health insurance, or worry that letting an employee go would increase their unemployment insurance taxes. They would no longer have to keep workers when business inevitably slowed, nor would they need to train new workers when business picked up again. They would no longer have to pay for vacations or sick days, nor would they be troubled by injury lawsuits and the rising cost of workers' comp. They would not even have to pay for lunchtime or bathroom breaks. Instead, temp leaders promised, business owners would gain "flexibility of personnel to the nth degree" and would be able to focus entirely on their main objective: making a profit.[4]

From a twenty-first-century perspective, this dual emphasis on profits and flexibility seems unremarkable. It is largely taken for granted that employers need workforce flexibility in order to keep up in a rapidly changing economic environment. And extra workers—like excess inventory—are generally considered a drain on the bottom line. Successful businesses are said to be "lean and mean," boosting profits by increasing efficiency and eliminating waste—in terms of inventory, machinery, and even people.

This has not always been the case. Over the course of the twentieth century, the view of workers as profit-draining liabilities repeatedly ran up against a very different management approach—the asset model of

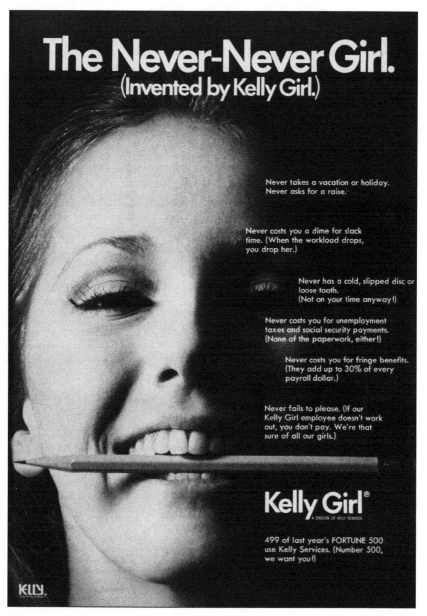

Kelly Services' Never-Never Girl, 1971 Source: *The Office,* January 1971, p. 19

work—in which workers were considered a key source of profits. In the postwar era, the asset model enjoyed widespread cultural support: Labor unions had institutionalized asset-model jobs for a growing number of workers, and, at the same time, management circles generally believed that tending to workers' welfare was profitable. But by the end of the century, this had changed. Not only had it become culturally acceptable for employers to see workers as little more than costly liabilities; it was considered sound business sense to do so.

Labor market scholars have traced the origins of this shift to what has been called the "Great U-Turn" in the American economy. This phrase, coined by economists Bennett Harrison and Barry Bluestone, describes a sharp about-face in the U.S. economy away from the booming prosperity of the postwar era to a time of economic turmoil and decline.[5] Economists and sociologists have explained this reversal by pointing to structural changes in the economy, such as deindustrialization, de-unionization, globalization, and economic recession.[6] These dynamic forces built on each other, leading to worsening conditions for American workers. The decline of manufacturing, for example, decreased the number of well-paying jobs in the unionized industrial sector, which in turn intensified the fall of union power. Meanwhile, the rising service economy replaced good jobs with so-called "McJobs"—low-wage, nonunion, service-sector employment. Scholars such as Paul Osterman and Annette Bernhardt have argued that, taken together, these changes led to stagnating wages and stymied upward mobility for workers.[7]

Workers were not the only ones suffering in the new economic environment. Business owners, too, faced severe challenges. Profit margins declined as America's global economic dominance gave way to intense international competition—what Harrison and Bluestone called an "invasion of foreign business."[8] This profit squeeze was further exacerbated by a series of deep economic recessions, triggered by the Vietnam War, the collapse of the Bretton Woods system of international monetary management, and the oil crisis of 1973. Employers responded to these exceptionally difficult times by cutting costs wherever possible: moving factories overseas, outsourcing non-core competencies, hiring contingent workers, and crushing unions.

Employers claimed that such actions were necessary to survive in the harsh new economic environment, but this is misleading. In truth, the business world of the 1960s and 1970s featured a number of alternative ideas about how best to organize work and boost profits, even during difficult times. Employers faced a choice, not an imperative.[9] The dominant theories of personnel management, in fact—those theories that were taught in business schools and promoted in management textbooks—did not advocate the "lean and mean" approach at all. Rather, by and large they promoted the view that workers were assets to the company's bottom line and could not be dumped without serious consequences. One of the best-selling management books of the era, for example, was called *Up the Organization: How to Stop the Organization from Stifling People and Strangling Profits*. Written in 1970 by Robert Townsend, former president of Avis Rent-A-Car, *Up the Organization* was a classic example of the asset model of work. Townsend disdained managers who made workers do all the "dog-work," as he called it, and he urged them to give workers the autonomy and authority to make decisions in "important matters."[10] What's more, Townsend strongly believed in fostering workers' skill development and advancement up the corporate ladder. *Up the Organization* quickly became a standard reference book for corporate executives, sitting on the *New York Times* nonfiction best-seller list for twenty-eight weeks—with seven of those weeks at the top.[11]

Thus, even the harsh economic climate of the 1970s was not necessarily hospitable to the temp industry's semi-permanents and Never-Never Girls. The need for disposable workers was not obvious; temp executives still had to explain and justify their new products. And for this purpose, the old Kelly Girl strategy would no longer serve. In fact, it might hurt the industry's campaign by suggesting that temping was only for "extra women." So industry leaders let "Kelly" go. In her place they came up with a modernized version of the liability model of work. The temp industry's new model was a direct descendant of much earlier versions of the liability model of work, most notably the nineteenth-century "Babbage principle," which maintained that skilled workers should be replaced by unskilled labor whenever possible.[12] But the temp industry's model went even further: All workers could be replaced by temps, regardless of their skill or status.

In the late 1960s and 1970s, temp executives launched their updated liability model of work with all the passion and ingenuity they had previously devoted to the Kelly Girl strategy. This campaign required a fundamental shift in strategy, however. First, industry leaders had to turn their attention away from selling jobs to housewives and focus instead on business owners. This did not mean that industry leaders never advertised to workers (or, specifically, women workers), but they expended little creativity on such ads, which were generally featureless announcements of job openings and wage rates. Nearly all of temp executives' considerable ingenuity and resources were dedicated to selling their model of work to business owners.

Second, instead of selling "extra women," temp executives sold "expertise" in personnel management. Indeed, they went to great lengths to establish themselves as authorities in this field, distributing booklets, holding seminars, and even offering on-site consultations, all of which proclaimed the temp industry's expertise (and business owners' incompetence) in workforce management. This need to establish their "expertise" is hardly surprising, however, given how fully the temp industry's liability model of work challenged other, well-accepted experts at the time.

This chapter examines temp leaders' campaign to sell a "semi-permanent" model of work, beginning with a look at the dismantling of the Kelly Girl strategy and the industry's successful expansion into new sectors of the economy. The chapter then turns to a closer look at these developments and their significance for the broader story of work in America. This involves, first, a careful dissection of the temp industry's new model of work, placed in the context of the leading management philosophies of the time. A final section takes an in-depth look at the temp industry's marketing campaigns that helped make the semi-permanent model of work a "normal way to do business." Without underplaying the significance of macroeconomic factors, this chapter seeks to acknowledge the importance of cultural campaigns in changing the nature of work in the American economy.

"We won't send a girl to do a woman's job": Dismantling the Kelly Girl Strategy

We left Chapter 1 with the temp industry's Kelly Girl strategy constructing temp work as the domain of white, middle-class housewives. With this campaign, industry leaders established temping as a legitimate sector of the economy. Indeed, the industry's remarkable success in the postwar era testified to the ingenuity and cultural power of the Kelly Girl approach. Yet by the late 1960s, the Kelly Girl strategy had begun to run up against real limits. Industry executives had so profitably legitimized temporary work that they were ready to move beyond the narrow niche of female secretarial work. In particular, they wanted to expand their already substantial inroads into the male labor force. And this would mean redrawing the face of temp work to include men and male "breadwinning" jobs.

The feminized names that most temp agencies had adopted in the 1950s were the first things to go. By the early 1970s, nearly all temp agencies had removed the word *girl* from their company names. In 1966, for example, Kelly Girl changed its name to Kelly Services. "Obviously, we can't call ourselves Kelly *Girl* Service any more," exclaimed Kelly leaders in a series of advertisements, noting the company's "big, strapping" male temps.[13] By the early 1970s, American Girl and Western Girl had followed suit, changing their company names to AGS and Western Services, respectively.[14] Manpower, meanwhile, discontinued its once-popular White Glove Girl campaign.[15]

This shift was captured perfectly in a series of advertisements from Olsten Temporary Services, which announced, "We won't send a girl to do a woman's job." Common among the many ads in this 1967 campaign were those featuring a young, trendy woman wearing white go-go boots and a short miniskirt. The headline of one such advertisement read: "We turned her down."

> She was young. And gay. But she couldn't swing with us. Because she couldn't do the work that our clients expect from an Olsten woman. So reluctantly we turned her down. (Although we did tell her, as we do with all our applicants, how to acquire the necessary skills.) When we send you a temporary employee, you can be sure she will get the job done. . . . We won't send a girl to do a woman's job.[16]

Had industry rhetoric simply replaced the word *girl* with *woman*, it would likely have been a reflection of changing gender norms rather than evidence of any real change in strategy. But although feminism clearly influenced industry advertisements, temp executives were, in fact, undertaking a much broader campaign. Beyond selling "women" rather than "girls," temp leaders of the late 1960s and 1970s were trying to move away from the image of temping as marginal, feminized work; they wanted to radically redraw the public face of temp work to include male temps and traditionally male occupations. For instance, although Dot Girls retained its feminized name longer than other temp agencies, in 1974 the company launched a major publicity campaign to promote its male temporary workers. With the tagline, "Some of the best Dot Girls are men," one of the advertisements read: "Our men go to work on the jobs you wouldn't ask our girls to do. In the stock room. Mailroom. Shipping. Any place you need men. They may not be as pretty as Dot Girls, but they're just as good."[17]

But moving into traditionally male employment required more than simply advertising male temporary workers. It required a new cultural justification for temp work. In the postwar era, industry executives claimed that temp work would permit women to walk the tightrope between the desire to work and cultural pressure against doing so. It would give them independence and self-fulfillment, without undermining the domestic ideal. By the 1970s, industry leaders had revamped their rhetoric to justify male breadwinners as temps. Foreshadowing later industry marketing campaigns that would portray temps as "free agents,"[18] industry executives of the 1970s claimed that temping would give men the "leisure time" and "flexibility" they desired.[19] In a 1974 article in the *Chicago Tribune*, for example, Manpower's Elmer Winter declared that the young adults of the 1970s did not even want permanent jobs; rather, they wanted "a commitment to themselves rather than to a corporation." Winter proclaimed that temping was just the ticket for this new, more self-concerned generation of workers.[20]

The most important reason to justify male temps was to break into traditionally male occupational sectors, which were higher paid than pink-collar work and potentially more lucrative for temp agencies. In the late 1960s and 1970s, temp agencies made a strong push into technical, medical, and engineering jobs, as well as high-level management positions. For instance, in 1968 Manpower created an entire subdivision—Manpower Technical Division—dedicated to supplying the technical sector with temps. As company executives frequently bragged to business owners in their 1970s advertisements, "We've expanded our work force to include the technicians, nurses, engineers, and other specialists your modern business requires."[21] Staff Builders, too, advertised temps in a number of traditionally male occupations, including technical, medical, and industrial jobs.[22] At the same time, both Western and Kelly Services began supplying temps to the health care and marketing sectors.[23]

It is important to note that abandoning the Kelly Girl image did not mean giving up strategic constructions of women in industry advertisements. In fact, many of the temp agencies that had dropped the word *girl* from their company titles retained feminized names for their office work divisions. Both Kelly Services and AGS, for example, continued to call their clerical temps Kelly Girls and American Girls, respectively, for many years. (Indeed, Kelly did so into the early 1990s.)[24] And although the white gloves and stiff coiffure disappeared from industry advertisements, they were replaced by highly sexualized images of women—the same images of skimpily clad women with wind-blown hair that populated a wealth of other marketing campaigns at the time.[25] "Get a free half hour with Kelly Girl," Kelly executives offered in an early 1970s series of advertisements portraying a tantalizing Farrah Fawcett look-alike staring intently into the camera.[26] Victor Temporaries had a similar proposal. Featuring a sultry woman better suited for a James Bond movie than an office, the 1968 advertisement asked: "Want to meet a calculating woman? She's got your number, and you can get hers. . . . Call on Victor Temporaries and you're in business."[27]

The temp industry's efforts to move beyond the Kelly Girl paid off. Employers began "demanding" their services, and throughout the 1970s temp industry employment grew rapidly.[28] In fact, over the course of the decade, temp industry employment more than doubled, despite several severe recessions. In 1970, the industry employed 185,000 temps a day.[29] Ten years later, that number had risen to over 400,000 workers every day—the same number employed annually in 1963.[30] The bulk of the industry's growth was outside the clerical sector. At the start of the decade, nonclerical temp work accounted for about one-third of temporary employment. Just ten years later, nonclerical temp work represented 45 percent of the temporary market—an increase of nearly 40 percent.[31]

In order to accomplish all of this, however, the temp industry needed more than just a cosmetic face lift. It needed a new model of work—one that would allow it to grow past its role as an ancillary niche of the labor market and recast it as a central fixture of the U.S. economy. As we will see, this would mean reviving and renovating the liability model of work and selling it as the industry's own.

The Temp Industry's Model of Work: The Semi-Permanent Employee

The underlying premise of the temp industry's new model of work was that employees were "expendable."[32] With "inventions" such as the semi-permanent employee, the Never-Never Girl, and more, temp industry leaders sold a model of work in which permanent employees were a "costly burden," a "headache" that needed relief.[33] "Stop paying help you don't use," advised Western Services in a 1969 advertisement. "Start using help you don't pay."[34] In fact, temp executives repeatedly argued that, instead of paying for workers, businesses should eliminate the human dimension of the employment equation altogether and "pay only for production."[35] As early as 1965, for example, Richard Kelly of Kelly Girl told *Financial World* that instead of having "typists waiting for something to type, machines waiting for something to machine, warehouses waiting for something to house," business owners should hire temps, lease equipment, and rent space in order "to reduce this high cost of unproductive time."[36]

This logic was pervasive in temp industry publications of the late 1960s and 1970s. In both articles and advertisements, industry leaders urged business owners to "rent" workers (temps), much like any other expensive office equipment, rather than "buy" permanent employees who were not continuously productive.[37] In a series of advertisements in the mid-1960s, for example, Olsten executives asked readers of the *Personnel Journal*: "Need only half a girl? Why pay for a whole one?"[38] "Whole" workers, they declared, were outrageously expensive, riddled with numerous "hidden costs," which included "exhaustive bookkeeping . . . umpteen payments to the government, state, this health plan, that insurance company . . . stretched coffee breaks, morning gab session, [and] afternoon washup time."[39]

Some industry leaders went so far as to explicitly liken workers to machines.[40] In the mid-1960s, for example, Victor Temporaries ran a series of advertisements that featured a highly sexualized woman, who was—perhaps incongruously—described as a "business machine."

New Victor business machine takes dictation, types, calculates, and cooks a delicious beef stroganoff. "Business machine" is actually too hard a description for anything as feminine as the girl you get from Victor temporaries. But she works as efficiently as a machine because she's been selected by Victor. . . . Find out what a hard day's work you can get from the softest of Victor's business machines.[41]

A few years later, in a widely published series of advertisements, Manpower also described its temps as machines. Depicting a woman sitting at a typewriter inside a large packing crate, the ad read: "The last word in 1970 office equipment! . . . Operationally, she's a beauty! Turn her loose on temporary workloads of any kind and watch the work disappear. She's the newest model in the world's most distinguished line of temporary office workers."[42]

Temp executives urged businesses to think of permanent employees as office equipment too. "Would you order twenty staplers every month, regardless of whether they were needed?" temp leaders rhetorically asked businesses. Why, then, should anyone keep twenty employees on staff when business is slow? Temp leaders repeatedly told employers to rethink the meaning of labor—to see it not as a fixed cost, like rent or utilities, but as a variable cost that could fluctuate with the business cycle. They argued that businesses should employ a "skeletal" core of permanent employees—perhaps just five—who could regularly be supplemented by ten, twenty, or even fifty temps when needed.[43] As one temp executive told the readers of *The Office* in 1970, employers should use temps to make labor "a variable expense [that] rides with the volume of work."[44]

The model of work that temp industry leaders promoted during this time period was a classic restatement of much earlier versions of the liability model of work. Employers from the late-nineteenth-century Gilded Age would have recognized the argument that workers imposed costly rigidities that detracted from businesses' primary focus—profits. But temp executives did not portray their model of work as a relic of the

The last word in 1970 office equipment!

She comes to your office after passing our rigid quality-control standards of testing, interviewing and checking. Operationally, she's a beauty! Turn her loose on temporary workloads of any kind and watch the work disappear.

She's the newest model in the world's most distinguished line of temporary office workers. Special Manpower training equips her to handle special assignments as if she were a permanent member of your staff. When it comes to temporary office work, she's "with it." She's responsible, uses good judgement and has fine skills. You don't find people like this easily or often. We've got over 100,000 of them throughout the world. Try us!

Manpower, Inc. Temporary Help Service

Manpower, "Last Word in 1970 Office Equipment!" 1970
Source: *The Office,* January 1970, p. 139

Gilded Age. They argued that the semi-permanent employee represented progress and modernity. Theirs was a "sophisticated" and "enlightened" approach to workforce management, in sharp contrast to what they called the "outdated" and "quaint" management styles of the past.[45] And perhaps there was an element of truth to this, in the sense that their ideas really did cut against the grain of mainstream management thought. Because this is so important, it is worth taking a closer look at dominant theories of personnel management of the late 1960s and 1970s.

Personnel Management in the 1960s and 1970s

The temp industry's model of work as embodied in the semi-permanent employee differed dramatically from the dominant theories of personnel management at the time. These theories can be categorized into two general groups: Human Relations and Administrative Management. The Human Relations approach to workforce management emerged in the late 1920s and continued to inform business circles through the 1970s.[46] In general, according to this theory, the best way to increase productivity— and profits—was to improve employee satisfaction. Adherents to this approach argued that workers would be more productive if they felt satisfied about their work environment. Thus, they recommended that employers improve workers' morale by listening and responding to their concerns, encouraging them to participate in administrative decision making, and enriching jobs to stave off monotony.[47]

The widely heralded "father" of the Human Relations movement was Elton Mayo, a Harvard Business School professor best known for the "Hawthorne Studies."[48] These were a series of studies conducted in the 1920s and early 1930s at a Western Electric plant outside of Chicago. First led by company engineers, and later by Mayo and his team of Harvard researchers, the studies sought to examine the impact of workplace environment on worker productivity. The most famous finding of this research became known as the "Hawthorne effect," which held that no matter how the workplace environment was manipulated— in terms of worker supervision, pay, rest time, length of the workday, etc.—productivity of the workers under study was always higher than the productivity of the rest of the workforce.[49] In short, Mayo asserted, workers were being positively influenced by the attention of the researchers themselves.[50] Although the Hawthorne studies were roundly criticized by scholars who objected to, among other things, their unscientific methods and Mayo's selective reporting of data,[51] the so-called Hawthorne effect was widely celebrated, and Elton Mayo became the leader of an influential new approach to workforce management based on tending to the psychological needs of workers. "The 'Cult of Mayoism,'" noted management scholar Thomas O'Connor, "became the predominant management philosophy in its day, as administrators everywhere sought to re-train their supervisors to play the role that Mayo's assistants played."[52]

By the early 1960s, the Human Relations philosophy had become conventional wisdom within management circles, although at the time the philosophy was more commonly known as the behavioral school of thought.[53] According to management historian Sanford Jacoby, business owners had generally begun to "approach management from a psychological point of view, rather than an economic one."[54] Throughout the decade and into the next, company executives widely adhered to the belief that satisfied workers meant greater profits, and they made efforts to incorporate this version of the asset model philosophy into their business practices. It is important to remember, however, that this asset-model approach was still a management philosophy, and its commitment to workers' well-being extended only so far as the bottom line. Nevertheless, Human Relations theories did hold that, because workers were central to a company's success, they should be treated as key assets rather than as costly liabilities.

Two well-known theorists led the Human Relations movement in the 1960s: Douglas McGregor and Frederick Herzberg. McGregor was best known for his "Theory X/Theory Y," which juxtaposed traditional and behavioral styles of management. According to McGregor, the traditional style of personnel management, which he called Theory X, assumed that people inherently disliked work and thus needed to be coerced, controlled, directed, and even threatened with punishment in order to be productive. By contrast, Theory Y management assumed that people did not inherently dislike work and that they would naturally be productive if they were committed to the goals of the organization. Theory Y managers thus allowed employees greater control over their work and encouraged their creativity instead of attempting to coerce or control them. McGregor believed that the way a manager treated employees was a self-fulfilling prophecy: If workers were regarded as lazy, they would be lazy; but if they were expected to take on greater responsibility and challenges, they would respond in kind.[55] McGregor's theories were quite influential among corporate executives, including Avis president Robert Townsend, who, as mentioned earlier, went on to write his own management guide based on this philosophy.[56]

Like McGregor, Frederick Herzberg argued that satisfied employees were more productive and profitable. But in order for workers to be truly satisfied, Herzberg argued, they needed more than decent wages and working conditions. They needed challenging work, recognition for accomplishment, autonomy and authority, and opportunities for growth. Herzberg maintained that when businesses provided their employees with both a minimum level of job satisfaction and opportunities for promotion and reward, they would reap the profits of a highly motivated and productive workforce.[57]

Although the link between worker satisfaction and greater profits pervaded management circles at the time, this asset model philosophy could not have been further from the temp industry's liability model of work. According to temp executives, employee satisfaction simply did not matter, because employers could get productive workers without having to attend to their psychological needs. Recall Kelly's description of the Never-Never Girl: "When the workload drops, you drop her."

The temp industry's view of workers was not only at odds with the popular Human Relations approach; it was also dramatically different from the Administrative Management approach—the other management theory that was well regarded at the time. The Administrative school of personnel management sought to boost productivity by controlling the workforce from the top down, in contrast to the Human Relations collaborative approach. The founder of the Administrative philosophy was Henri Fayol, a French theorist whose early-twentieth-century writings were largely ignored in the United States until after World War II. Fayol outlined fourteen principles of management that he believed were necessary for the efficiency (and thus success) of any organization. His list was extensive, including, on the one hand, the need to control and discipline workers and, on the other hand, the importance of worker innovation, low turnover, and esprit de corps. Although his overriding emphasis was on top-down control, Fayol highlighted the importance of each worker's unique contribution to an organization, even when it came to the need for centralized management. Perhaps unintentionally evoking Karl Marx's critique of nineteenth-century class structure, Fayol wrote: "Each employee, intentionally or unintentionally, puts something of himself into the transmission and execution of orders. . . . He does not operate merely as a cog in a machine."[58]

But cogs in a machine were exactly what the temp industry was selling. With the "invention" of the semi-permanent employee and the Never-Never Girl, temp executives rejected the widely held belief that workers' unique skills, commitment, longevity, and creativity were vital to a company's success. Instead, they sought to revitalize a nineteenth-century style of employment relations in which workers were considered liabilities rather than assets. It was a style in which a company's success was in opposition to workers' welfare rather than dependent on it.

Selling the Semi-Permanent Employee

Perhaps because the temp industry's model of work clashed so unambiguously with prevailing views of workers, temp leaders of the 1960s and 1970s expended substantial money and effort trying to sell it. The challenge they faced was actually quite similar to the one they met in the 1950s, when they had to legitimize the industry in the face of opposition from unions and social activists. This time, the potential for outright resistance to the industry was much lower, but the stakes were just as high.[59]

Selling the semi-permanent model of work was a major undertaking. It was a lengthy campaign that carefully and strategically introduced new concepts that built on each other over time. First, industry executives successfully styled themselves as "experts" in the field of personnel management. Then, banking on their self-proclaimed expertise, they sought to convince employers that ordinary management issues such as the ebb and flow of the business cycle were major profit-shrinking problems. Finally, temp leaders argued that temporary workers were the perfect solution to such problems, and they marketed four inventive ways for businesses to replace permanent employees with temps. The sections that follow examine each of these steps in turn.

"Every smart businessman is wrong": Experts in Personnel Management

The first step in selling the semi-permanent model of work was to establish the temp industry's expertise—and business owners' incompetence—in the realm of personnel management. This theme was nearly ubiquitous in temp industry advertisements in the late 1960s and 1970s. Instead of featuring pictures of temps, industry ads more often featured temp agency "expert" managers, who were said to be "highly trained" in personnel management.[60] Alternatively, they portrayed befuddled business managers saddled with rising costs and declining profits, clearly in need of some expert advice.[61] Many temp advertisements eschewed pictures altogether in favor of lengthy text describing the industry's expertise in dealing with "complicated workforce problems."[62]

Consider a typical advertisement from Olsten, which introduced business owners to one of the company's "pro" managers. Featuring a man holding a body-sized pair of scissors, the text read: "Meet Tom Chalmers . . . Olsten's Cost-Cutting 'Pro.' When it comes to temporary personnel problems, his *free* advice and guidance can save you thousands of dollars. He's a 'pro'—intensively trained like all Olsten's managers to act as your permanent personnel consultant."[63]

A few years later, Olsten took a different tack on the same theme, with a number of advertisements portraying business owners in distress. One such ad depicted a businessman wearing only a barrel, presumably having lost the shirt off his back. He held a large graph that showed increasing profits—and increasing costs. "A Successful Year Could Ruin You," the headline warned. "All those nice, fat orders are flowing in and business couldn't be rosier. Right? But a few more people on the payroll means more bookkeeping cost, fringe benefits, insurance, pension fund, major medical, hospitalization, overtime and—oops. There goes your beautiful year right down the drain. It's time to act with resolution and vigor. Come to Olsten."[64] Olsten asserted that employers needed to be careful even when things seemed to be going well—and Olsten was the authority on the matter. "Such good thinking," the ad declared, "has made Olsten one of the fastest growing, most trusted services in America."[65]

Industry leaders went to great lengths to establish their "expertise" in workforce management. In addition to publishing many similar advertisements in both popular magazines and trade journals, temp executives distributed brochures, led seminars, and even offered on-site consultations to "educate" employers on the best ways to cut costs and boost profits.[66] For example, in virtually every advertisement Olsten offered business managers a "free money-saving booklet" that promised to explain "how to save as much as 28% in 'hidden personnel costs' by using Olsten Temporaries." Meanwhile, Manpower and Staff Builders distributed nearly identical "cost-saving" brochures, and both AGS and Dot Temporaries sent their business clients free slide rules that would calculate the "hidden costs" of permanent employees.[67]

Several temp agencies took an even more proactive approach to selling their "expertise" by conducting how-to seminars for personnel managers. For instance, in the early 1970s, Office Overload led a series of "Clerical Cost Control Seminars" that were said to address "setting workplace standards, determining areas of overstaffing or understaffing, measuring clerical output, and finally balancing the workforce with an eye to the economic use of temporary personnel."[68] Office Overload was not alone. In fact, Manpower had three full-time lecturers on staff who regularly gave seminars to business owners on "management methods." These personnel consultants were reportedly quite successful. According to a 1972 article in *Industry Week*, they were regularly booked months in advance.[69]

Temp leaders' most aggressive tactic to establish their "expertise" in personnel management was on-site consultations. Industry ads frequently offered to send a "team of specialists" that would visit any business, free of charge, and "analyze" its personnel needs.[70] Staff Builders made such an offer in a 1971 advertisement in the *Personnel Journal*:

> If you think your business isn't running at maximum efficiency, we have a personnel expert who'll help you analyze your various departments—Free! (Maybe you don't need a full staff at all times). . . . Would you like to find out how to reduce your spiraling unemployment insurance and workmen's comp rates? That, too, is part of Staff Builders' personal attention policy, and again, Free![71]

Olsten, "A Successful Year Could Ruin You," 1968 Source: *Personnel Journal,*
September 1968, inside front cover

The message that temp executives were the experts in managing workers—not business owners—was clearly conveyed in a series of advertisements from AGS with the headline "He asked for a steno and we said no." As the text went on to explain, "We told him he really needed a clerk, and he saw the point right away. He saved the difference ($8.75 per day) and that made the point even clearer."[72] Likewise, a 1970 series of advertisements from Manpower proclaimed in large, bold print: "Every smart businessman knows: when the crunch is on, you cut back on temporary help. Every smart businessman is wrong." Manpower told business managers to "try thinking of temporary help as a way to help you cut costs and protect profits. That's what *The Manpower Idea* is all about . . . a whole new concept in staffing alternatives designed to reduce costs and maximize profits."[73]

Temp leaders' efforts to be seen as experts in personnel management were quite successful. Over the course of the 1970s, temp executives were called on nine times to testify in congressional hearings on topics as diverse as equal opportunity, retirement, and policies affecting middle-aged women.[74] Manpower in particular came to be seen as a leading authority in business management. In addition to giving expert witness at a 1970 congressional hearing on the impact of franchising on small businesses, Manpower executives launched an entirely separate division of their company—called Franchisepower—dedicated to offering businesses their expertise on expansion through franchising.[75] And, perhaps most importantly, Manpower began conducting quarterly employment surveys, the results of which were cited in newspapers across the country.[76] Thus, by the end of the decade, Manpower and other temp leaders had positioned themselves as experts on a remarkably diverse array of management issues, from women re-entering the workforce to alternatives to retirement, and from the franchising business model to national employment trends.

The "Dangers of Overstaffing": The Problem and Its Solution

Having established themselves as management experts, temp leaders sought to convince business owners that the ebb and flow of the business cycle was a "dangerous problem."[77] Temp executives maintained that when business was flowing, employers had to pay for overtime or hire new workers to get everything done; and when business was down, there were too many workers with too little to do. Temp leaders declared that this was a "problem of overstaffing," and they repeatedly advised managers that it could ruin their business, even in good economic times.

For example, in a 1969 advertisement, Olsten warned business owners: "If you're staffed to handle business at its busiest, (you're overstaffed.) . . . What are some of your people doing when business is not all that busy? Draining away profits in salaries, benefits, overhead. Better keep your permanent staff small and call in capable, experienced Olsten Temporaries."[78] In another of the many similar advertisements on this theme, Olsten cautioned business managers in oversized print: "You May Have a Severe Swelling of the Payroll." Depicting an ill man with a thermometer in his mouth and a towel wrapped around his head, the ad read:

> A very painful condition, this.
>
> As you add new people to your staff things get worse. Up go your fringe benefit costs, bookkeeping costs, overtime costs. Down go your profits.
>
> That's when it really hurts. After all, new people are supposed to help add to profits, not reduce them. So what should you do? . . .
>
> . . . Come to Olsten Temporary Services. . . .
>
> We'll take care of the payroll and fringe benefit nonsense.
>
> That makes us practically painless.
>
> Businessmen. Take the cure. Call Olsten.[79]

The theme of worker-induced profit loss was evocatively captured in a series of advertisements from Uniforce Temporaries, a New York City temp agency. Depicting three workers chatting around a water cooler, the headline of the 1970 advertisement read: "They're Drinking Up the Profits."

> They're not thirsty. They're bored. Not enough to do. Those sounds you hear are profits gurgling down the drain in salaries, overhead and all those extra payroll expenses and employee benefits. That's

what happens when you're staffed up to handle peak volume business. Modern management stops the profit drain with UNIFORCE guaranteed temporaries. Creatively used to augment a permanent nucleus in peak periods. It's the one way to make sure you have all the people you need only when you need them. The result: greater efficiency and greater economy. And we'll all drink to that![80]

Similar to the ad featuring the businessman who had lost the shirt off his back during a successful year, these ads warned businesses that permanent employees were little more than profit-busting liabilities—even in good times. Industry leaders thus constructed a zero-sum equation between workers and a company's success: More workers meant fewer profits.

Kelly Services promised to make "costly overstaffing a thing of the past." In a 1969 advertisement with the headline "Here we are in the computer age . . . and office staffing is still in the gaslight era," Kelly urged business owners to use temps to avoid "unproductive work hours":

Businesses are investing in sophisticated office machines that save time and money. And losing it on outdated personnel practices. After all, a permanent office staff (like an expensive office machine) has to have work to do in order to give you a fair return on your payroll investment. But most offices have a fluctuating work load. It results in paying full-time wages for part-time work on slow days. Unavoidable overhead? Not anymore. Today, there's a new plus-service from the Kelly Girl temporary help people. It's the first practical way to match your work force to your work load. With no unproductive work hours. You use Kelly Girl temporary services to supplement your basic staff. That way, you can make your staff as large or as small as necessary. . . . This is the year when you can make costly overstaffing a thing of the past.[81]

Kelly and other temp leaders argued that workers were like expensive office machines: They needed to be fully productive in order to justify their expense. Yet permanent workers could not be productive at all times—business slowed, and workers got sick or went on vacation.

Olsten, "You May Have a Severe Swelling of the Payroll," 1968
Source: *Personnel Journal,* October 1968, p. 693

Industry leaders proclaimed that such unproductive time used to be considered an "unavoidable expense"—but not anymore. Temporary workers would allay the "dangers of overstaffing."[82] Toward this end, temp executives developed and aggressively marketed four new strategies for using temps. Underlying each strategy was a single goal: Replace permanent employees with temps.

The first strategy was called "downstaffing." Temp leaders argued that business owners should reduce staff levels to a minimum ("skeleton staff") and fill formerly permanent positions with temps.[83] This advice was often implicit in industry publications that relentlessly warned against making a "premature commitment" to permanent employees.[84] Yet many temp leaders also explicitly encouraged businesses to replace permanent workers with temps.[85] For instance, in a 1971 series of advertisements with the headline "How will we ever replace Judy?" Kelly responded, "Maybe you shouldn't. . . . Now's your chance to conquer rising costs . . . to save most of Judy's pay plus *all* her fringe benefits. Simply divide her work. Between your employees—and a twice-weekly Kelly Girl temporary. (Divide and conquer!) . . . Temporary slowdown? Out she goes. No pink slip. No red tape. Or red eyes. When things look up, call us."[86] Michael Notaro, president of the temp agency Task Force, offered similar advice: "Don't be too quick to fill a position when a vacancy occurs," he told business executives in a 1971 article in the *Personnel Journal.* "What may seem to be a full time job can be filled by someone working only three days a week while your company pockets the 40% savings."[87] Likewise, a 1971 advertisement from Manpower advised, "It just doesn't pay to fill certain jobs with permanent personnel. . . . The next time an employee leaves, save yourself the cost of a replacement."[88]

Downstaffing was recommended not only for downturns in the business cycle. Temp leaders argued that it was a good idea during boom times as well. As Western Services told businesses in a 1971 ad, "You've trimmed the fat. Now, *stay* streamlined. . . . There's no need to fatten up your staff when things start to pick up again. Instead, use temporary help."[89]

Such appeals could be quite successful. According to the trade journal *Industry Week*, in the early 1970s Manpower successfully convinced one insurance company that all of its departments were "overstaffed."

Manpower advised the company to trim its workforce to the lowest possible level and use temps to cover its ten busy days every month instead of staffing for the "rush period." The company did so, and Manpower's Elmer Winter boasted that it saved $400,000 in the first year the plan was implemented.[90] Several years later, Manpower successfully sold this strategy to a West Coast company that produced health care products. As a top Manpower executive told *The Office* in 1976, the health care products company was in a bind because demand for its products had grown but the availability of raw materials was unpredictable. Manpower advised the company to rely entirely on temps instead of hiring a permanent workforce (which would put them at risk of having too many or too few employees). Company leaders agreed to do so, and Manpower was soon sending between five and seventy-five temps, along with supervisors, for several shifts every day.[91]

Perhaps the best example of the industry's success in selling downstaffing came a few years later with Motorola. By the start of the 1980s, Motorola had fully embraced downstaffing as a management strategy: It employed a small core of permanent employees that was heavily supplemented by temps. When the severe recession of 1981 hit, the strategy paid off. While other large companies faced public indignation for mass layoffs, Motorola preserved its well-publicized "no layoff" policy—and its reputation—simply by dropping three hundred temporary workers, a move that got almost no media attention.[92]

The second strategy that industry leaders sold was called "permanent temporaries," which involved using temps on a permanent basis. In fact, as early as 1962, Kelly had urged personnel managers to "get the Kelly Girl habit . . . put temporary help on permanent call."[93] Within a few years, Kelly had devised a catchy slogan for the permanent use of temps: "the right P.T.M. (Permanent-Temporary Mix)"—that is, the optimal ratio of permanent workers to temporary workers in an organization.[94] By the end of the decade, Kelly and other industry executives frequently counseled businesses to move beyond what they called the "original 'fire engine' concept" of temps: using temps as stop-gap, short-term replacements for permanent workers. Instead, they advised companies to use temps on a long-term basis.[95] In a 1968 advertisement in *Nation's Business*, Olsten executives declared the idea that temps are needed only at desperate times to be "the most dangerous myth of all." They therefore advised business readers to "use Olsten temporaries regularly and you can cope with any situation. . . . That's why so many companies are joining the Olsten Revolution."[96]

Temp leaders had remarkable success selling "permanent temporaries." As early as the 1960s, in fact, some business owners had already begun to use what industry observers today would call "permatemps." For example, as reported in the *Wall Street Journal* in 1963, the American Motors Corporation had replaced five full-time employees with five permanent temps. As a result, the journalist boasted, the car company saved eighty hours a week in wages.[97] A decade later, Shell Canada was using five to seven temps every day on a permanent basis simply to open envelopes. "You can't hire people to do that full-time," explained a company representative.[98]

The third staffing "solution" that industry leaders sold involved more than simply hiring greater numbers of temps. It called for turning permanent employees into temps—a move that industry leaders called the "transfer of personnel" or "payrolling."[99] An industry executive explained to readers of the *Management Review* in 1974 that workers would "go to work exactly as if they were company employees. But there is one very important difference: They are employed by a temporary-help service rather than being put on the company's own payroll."[100] The strategy was perhaps most succinctly described in an early 1970s series of advertisements from Western Services: "Just say goodbye . . . then shift them to our payroll and say hello again!"[101]

Industry leaders had begun promoting payrolling as early as the mid-1960s. In 1965, Robert Miller, president of Employers Overload, described it as a strategy with great potential for both business owners and temp industry leaders, but one that as yet had been "literally untouched."[102] By the mid-1970s, industry executives were marketing the strategy widely. They argued in countless advertisements and articles that turning permanent employees into temps had several key advantages: "The employees do not affect the unemployment insurance rate if they have to be terminated, they do not add to the cost of fringe benefits or payroll maintenance, and they are outside the company's normal policy requirements for personnel."[103] A 1977 article in *Administrative Management* was even more forthright in describing the benefits of this strategy: " 'Payrolling' is . . . used whenever a firm wants to avoid the ever-increasing expenses of hiring a permanent employee."[104]

In the 1970s, W. Robert Stover, president of Western Services, was the leading proponent of this particularly imaginative strategy. Time after time, in both business journals and advertisements, Stover promoted payrolling as a way to cut permanent workers and replace them with temps. Stover argued, for example, that payrolling was especially useful when applied to new hires. By putting new employees on a temp agency's payroll, he claimed, businesses would easily be able to undo a "hiring mistake."[105] Those employees who sufficiently "demonstrated their value," Stover maintained, could eventually become permanent employees and get a "psychological lift" in the process.[106] This was the theme of a 1971 series of advertisements from Stover's company, then known as Western Girl. "*Don't* hire a loser!" the headline commanded. "Instead put your prospective employees on Western Girl Inc.'s payroll for the probationary period. Let them prove themselves. *Then* transfer them to your company payroll."[107]

But payrolling was not intended to be used only for new hires. It was also said to be an "excellent approach" for long-term employees, including those who had been laid off. By bringing "a company's laid-off employees back on the payroll of a temporary personnel service," argued Staff Builders in a 1975 article in *The Office*, "the employer is helping re-employ his older workers, is reducing his unemployment rolls, yet is not increasing his fixed labor costs as quickly, or creating further unemployment liabilities in the event he must make further layoffs."[108] In other words, payrolling would allow an employer to have all the benefits of a permanent workforce—including company-specific experience and expertise—without any of the costs.

Industry leaders argued that payrolling, like the other staffing strategies, was profitable in boom times as well as during economic downturns. Manpower's Elmer Winter advised that during recessions, business owners should use payrolling to avoid the "burdensome employer obligations and hidden costs" of permanent employees.[109] And "when business is expanding," said Western's W. Robert Stover, "the same approach can be used . . . before a permanent commitment is made to increase the regular staff."[110]

The fourth strategy that industry leaders sold was similar to payrolling in that it involved turning permanent workers into temps. However, this strategy called for outsourcing entire departments to the temp industry. Temp leaders argued that outsourcing, variously called "contract staffing" and "facilities management," would let business managers avoid the "headache" of employer responsibilities and give them "undreamed-of flexibility to help cope with any business condition."[111]

Manpower called the strategy "contract staffing." According to company leaders, it was "the ultimate staffing service": "a full-time work force employed, supervised and administered by us, for you, wherever, whenever, and for as long as it's needed."[112] Manpower's extensive description of this outsourcing strategy—published repeatedly in a widely distributed series of advertisements in the mid-1970s—is worth quoting at length:

> Manpower is . . . solving today's more complicated and expensive staffing problems through contract staffing. We'll employ full-time workers for you . . . for any length of time . . . for any task that needs doing. We'll help you plan, set goals, define objectives, and set specifications. Then we'll hire, train, and supervise the staff you need to meet your goals. And we'll handle the administrative details to keep the business flowing. What's most interesting about Manpower contract staffing is that you're free of the paperwork, administrative costs, hiring problems, and all the management burden for a whole staff . . . from one crew to a staff of thousands. That's Manpower today, a total staffing and management resource that can be more help to you in more ways than you may have thought. Call us. Let's talk about how we can be of the most help in solving your staffing problems.[113]

The advertisement incorporates themes that reverberated throughout temp industry publications of the time period: The temp agency was the management expert, workers were an expensive burden, and the employer's sole goal was profit. Contracting out entire business functions reified each of these assertions. Manpower would take over every aspect of staffing, from planning production to hiring and managing thousands of workers, all of which—according to the temp "experts"—were profit-draining burdens.

These themes were captured perfectly in an early 1970s series of advertisements from Olsten, which also promoted the imaginative (and rather extreme) strategy of outsourcing. "Forget the rules," the headline read. "We'll help you build profits. Not overhead."

> 1971 is the year to discard a lot of notions about running your business. Costs are up. New business is tough to get. Certainly profits have been hard to come by. Olsten Temporary Services can help you make '71 look a lot better in the profit department. If you're already using temporary help, you know how they can save you money . . . and headaches. . . . It's time to take the next logical step. *Multiply* your savings. Not just a secretary to two from Olsten. Or a file clerk. But a *whole* department of people to do your shipping, filing, computer work, assembly. Whatever you do, we do.[114]

As these advertisements reveal, industry leaders asserted that any kind of worker could become a temp. And the responsibility for workers—those costly "headaches"—should be borne by the temp industry, not employers.[115]

In the 1970s, temp industry leaders encountered some success in selling outsourcing to businesses. The best example was Manpower's creation of the Manpower Petroleum Division in 1975. According to company executives, its purpose was to operate gas stations for petroleum companies across the country. *Business Week* reported that within the first year, Manpower was staffing and supervising seven hundred different gas stations, earning more than $2 million a month in profit in this division alone. Manpower president Mitchell Fromstein declared that Manpower Petroleum was "only the first wedge in what will be a rapidly expanding market for permanent help supplied by companies like Manpower. . . . In the future," he added, "I think our industry will be handling jobs that traditionally went to full-time employees."[116] Although Fromstein's aspirations were, perhaps, never entirely realized, temp industry leaders continued to market their outsourcing strategy to business owners with gradual but evident success. In fact, by the 1990s, as shown in Chapter 4, several industry leaders—including Kelly, Olsten, and Western—had established outsourcing divisions dedicated to taking over entire departments for businesses—workers, supervisors, and all.

By the end of the twentieth century, these four temp industry strategies—downstaffing, permatemps, payrolling, and outsourcing—had become common, legitimate uses of temps in the business world. Indeed, it was these kinds of practices that helped make the temp industry the poster child for the "leaner and meaner" business model at the time. And yet they were not recent innovations; industry leaders had been marketing them since the 1960s.[117] As industry executive Samuel Sacco wrote in *Office Systems* in 1993, "Office managers, human-resource managers, and small-business owners didn't just wake up one morning and decide they wanted to use temporary employees in new and different ways."[118] He was right. Business owners did not just wake up one morning and realize that they wanted to outsource the mailroom to Manpower or put their permanent employees on Kelly's payroll. But while Sacco attributed the expanding use of temps to "competitive pressures," it was in fact the temp industry's long-term, aggressive marketing campaigns that led employers to replace permanent workers with temps.

Conclusion

The underlying philosophy of each of the four strategies was the same: Permanent employees were a costly and unnecessary burden that could be easily remedied with temps. Boiled down to its essence, the philosophy was a revival of a liability model of work that hearkened back to the Gilded Age of the nineteenth century. Yet the business world of the 1960s and 1970s was dominated by a very different approach to workforce management that was far removed from the Gilded Age. And although prevailing theories of personnel management of the 1970s did not embrace the union-based asset model, which actually included worker welfare in the definition of a company's success, they did agree on one thing: Workers were key assets to a company, and the best way to boost productivity and profits was to take care of workers. But in the temp industry's model of work, the employer–employee relationship—considered vital to a company's success by both the Human Relations and Administrative schools of personnel thought—became irrelevant. The lower cost of temps prevailed over the skills, loyalty, and stability of permanent employees.

The temp industry's hard-driving and successful campaign to spread its ideas was not contained to a small sector of the economy, the way it had been in the 1950s when it advertised temp work as a way for housewives to earn pin money. By the 1960s and 1970s, temp agencies were openly recruiting men and selling temp work in a variety of male "breadwinning" jobs. In spreading this fractured employment relationship to the primary sector of the economy, temp industry leaders heralded a fundamentally new understanding of the role of personnel management in business; it was one that pit profit margins against worker welfare rather than recognizing the two as interrelated. This understanding would become a guiding principle for a new generation of business leaders in the 1980s.

3 | THE TRANSFORMATION OF WORK

In 1981, Jack Welch took over as CEO of General Electric (GE) and became an instant icon—the ringleader of a new generation of "leaner and meaner" corporate executives. Within just five years, Welch cut 120,000 employees, one-quarter of GE's workforce. "What made Welch's reductions notable," observed biographer Thomas O'Boyle, "was that his actions had been taken not to curtail losses but to enhance profitability."[1] The business world responded to Welch with awe and perhaps a little fear. In 1982, *Newsweek* dubbed him "Neutron Jack" (he destroyed people but left buildings standing), and in 1984 *Fortune* magazine named him the "toughest boss in America."[2] By the end of the decade, the trepidation Welch roused in people had turned into admiration. In 1989, *Fortune* called Welch "manager of the century," and a few years later *Business Week* described him as "the gold standard by which other CEOs are measured."[3]

Both cutting edge and cutthroat, Welch was a unique character. His management style, however, was hardly unique. By the end of the 1980s, it had become the normal way to do business. Other executives followed in his footsteps, including "Chainsaw" Al Dunlap, whom *Newsweek* called "America's most notorious employee killer."[4] Business leaders were not the only ones embracing a cutthroat approach. Throughout President

Ronald Reagan's administration, government officials championed the need to cut employees in the name of greater efficiency and less bureaucracy.[5] In 1984, even the National Labor Relations Board (NLRB) advocated the new conventional wisdom. "Everybody likes to make a good wage," the chairman of the NLRB told the *New York Times*, "but if your wage and benefit package is one that makes your employer go under, that's part of the picture, too."[6]

Jack Welch, Al Dunlap, and the National Labor Relations Board could say what they said—and do what they did—because of a broad change in American culture, a transformation they not only helped create but also benefited from. By the mid-1980s, the cultural battle between the asset model and the liability model of work had, for the most part, been won. Workers were generally considered profit-limiting liabilities rather than the profit-boosting assets that management gurus such as Robert Townsend had championed just a few years earlier.

Mainstream journalists represented the newly dominant liability model of work as fresh and innovative, and Jack Welch and his peers were hailed as iconoclastic heroes.[7] But the understanding of workers as liabilities was hardly new, although it was being reconstructed in novel terms. Even in the postwar heyday of the asset model, there were plenty in the business world who championed the idea of workers as costly burdens. And one of the loudest and most persistent of these voices was the temp industry's. It was not the only force working to revitalize the notion of workers as liabilities, however; the temp industry cannot be credited with causing such a broad social transformation single-handedly. But, as illustrated in Chapter 2, temp leaders played a key role in revitalizing the liability model of work and delivering it in an easy-to-use package to thousands of businesses throughout the 1970s.

If the temp industry helped to promote and circulate the liability model of work, it also stood to gain from that model's success. Notions of workers as "fat" to be "trimmed" by aggressive management helped the industry flourish in the 1980s. The number of temps rose dramatically, and the industry expanded into virtually every sector of the economy. Its reach was so pervasive, in fact, that it became an economic institution in itself, carefully watched by economists gauging broader economic trends and used extensively in both the private and public sector. As temp executive Robert Half proclaimed at the end of the decade,

"We are in the midst of what might be called 'the age of the temporary worker.'"[8]

By the 1980s, the temp industry no longer faced a skeptical audience that needed to be convinced of the benefits of the liability model of work. Employers, the government, and even many workers seemed to have accepted it as common sense, thanks at least in part to the industry's campaigns. Such success meant important changes for the temp industry. For the first time since the industry's founding, temp executives did not need to engage in a cultural battle to defend and justify the temp industry's existence. Gone was the 1950s need to legitimate temping through Kelly Girl campaigns; gone too was the 1970s need to justify the industry's expansion into primary sector work. By the 1980s, the vast majority of companies already used temps, and not just every once in a while. As the U.S. Department of Labor's Women's Bureau reported in 1988, "Today a company that lacks a built-in budgetary line item for temporaries may be the exception rather than the rule."[9]

The 1980s thus marked a turning point in the temp story. Temp industry marketing campaigns, which had played such an important role in cultural battles over work from the 1950s to the 1970s, became much more muted. Instead of seeking to convince employers to think of work and workers in a new way, temp ads of the 1980s generally sought to gain market share: Manpower executives wanted employers to choose them over Kelly Services, Kelly leaders wanted employers to use them rather than Olsten, and so on.[10] The real story of the 1980s lay elsewhere—in what the temp industry did with its success. Industry leaders leveraged their cultural triumph into even greater growth for themselves and their model of work. Temp executives were key creators, and key beneficiaries, of the newly dominant liability model, and they aggressively explored every way to maximize and institutionalize its dominance. In doing so, they helped transform the experience of work not only for temps but for all workers in America.

Understanding the transformation of work requires widening the narrative lens. Pulling focus away from temp industry publications and advertisements, we now turn to the broader story of workplace change and conflict, analyzing how temping became institutionalized in the American economy. The story unfolds along three axes. The first is temp industry expansion in the 1980s: The industry not only tripled in size but also began taking on a structural role in the United States labor market. Second is the institutionalization of temp work: The industry played a surprisingly important role in the wave of corporate restructuring that swept the business world of the 1980s. Last is the introduction of temporary work into two long-standing holdouts of the asset model: the unionized sector and the U.S. civil service.

The changes introduced by the temp industry during this time period were dramatic and, in some cases, even shocking. Temp leaders helped pioneer and institutionalize some of the most controversial elements of the new economic order. But it is important to note, again, that the temp industry was not alone among proponents of the new liability model, and despite its strategic importance and explosive growth, the industry was hardly a dominant economic player. In fact, by the end of the 1980s, it accounted for just 1 percent of U.S. employment.[11] Yet this 1 percent should not be dismissed: It represented an enormous number of employees—far more than most other industries. Temping was no bit player. Moreover, the temp industry had a ripple effect on many workers beyond the relatively limited circle of actual temps. Recall that corporate executives had learned to lay off workers—in some cases, thousands at a time—and replace them with temps; some even forced their permanent employees to become temps. Such actions helped create a climate of insecurity even for those workers who did not lose their jobs. Even more important, perhaps, is the fact that employers started using temporary workers as new and powerful weapons against labor unions. As employers increasingly used temps to replace permanent employees during labor disputes, the bargaining position of all unions was weakened, not only those whose strikes were broken by temps.

In the 1980s, the temp industry's model of work thus became a powerful cultural story about what *could be* for American workers. The industry's campaigns helped redefine common sense about work for everyone, not just for temps. Even if employers did not adopt all of the temp industry's aggressive strategies, the temp model was available to them—and workers knew it. Just as the cultural strength of the asset model had real consequences for workers in the postwar era, the cultural strength of the liability model had real consequences for workers in the 1980s, not only in terms of increased job loss and lower wages for some workers but also in heightened fear and anxiety for many more.[12] The temp industry was actively and aggressively helping to bring about the rise of the new liability model, even as its leaders maintained they were simply passive beneficiaries of economic change.

"The Age of the Temporary Worker": Expansion of the Temp Industry in the 1980s

In 1981, the United States entered a severe recession, and by the end of 1982 national unemployment levels had reached 10.8 percent, the highest since the Great Depression.[13] But even as the national economy slumped during the two-year downturn, the temp industry grew—as much as 9 percent a year. "This counter-cyclical growth," observed labor market scholars Nik Theodore and Jamie Peck, "suggested that the temp sector had come to perform more than simply a 'shock absorber' function and instead was beginning to establish an *ongoing* role within a restructuring economy."[14] Hiring temps was no longer just a way for employers to weather the business cycle, dumping temps when the economy took a nosedive and hiring them back when it recovered. The temp industry was already a well-established economic sector and an increasingly popular tool for implementing the newly revived liability model of work.

When the recession ended, the temp industry's growth only intensified. In the first year of economic recovery, national employment grew less than 1 percent; temp employment spiked 17.5 percent.[15] In fact, at the time, it was the fastest-growing industry in America.[16] For the remainder of the decade, temp industry employment grew, on average, a remarkable 15 percent a year.[17] As a result, during the 1980s, the size of the temp industry nearly tripled—from 400,000 workers a day at the start of the decade to more than one million workers a day by the end.[18]

Vast numbers of temp agencies, many too transitory to be counted, popped up across the country. In 1980, industry observers estimated that there were somewhere between twenty-five hundred and five thousand agencies in the United States; by the end of the decade, estimates ran from seven thousand to more than ten thousand.[19] Despite the growing number of agencies, the larger, better established agencies—Manpower, Kelly, and Olsten, along with newcomer Adia, a Swiss temp agency—continued to dominate the industry, controlling about 35 percent of the market at the end of the decade.[20] Throughout the 1980s, Manpower maintained its long-held position as industry leader, both in the United States and abroad. At the end of the decade, with 830 offices in the United States and 1,450 offices worldwide, Manpower employed more than 550,000 workers annually and banked $3 billion in sales.[21]

Yet the influence of the temp industry as a whole far outreached even Manpower's impressive numbers, in part because temp workers were distributed widely among many businesses. Manpower alone provided temps to some 300,000 different employers every year.[22] According to a 1980 survey conducted by the business magazine *The Office*, 86.4 percent of companies used temps.[23] By 1986, 100 percent of companies surveyed used temps, although by the end of the decade that number dropped to a perhaps more realistic (but still astounding) 90 percent.[24] Not only were more companies using temps; they were using them more often. In 1980, just over 5 percent of *The Office* survey respondents employed temps "continually," either by retaining some temporary workers on a long-term basis or by continuously using a variety of temps in certain jobs.[25] By 1988, however, 13 percent of companies said they hired temps continually—an increase of 160 percent.[26] In just eight years, the continual use of temp workers had skyrocketed from one out of twenty companies to one out of eight.[27] Not surprisingly, the length of temps' assignments also increased dramatically.[28] At the start of the decade, the average temporary job lasted just one week; by 1990, it had more than doubled in length—and many lasted much longer.[29] In 1984, the senior vice president of Western Temporary Services told *Office Administration and Automation* that "long-term assignments are definitely the trend. In fact, most national contracts are now for a year. We used to have assignments that lasted only one week, but now, we are even starting to see two-year contracts."[30] In fact, at one New York temp agency, fully 80 percent of the temporary assignments were long-term positions, usually lasting a year or more.[31]

In the 1980s, the temp industry expanded across all sectors of the economy, reporting strong growth in all three of the major occupational categories—pink-, white-, and blue-collar.[32] In particular, industry leaders moved into the more lucrative white-collar sector, with its higher wages and potentially higher profits. The move was evident in the proliferation of new temp agencies that specialized in highly skilled professions such as law (The Lawsmiths), medicine (Locum Tenens), accounting

(Accountemps), and corporate business (Corporate Staff Inc.). Meanwhile, older temp agencies continued to diversify, creating divisions that specialized in a variety of white-collar occupations, particularly in health care. Norrell Temporary Services, for example, entered the medical field in 1981, and by the end of the decade medical staffing accounted for 25 percent of its business.[33] Olsten likewise expanded its already well-established health care division so aggressively that by the end of the 1980s it represented more than 30 percent of company sales.[34] Even with the push into white-collar jobs, however, the industry continued to derive most of its profits from its old standby—pink-collar work.[35]

Helping to justify the industry's multifarious expansion was a new public relations campaign casting temp work as highly skilled, family-sustaining employment. As in the postwar era, temps were described as "highly skilled professionals," "experts," and "specialists." Unlike the postwar era, however, industry ads often targeted highly skilled, traditionally male occupations. A 1981 advertisement from Dunhill Personnel Services, for example, sold engineers rather than "gal Fridays." Featuring a picture of Isaac Newton holding an apple (with a band-aid on his forehead), the ad asked: "Is he right for that job in engineering?"

> Searching for that unique talent to work in your engineering department is a matter of gravity. Make the right choice and your company's future may be assured. Make the wrong choice and it could be costly. Our research has shown that it may cost an employer as much as $15,000 or more to find one qualified $25,000 professional. . . . Would you settle for anyone but the best in that R&D or engineering slot? Would Sir Isaac have discovered gravity if he'd been hit on the head with a fig?[36]

Likewise, Accountemps marketed their temps as "slightly overqualified specialists." With the tagline "Rent an Expert," one of their advertisements read:

> Accountemps employees are specialists . . . Ask for a bookkeeper, and we'll send you a highly qualified one. Ask for several accountants, and you'll get the best for your purpose. Ask for six auditors, and you'll have thoroughly trained professionals. . . .

For a day, a week, a month or longer. Call any one of 80 offices in the United States, Canada and Great Britain. We'll have one or more slightly over-qualified specialists at your place of business—immediately.[37]

The arguments were not new, but openly pushing temporary work in high-wage, primary sector jobs was new indeed. Temp executives were no longer confined to a narrow corner of the secondary labor market by their murky reputation or fear of union antagonism. By the 1980s, the widespread resurgence of the liability model of work left industry leaders free to move across the economy, spreading employment norms once associated with women's work—secondary jobs not intended to support families—into the primary sector. According to some labor market scholars, most notably Leah Vosko, such expansion pointed to a more fundamental "feminization" of work in the American economy.[38] Even in the 1980s, industry observers noticed the transformation. As one expert told the *New York Times* in 1986, temp work (and contingent work more generally) was "reminiscent of women's work. Women have always had these kinds of jobs."[39]

The temp industry's campaign to expand into the white-collar sector presented an interesting dichotomy: On the one hand, industry leaders described temping as legitimate, family-sustaining employment; on the other hand, they portrayed temps as workers who wanted to be free of the typical constraints of regular jobs. In the first case, industry executives repeatedly claimed that temping was a legitimate "career."[40] "If you have always associated this industry with bored housewives, starving actors, or secretaries who pinch-hit while the regular employee is on vacation, you need to be reeducated," wrote the executives of Career Blazers in their 1988 book *The Temp Worker's Handbook: How to Make Temporary Employment Work for You.* "Today you will find temps who are highly skilled, many with college diplomas and advanced degrees. . . . For many, temporary employment offers permanent career satisfaction."[41] In the second case, however, industry leaders argued that many workers of the 1980s wanted emancipation from the nine-to-five regimen. They repeatedly described temps as "gypsies," "Lone Rangers," "freelancers," and "workplace nomads"—workers who craved the autonomy that temping offered.[42] Robert Half, founder of Robert Half International and Accountemps, told readers of *Management Accounting* that temping satisfied workers' desire for "a more entrepreneurial life."[43]

The portrait of a new generation of workers who "demanded" autonomy and flexibility—in contrast to previous generations who desired security and stability—was widely accepted by the popular media. Story after story in newspapers and magazines extolled the sovereignty of this new class of professional temps.[44] A 1987 *Forbes* article, for example, declared that these "Lone Rangers" preferred their "freelance" lifestyle:

> What about the freelancers themselves? Do they feel neglected, exploited, left out? Are they simply a new variation of Marx's army of unemployed labor, created by the capitalist bosses to keep wages down? Some may yearn for the security of a big company payroll, but most do not. An increasing number . . . prefer the flexibility and freedom of the freelance life. It makes them feel like the Lone Ranger, rather than just a cog in a machine.[45]

One of these happily emancipated temps appeared in *Newsweek* in 1988. He was a former marketing executive who had become a temp after losing his job at (Jack Welch's) General Electric. But he was "content with his gypsy life," the article observed: "As he puts it, [temping] gives you the flexibility to go to the Caribbean when you want."[46]

Although success stories dominated popular media coverage of professional temp work, there were occasional exceptions to the rule— white-collar temps who longed for the security (and paychecks) of permanent work. For instance, in 1987, *U.S. News and World Report* told the story of Frank Heary, who had been laid off from his $44,000-a-year job as an accountant. Two years later, he was earning just ten dollars an hour as a temporary accountant. "I'm delivering a Cadillac for a Volkswagen price," he lamented.[47] And in 1986, the Washington, DC–based Bureau of National Affairs publicized the story of Walter Marty, who had been laid off from his job at a small computer design firm in Silicon Valley. Unable to find permanent work in the depressed region, Marty had started temping at Apple Computer. "I would rather be permanent," he told the Bureau of National Affairs. "I don't see any flexibility as a temporary. There is no security, no insurance, no company benefits."[48]

Such stories reveal the somewhat ambivalent embrace of white-collar temping, but they highlight something else, too: the way temping had expanded across the economy, even into the narrowest "niche" markets such as accounting and software design. The temp industry even reached such exotic corners as the nuclear power industry. Temp agencies Dillin Nuclear Inc. and Atlantic Nuclear Services (affiliated with Manpower) specialized in providing nuclear plants with "jumpers"— temporary workers who would be exposed to high doses of radiation over short periods of time. Because workers' exposure to radiation was limited by federal regulations, nuclear plants regularly employed temps to do their high-exposure "dirty work." And it could be quite profitable for workers: Temps could earn fifty to seventy-five dollars a day, sometimes for just a few minutes of work. The *New York Times* interviewed one temporary jumper, who was also a part-time college student and part-time cab driver. "I don't want to jump anymore," he told the *Times*. "I've just got a feeling that maybe I had too much. I don't say I wouldn't work in a nuclear plant again, doing something else. I'm not scared of radiation. But I'd rather not jump again." He paused. "Unless I get really hard up for the money. They do make it lucrative."[49]

Ironically, the temp industry's reach was perhaps best illustrated by those businesses that *stopped* using temp industry services. By the 1980s, a number of large corporations had come to rely so heavily on temps that they decided to stop using outside temps and launch their own in-house temp services instead.[50] Georgia Pacific provides a perfect example. As reported in *Fortune* magazine, in the early 1980s Georgia Pacific was using temps from twenty different agencies to staff its high-turnover clerical department when CEO Pete Correll decided to end this "costly reliance" on outside temps. However, instead of reducing turnover by turning the clerical jobs into well-paying, permanent positions, Georgia Pacific embraced the temp industry's model and established its own in-house agency called Georgia Temp. Company executives told *Fortune* that, as a result, turnover among the company's clerical temps dropped from 40 percent to just 9 percent. The agency was so successful, in fact, that Georgia Temp managers began marketing their services to other companies in the Atlanta area. By the mid-1990s, Georgia Temp was providing 250 temporary workers a day to Georgia Pacific and another 250 temps to various companies around the city.[51]

Bank of America took a similar course. According to a report by the Bureau of National Affairs, in the mid-1980s the bank was relying on numerous temp agencies to deliver as many as eight hundred temps a month. But in 1985, company executives decided to end their "long-standing reliance" on outside temp agencies, asserting that they had become "more entrenched than they should be" in the bank's operations. Instead of eliminating (or even diminishing) its reliance on temp work, Bank of America internalized the temp industry's model and created its own pool of 250 temporary workers, called B and A temps. Bank executives told the Bureau of National Affairs that the venture was a great success: Not only did they save money; they also secured a steady pool of temporary workers who were more committed and productive than traditional temps.[52]

Thus, after investing very large sums of money, Georgia Pacific and Bank of America gained many of the benefits associated with full-time, permanent employees—low turnover, longevity, and even loyalty—without any of the commitments to workers that traditional employers assumed, such as health and pension benefits, payroll taxes, and unemployment taxes. By bringing the temp industry's model of work "in house," these cases revealed just how deeply the temp industry had become rooted in business practices in the 1980s.

"A Safeguard in These Unpredictable Times": The Institutionalization of Temp Work

As the examples of Georgia Pacific and Bank of America suggest, temp work had become entrenched in the American economy in the 1980s. But hiring temps was more than just the "normal" way to do business. The temp industry had become what sociologists call an economic institution, playing a key role in the inner workings of the economy. This can be seen in the way the industry was used in the wave of corporate restructuring that swept the business world in the 1980s. During this time, corporate executives such as Jack Welch were unapologetically laying off workers, cutting training programs, and outsourcing non-core departments—all in the name of greater flexibility in order to compete in the newly globalized economic environment. Welch and his followers very publicly proclaimed that American businesses needed to be "leaner and meaner." Yet lean and mean companies still needed workers, and they found those workers in temps.

The most direct role that the temp industry played in corporate restructuring was in implementing what the business world at the time called the "ring-and-core" approach: maintaining a small core of permanent employees surrounded by a wide ring of contingent workers that could be adjusted according to the business cycle.[53] Yet, as illustrated in Chapter 2, temp industry leaders had been marketing this management strategy since the late 1960s, advising businesses to keep only a "skeletal" core of permanent employees and use temps for the rest.[54] In the 1980s, temp executives adopted the ring-and-core rhetoric as their own, urging employers to create a two-tiered workforce using temps. In 1985, for example, Manpower president Mitchell Fromstein told the *New York Times* that "management [should] build a core work force that it can pay full benefits, and commit itself to without layoffs. Temporaries are the people who support that core."[55] Likewise, a typical advertisement from Kelly told businesses "How to Beat the Hire/Layoff Cycle": "Call Kelly Services. Your business seems to be beginning to pick up. For the first time in a long time, you're looking to hire. But you hesitate. Is now really the time to hire full-time? What if that 'growth' doesn't really materialize? Will today's hiring merely trigger layoffs tomorrow? Kelly Services can be a safeguard in these unpredictable times."[56]

Temp leaders argued that the ring-and-core strategy would not only boost profits; it would also protect permanent employees from the layoffs that had caused widespread fear and anxiety earlier in the decade. Thus, in an ironic twist, industry leaders were using asset model rhetoric to institutionalize their liability model of work. For example, in a 1984 advertisement, Kelly told readers of the *Personnel Administrator* that supplementing permanent employees with temps would "protect" both profits and "the people who make your company profitable."[57] Industry leaders maintained that permanent employees thus shielded from layoffs would be more productive because they would feel "more secure about their jobs."[58] Likewise, Norrell assured business owners that the ring-and-core strategy would increase productivity because permanent employees would feel less "stress" and "strain." Depicting two older men fishing, the headline of one Norrell advertisement read: "Since he started using Norrell, Alan Parker spends Saturdays fishing his favorite stream."

He used to worry about how the unexpected overtime and stress affected his staff. Turnover and absenteeism usually increased after particularly high volume weeks. But then he learned about a management tool from Norrell called Peak Period Staffing. Working with his Norrell branch manager, Alan developed a job description of what was expected during the high volume times. Norrell searched out the qualified employees and made sure they were trained to handle the job so they could immediately step into the situation. The result is that now Alan knows his permanent staff can be counted on for the routine work, and that when the unexpected workflow begins, qualified help from Norrell is a phone call away. The work is done faster, at less strain on his star employees—so he keeps them longer. And Alan is able to relax.[59]

It is important, however, not to overlook the fact that permanent workers were stressed, at least in part, because of the liability model that temp agencies such as Norrell and Kelly had worked so hard to sell. Embracing the notion of workers as liabilities, many companies had downsized dramatically. As a result, the remaining employees had to take on more work. What's more, when business increased, many companies quite literally did not have enough employees. The institutionalization of the liability model thus required greater reliance on temporary workers, reifying the strength of both the temp industry and its model of work.

Industry leaders' use of asset model rhetoric about "protecting" permanent workers was highly strategic: It was an effort to capitalize on employers' fear of public backlash against corporate layoffs. And, for a growing number of companies, it worked. Businesses such as Hewlett-Packard and Motorola were able to ride the considerable ebbs and flows of the high-tech economy without committing the large-scale layoffs for which many other companies—including Chrysler, General Motors, and General Electric—had been vilified earlier in the decade. How so? Simply by hiring and then "letting go" hundreds of temps at a time.[60]

Other major corporations followed their example. For instance, at Apple Computer, temps accounted for as much as 30 percent of the workforce in the mid-1980s.[61] In explaining this remarkably high percentage, a company executive echoed temp industry rhetoric: "We are basically trying to protect our full-time jobs," he told *Business Week* in 1985.[62] Perhaps the strategy worked, at least in terms of the company's reputation: When Apple faced a downturn the same year, the layoff of seventy-five permanent employees across three factories in Los Angeles made newspaper headlines. But there was only brief mention, buried deep in a *Los Angeles Times* article, that 850 temps had already been "trimmed" at just one of those factories.[63] Indeed, the role that temporary workers played in avoiding layoffs and saving Apple's reputation was no secret. In 1988, Apple's director of human resources told *Fortune* magazine:

> A layoff is devastating. This company never wants to have one again. It affects every single person in the organization. The people who remain feel guilty that they were the ones who stayed and anger at management for letting the layoff happen. Gaining the ability to avoid all that clearly outweighs the extra administrative cost and effort that's required to manage a temporary work force.[64]

Apple Computer, Motorola, and Hewlett-Packard were not alone in the 1980s. Major corporations, including IBM, Lockheed, USAir, and Ford, cut their permanent workforces and replaced them with temps.[65] And by the end of the decade, companies such as Xerox, Westinghouse, and General Electric were spending more than $20 million a year on temporary workers.[66] For these corporations and many others, the temp industry had become an essential tool for reorganizing production according to the newest employment paradigm—the updated liability model, articulated and sold by the temp industry and other advocates of the new economic order.

Beyond operationalizing corporate restructuring, the temp industry also built itself into an economic institution by becoming a leading purveyor of worker training. Not only were corporations of the 1980s lowering labor costs by cutting workers; they were also cutting training programs. Early in the decade, temp industry leaders took note and began offering free training programs to temps, particularly in the fast-changing field of office automation. Manpower was the first and arguably the most successful to do so. In 1982, with an initial investment of

$15 million, Manpower launched "Skillware," a self-paced, interactive training program that allowed its temps, free of charge, to gain skills in a variety of computer hardware and software systems. By the mid-1980s, Manpower had become a major training provider, not only for temps but for permanent workers as well.[67]

As beneficial as such training was—for workers in need of skills and employers in need of skilled workers—it also had significant downsides. The temp industry's promise of a ready supply of skilled workers enabled employers to cut both permanent employees and training programs even more. It thus sparked a self-reinforcing cycle: Businesses downsized their workforces and cut training; temp agencies developed state-of-the art training programs and offered free training to temps; then, with the expectation of getting skilled temps at no extra cost, businesses cut their workers (and training) even more; temp agencies ramped up their training programs to get more business; and employers relied ever more on temps. For some companies, in fact, it was training rather than price that convinced them to go with one temp agency over another. This was particularly true for Westinghouse, one of the companies spending more than $20 million a year on temps.[68]

In sum, in the 1980s the temp industry became a fixture of the new economy by helping companies implement a two-tiered workforce and by becoming a crucial provider of skills training. Temp leaders may not have invented the new liability model of work, but they went a long way toward implementing it for American employers. "Neutron Jack," the corporate icon of the time period, might also have been called "Temping Jack": His company spent some $20 million a year on temps. And while Jack Welch was clearly no temp industry puppet, he could not have done what he did without temps or, more importantly, without the temp industry's cultural influence in both modernizing and legitimizing the view of workers as costly liabilities.

The Temp Industry and Redoubts of the Asset Model in the 1980s

The temp industry had such success with its new liability model of work in the 1980s that it was even able to make inroads into two long-standing holdouts of the asset model: the unionized sector and the U.S.

civil service. These sectors of the economy had retained many of their founding asset model principles longer than most. While the liability model of work offered employers tremendous flexibility in acquiring and dismissing workers, in the unionized sector there were relatively strict rules about hiring and firing employees. And while the liability model emphasized the lack of obligation between employers and workers, the union system was anchored in the reciprocal, long-term commitment between the two. Worker longevity was also the basis of the civil service employment model. Founded in the nineteenth century, the U.S. civil service had been created to establish a large and stable federal workforce that would endure despite administration changes in the White House. Instead of rewarding workers for their political connections (the so-called spoils system), the civil service rewarded workers for their merit. Government workers were required to pass rigorous exams, and in return they got good wages and job security.

The fact that the asset model had survived in the unionized sector and in the U.S. civil service was a testament to the long-term efforts of labor unions and workers. Amid the economic and cultural conservatism of the 1980s, however, many forces pushed against these holdouts. The temp industry proved crucial in eventually cracking them open. This reveals another dimension of the temp industry's success in the 1980s and its role in spreading and implementing the liability model of work.

"The Beginning of a More Viable Management–Union Relationship": Temps and Labor Unions

In the 1980s, the temp industry helped rewrite the rules of engagement in the battle between labor and capital. In the first place, a ready supply of temps made it far easier for businesses to replace striking workers, and this quickly became a powerful new weapon against organized labor. In 1981, for example, Blue Shield in San Francisco hired temps to replace eleven hundred striking workers.[69] And in 1986, AT&T hired some six thousand temps to weather a twenty-six-day strike.[70] Such replacements had become common by the mid-1980s. As one union official told *Work-*

ing Woman in 1986, "Everywhere we have a picket line . . . temporary workers are brought in."[71]

In truth, the practice of replacing strikers had long been sanctioned by U.S. labor law. In a highly controversial decision, the U.S. Supreme Court ruled in 1938 that employers could hire striker replacement workers and did not have to discharge them when the strike came to an end. In essence, the decision known as the Mackay Doctrine allowed employers to hire permanent replacements for strikers. According to critics of the Mackay Doctrine, the ruling effectively allowed employers to fire striking workers. Employers rarely exercised this power before the 1970s, but they began to adopt the more aggressive response to strikes and, after President Ronald Reagan famously fired and replaced striking air traffic controllers in 1981, it became common practice.[72]

Temp agencies originally played only a minor role in this development. Until the mid-1980s, industry leaders had explicitly banned agencies from supplying temporary workers to break strikes; in fact, this had been a provision of the industry's code of ethics since the 1960s. Although there was ample evidence that the restriction was not always enforced (see, for example, the 1981 strike at Blue Shield mentioned earlier), temp industry executives at least outwardly maintained their respect for picket lines. But in 1985, the Federal Trade Commission (FTC) filed a formal complaint against the temp industry's ban on supplying striker replacements, calling it "an illegal restraint of trade."[73] In response, according to a report by the Federal Trade Commission, "the National Association of Temporary Services, Inc. (NATS) agreed to amend its code of ethics so that the code would *not* restrict its members from . . . providing services to firms involved in a strike or a lock-out."[74]

A year later, the use of temporary workers during labor disputes was further legitimized by the National Labor Relations Board (NLRB). In its 1986 *Harter Equipment* decision and in subsequent rulings upholding it, the NLRB found that "absent specific proof of antiunion motivation, an employer does not violate [the National Labor Relations Act] by hiring temporary replacements in order to engage in business operations during an otherwise lawful lockout," even if the lockout was not compelled by the threat of a strike.[75] In short, the NLRB ruled that employers could legally lock out their permanent employees and replace them with temps if bargaining was not going their way.

Support from the FTC and the NLRB made temporary workers a powerful weapon against organized labor in the 1980s. In the *Harter* case, for example, a New Jersey–based company and officials of Local 825 of the International Union of Operating Engineers began negotiations for a new contract in 1981. Company executives told the union that Harter was experiencing "grave financial difficulties," and, as a result, they "sought reductions in wages and changes in the union-security clause."[76] Union leaders rejected their proposals but offered to extend the current contract for six months so that negotiations could continue. Company executives would not allow the extension, nor would they permit employees to work without a contract. Instead, they locked out the workers and replaced them with temps. In a precedent-setting decision, the NLRB ruled in favor of the company. Arguing that the use of temps during a lockout had only a "comparatively slight" impact on employees' rights—the right to bargain collectively, to strike, and to engage in union activities—the NLRB ruled that the use of temps was a "legitimate employer weapon."[77]

Also in 1981, negotiations between Marquette Company, a cement manufacturer in Catskill, New York, and the company's clerical employees came to an impasse. As in the *Harter* case, Marquette locked out its workers and used temps from Kelly Services to maintain normal production levels until union leaders conceded to a more favorable contract. An administrative law judge initially ruled against the company, arguing that the "prolonged lockout with the use of replacements was inherently destructive of employee rights" and was "so inherently prejudicial . . . that no proof of antiunion motivation [was] necessary." But in 1987, the NLRB reversed this ruling. Citing the *Harter Equipment* case, the board found that the company's "use of temporary replacements was 'a measure reasonably adapted to the achievement of a legitimate employer interest.'"[78]

Other companies used temps even more aggressively. When workers started a union drive in 1984 at Middle Earth Graphics, a small printing firm in Kalamazoo, Michigan, company executives shifted nearly all of their workers to Manpower's payroll—essentially firing them and rehiring them as temps. If the workers refused sign up with the temp agency, they were fired; the most strident of the union organizers were fired outright. Manpower subsequently supplied the company with nineteen Middle Earth employees-turned-temps along with twelve newly recruited temp workers. Middle Earth's astonishing use of temps did not stop there, however. Six months later, when an unfair labor practices settlement required the company to reinstate the fired union organizers, Middle Earth executives transferred nine of their Manpower temps *back* to the company's payroll. According to the NLRB, the company was trying to "pack a prospective bargaining unit with employees of another employer (Manpower) to offset the return of union sympathizers." This time, the NLRB ruled against the company.[79]

Company executives at M.P.C. Plating in Cleveland, Ohio, employed a similar strategy. When M.P.C. workers started to organize a union in 1985, the company's president told them that they would be fired unless they signed up with a temp agency.[80] Only two of the workers agreed to become temps, however, and the company barred the rest of the employees from the workplace. The next day, the barred workers started a strike that lasted several months and ultimately cost most of them their jobs. Within a week, M.P.C. hired temps to replace the strikers and, a month later, hired permanent replacements. However, like the executives at Middle Earth, their use of temporary workers did not end there. Six months later, M.P.C. executives compelled their new "permanent" employees to sign up with the local temp agency; as before, they would be fired if they refused. As in the Middle Earth case, the NLRB ruled against the company and ordered M.P.C. to reinstitute a permanent workforce and bargain in good faith with the union.[81]

The above cases were only a few of the many in which companies used temporary workers to undermine unions in the 1980s.[82] Temps were employed to break up union-organizing drives, to put additional pressure on workers during lockouts, and to come through employee strikes unscathed. Indeed, by the end of the decade, these practices had become so widespread that at least one temp agency started specializing in strikebreakers. In 1989, Daniel Mordecai founded U.S. Nursing Corp., a temp agency dedicated to providing temps to hospitals whose employees were on strike.[83] As a consequence, strikes lost power as negotiating tools for labor unions. In fact, because of the ready availability of temps, strikes could even be a boon to employers. As management professors John Kohl and David Stephens explained in the *Personnel Journal* in 1986, employers no longer needed to make concessions in negotiations with unions. Instead, they could simply let workers go on strike—and then hire temps. "Rather than 'the end,'" Kohl and Stephens wrote, "a strike may actually be a beginning of a more viable management-union relationship."[84]

"A Simple Management Decision": Temps and the U.S. Civil Service

In the 1980s, the temp industry also made inroads into the other redoubt of the asset model of work, the U.S. civil service. In 1985, the Office of Personnel Management (OPM) took the first critical step by significantly expanding federal agencies' ability to hire temporary workers instead of qualified civil servants. Specifically, the new policy increased the maximum length of temporary appointments in government jobs from two to four years, and it allowed federal agencies to hire temps to fill much higher-level white-collar positions than before.[85] Although the policy involved direct-hire temporary workers—short-term workers hired directly by government officials—and not temps from private agencies such as Manpower and Kelly, it opened the door for federal agencies to hire significantly more temporary workers for civil service positions.[86] In fact, according to a 1988 report by the U.S. General Accounting Office, the new guidelines "encouraged agencies to use temporary employees in any situations they deemed appropriate."[87] Furthermore, as we will see, the policy laid the groundwork for government officials to authorize the use of private-sector temps a few years later.

A closer look at the 1985 policy suggests that, with the new guidelines, government officials were formally sanctioning the liability model of work. For instance, the language OPM officials used to justify having more temporary workers in the federal government was the very same rhetoric temp executives used in their own marketing campaigns: "Temporary employment is one extremely important element in a comprehensive staffing policy and one which is very cost efficient. This type of employment gives agencies flexibility to deal with workload peaks and at the same time can be used to protect the jobs of career employees who are serving in activities facing cutbacks."[88] The similarity to temp ads is remarkable. The main themes of the statement—the indispensability of temps in a "comprehensive staffing" plan, the need for cost efficiency along with flexibility, and the importance of protecting permanent employees—were virtually ubiquitous in temp industry advertisements of the time period.

As in the private sector, underlying this rhetoric was the desire to save money by hiring temps rather than permanent employees. An OPM internal memo, made public by the *New York Times* in 1985, described the incentive quite clearly: "Temporary employees have significantly fewer rights and benefits than career employees." For instance, the memo went on to explain, temps were not eligible for federal health benefits and could be dismissed at any time without government liability.[89] Although OPM officials were not quite so candid in their public statements, they did draw parallels between private and public sectors in justifying their decision. For instance, OPM director Donald Devine told the *Los Angeles Times* that the policy was a "simple management decision" to help government do what private industry had done using the temp industry.[90] "Recent trends in Federal agency staffing show a disturbing growth in full-time permanent employment at the expense of temporary, part-time and intermittent staffing," Devine told reporters in another *Los Angeles Times* article. "Automatically filling every position with a career-conditional employee makes little sense when operations are being cut back."[91]

However, although this "simple management decision" had become standard in the private sector, it was far from routine in the public sector. In fact, the U.S. civil service's decision to expand its number of temporary workers represented a radical break from its long-standing model of employment. This fact did not go unnoticed by government officials. Indeed, as reported by the *New York Times*, another confidential memo prepared for Devine admitted that the decision could be seen as "a reversal of longstanding policy."[92] Publicly, OPM used somewhat more tempered language, describing it as a "big change, a significant turnaround in this area of personnel policy."[93] The U.S. General Accounting Office agreed, calling the policy a "major revision" of the government's employment practices, and undertook several major studies to examine its consequences for civil service workers.[94] These investigations revealed that 25 percent of temporary appointments in federal jobs were improperly used to fill permanent positions; moreover, in some federal agencies up to 20 percent of temporary workers were "making a career" out of temp work, working continuously in one temporary appointment after another, year after year.[95]

To many observers in the business community, however, the decision to hire more temps was long overdue. Soon after the OPM issued the new policy, the editors of *The Office* published the following statement of support: "Federal government officials for years have been criticized for failing to conduct business more in line with practices used in private industry. By so doing, the government would spend less money and also increase productivity, critics have commonly claimed. Now, at long last, there are indications that Washington is beginning to pay heed."[96] However, *The Office* editors encouraged government officials to turn to the temp industry instead of recruiting temporary workers on their own. The editorial continued,

> At present, the government plans to hire temporaries through public notice. . . . A much more prudent step would be for officials to contact the National Association of Temporary Services in Alexandria, Virginia, and discuss hiring help through temporary employment services around the U.S. This way, the government could assure itself of enough manpower during heavy work periods, knowing that the temporary is of high quality and performs well in the office.[97]

Sam Sacco, executive director of the National Association of Temporary Services, agreed. "There are thousands of examples of how temporary help workers have aided private sector companies in their staffing needs," he declared. "But more pertinent to the federal government's decision to expand the use of temporaries, are the . . . cases where private sector temporary help companies have aided state and local governments with their staffing needs."[98]

In 1988, the OPM followed these suggestions by recommending that federal agencies be allowed to use private-sector temps. Using language remarkably similar to Sacco's, OPM director Constance Horner wrote:

> For decades, private companies have turned to temporary help firms for services in emergencies, illnesses, or other

interim circumstances when it was impractical to use their own employees. . . . State and local governments have successfully used temporary help firms without detriment to their civil service system. It appears the same services could be utilized by the Federal sector without compromising the civil service.[99]

A year later, OPM officials ruled that the federal government could use temps from private agencies such as Manpower and Kelly, just like "every other type of organization in the United states."[100] And several years later, as described in Chapter 4, OPM officials greatly expanded federal agencies' ability to use private-sector temps, successfully bringing the government's employment policies "more in line with practices used in private industry"—and the new liability model of work that was flourishing there.

Conclusion

The 1980s saw both a vast expansion of the temp industry and a fundamental transformation of its role in the American economy. Not only were more employers using greater numbers of temps; they were using them to change the very organization of work. In the process, many employers embraced the liability model of work that the temp industry had worked so hard to sell. This contributed in important ways to a broader transformation of the American economy—away from the postwar labor market that saw workers as assets, toward the liability model economy of corporate executives such as Jack Welch. Temp executives had long pushed for such a shift, claiming it was necessary to their business plan; and they were not wrong: The newly favorable climate helped the temp industry and its model of work make inroads into two of the last significant holdouts of the asset model—the unionized sector and the U.S. civil service. The temp industry's expansion into these sectors was neither swift nor complete, but by the end of the decade, both unions and the civil service had been weakened to the point that they no longer posed a viable challenge to the newly dominant liability model of work. The temp industry's triumph seemed nearly complete, and the "new economy" seemed to offer it nothing but even better days ahead.

4 | BOXING IN THE TEMP INDUSTRY

In the early 1990s, Manpower replaced General Motors as the largest employer in the United States, and the temp industry was one of the fastest-growing sectors of the economy.[1] By all accounts, the temp industry's liability model of work was poised to become the new norm. "Chainsaw" Al Dunlap and his aggressive management style—captured perfectly in the title of his best-selling book *Mean Business*—were widely acclaimed. Reports in the popular media announced the "temping of America" and the rise of the "disposable workforce."[2] Books such as *The Temp Track: Make One of the Hottest Job Trends of the 90s Work for You* offered workers "positive, practical advice on using temporary work to its fullest advantage."[3] Meanwhile, magazines such as *Temp Slave!* documented the travails of temporary workers with bitter humor, garnering a remarkably widespread following and even inspiring a musical comedy by the same name. And on the silver screen, movies such as *Clockwatchers* portrayed temps' mind-numbing alienation, and *The Temp* described one temporary worker's deadly plot for advancement ("Don't Get Mad, Get Promoted," ran the movie's tagline).

Yet, perhaps because of the remarkable ascendancy of the temp industry at the time, organized opposition against it began to emerge. Temps, community activists, union leaders, and political reformers launched their own battles against the industry in an effort to protect workers' interests by promoting permanent jobs and improving temporary ones. Their efforts challenged the temp industry in two key ways. First, there was a strong movement to redefine the very meaning of employment. A variety of activists, including temporary workers, politicians, and labor organizers, began to question the temp industry's long-standing assertion that the employer–employee relationship was defined by remuneration—that is, by who issued the paycheck.[4] They sought to broaden the definition of employment to include questions of place, time, control, and autonomy. This expanded definition was undoubtedly more complex and, as a result, could not be reduced to a simple, easy-to-use legal formula. But in some ways it offered a more straightforward understanding of employment. Someone who worked every day for years at a time at a single company, under the supervision of that company's managers, was to be considered that company's employee, even if his or her paycheck was signed by a temp agency. With the new definition of employment, employers could retain the flexibility of using temps, but they would not be able to exploit temporary workers by treating them as second-class, full-time employees.

For those who were truly "temporary" workers, employed by their agencies rather than the companies where they worked, a second set of campaigns sought to make temping a decent job in its own right. On the whole, temporary work, with lower wages, fewer benefits, and less job security than permanent employment, was a "bad" job.[5] However, a variety of social and political activists maintained that temp work need not be intrinsically "bad," and they sought to improve it by using three basic strategies. First, they worked to improve temps' wages, benefits, and working conditions. Second, they promoted unions for temporary workers. Finally, they sought to confine temping to truly *temporary* jobs. In their view, long-term temporary work was an exploitative oxymoron.

The goal of both these campaigns—to redefine employment and to improve temp work—was to diminish the downsides of temporary employment. Long-term temps were to be considered the employees of the companies where they worked and were to be compensated as such; temp agencies were to become decent employers in their own right. This would improve the work lives of temps and, perhaps more importantly, diminish the temp industry's downward pressure on labor market standards for all workers.

Neither of these campaigns was entirely successful, however. They were hampered by existing laws and the slow pace of legislative change, the political clout of the temp industry, and the inherent difficulty of organizing temporary workers. Their efforts were also limited because they focused on the more extreme abuses of the temp industry rather than the liability model of work that underpinned it. Nonetheless, their efforts were significant—not necessarily for their achievements, which were few, but for their potential. Outright successes may have been scarce, but taken together these challenges to the temp industry succeeded in drawing the blueprint for a very different model of work—one built on labor union approaches to work and workers as well as management theories such as the Human Relations approach. Instead of being treated as costly liabilities, workers were to be treated as assets, respected for their skills, dedication, and humanity. And instead of severing the employment relationship—detaching workers from employers, and work from the workplace—employers were to regain responsibility for their workers, and work was to be rooted in a particular place and community. These campaigns, in short, pointed the way toward an updated version of the asset model that would counter the temp industry's newly dominant liability model of work. Although this new model has yet to be implemented, the critical first steps have been taken. Only human action—similar to that of the temp industry on behalf of its liability model—will translate these early efforts into a persuasive and transformative model to put into practice.

This chapter begins by examining the extraordinary expansion of the temp industry in the 1990s. Industry leaders penetrated deeper into firms' business practices, assuming management positions and even taking over entire departments—the culmination of several decades of intense advertising campaigns. Meanwhile, the industry continued its expansion across the labor market spectrum into highly skilled white-collar jobs and, even more, into low-skill industrial work. Perhaps most importantly, the temp industry spread across the globe, merging with overseas competitors and pushing foreign markets to legalize temporary work.

This expansion also brought its own limits, however, including increased competition and declining profit margins. These internal dynamics imposed considerable constraints on the industry's growth. But the real potential for limiting the temp industry, I contend, came not from market forces but from the many people who challenged the temp industry during this time. Thus, the lion's share of the chapter will examine the two campaigns to redefine the meaning of work in the 1990s, drawing out their blueprint for a modernized asset model of work.

The Rise of the Temp Economy: Expansion and Its Limits

The organized resistance to the temp industry that emerged in the 1990s was especially striking because the industry continued to grow and gain strength throughout the decade. Between 1990 and 2000, employment in the U.S. temp industry nearly tripled, accounting for about 10 percent of the nation's employment growth.[6] The number of people employed as temps on a daily basis also tripled, from less than one million workers a day at the start of the decade to nearly three million by 2000.[7] Industry sales increased even more, quadrupling from $15.6 billion in 1990 to $64.3 billion in 1999.[8]

This spectacular growth can be attributed to three modes of expansion: penetrating deeper into firms, pushing into new occupational sectors (as well as existing strongholds), and extending across the globe. Although these strategies also introduced limits to the industry's growth, altogether they resulted in a massive global industry with considerable political clout in the United States and abroad.

First, the industry expanded by deepening the role that temp agencies played in their corporate clients' everyday affairs. In order to gain an edge in the increasingly competitive market of the 1990s, industry leaders began promoting a variety of "new" services that extended their reach into the business practices of their clients. These services included "vendor-on-premise" (VOP) arrangements, in which an agency supplied not only temps but also supervisors to manage a company's temporary workforce; "in-house outsourcing," in which a temp agency assumed control of an entire department for a client company; and "master vendor" contracts, in which one agency became a company's "preferred supplier" of temporary workers. At least in terms of vendor-on-premise arrangements and outsourcing, however, these were not "new" services at all. As described in Chapter 2, temp leaders had been promoting these uses of temps since the 1960s (recall their ads for "contract staffing" and "facilities management"). These services had been only a trivial portion of industry sales until the 1990s, however, when industry leaders repackaged and advertised them under new trade names—VOP and outsourcing, respectively.

The growth of these market-enhancing strategies profoundly affected the nature of the employment relationship both for temps and for their permanent counterparts. In VOP arrangements, for example, temp agencies typically provided a large number of temporary workers as well as supervisors to oversee them. The agency thus might set up shop on a company's premises, recruiting, interviewing, hiring, training, and overseeing the workers.[9] For example, as described in a 1993 article in the *Personnel Journal*, the leaders of the Atlanta temp agency Norrell Corp. ran what they called a "mini-branch of Norrell" inside a Michigan automotive plant. As a result, said a Norrell manager, "the company doesn't have to deal with managing the contingent work force; the responsibility falls on Norrell." The *Personnel Journal* reported that outsourcing both workers and supervisors to oversee them was very attractive to the automotive company: Fully half of its workforce was temporary.[10]

Olsten Temporary Services provided similar services to the software company Lotus Development Corp. As described in a 1996 article in the *Management Review*, Lotus had only six full-time employees at its manufacturing plant in Massachusetts, but during peak production times the company needed as many as 250 workers. Olsten not only supplied the company with those 250 workers at a moment's notice; it also provided managers to oversee them. "An on-site manager takes responsibility for Olsten employees and is the first line of contact with the client," an Olsten executive told *Management Review*. "Olsten does the packing and shipping [of the software] so that Lotus can focus on its core business: software development."[11]

This arrangement was quite attractive for many business owners in the 1990s, especially as labor markets grew tighter toward the end of the decade. Even so, the rise in the number of VOP contracts was astonishing, growing by more than 2,000 percent over the course of the decade. VOP sales increased nearly as much, bringing in over $10 billion by the end of the 1990s.[12]

VOP arrangements were arguably the apotheosis of the liability model of work that the temp industry had been selling since the 1960s. Not only did business owners not have to recruit or hire their workers; they did not even have to interact with them. With a simple phone call, they were able to get as many workers as they needed, whenever they needed them, along with managers to oversee them. No recruiting, no interviewing, no training, no paperwork, and virtually no legal obligations to the workers—only a single bill from the temp agency. And when temps were no longer needed, another quick phone call and the temps would disappear, no strings attached. The employer–employee relationship was "effectively severed."[13]

The second way industry leaders deepened their role in clients' business practices was by taking over entire departments, or "in-house outsourcing." In 1994, one industry observer explained to *Purchasing* that under this arrangement, temp agencies provided "full-time, permanent employees to companies that no longer want to staff and manage noncore departments, such as the mailroom and accounts payable."[14]

The temp industry had been selling this strategy for decades, but, because of the widespread acceptance of the liability model of work in the 1990s, industry leaders were able to be more candid in their promotional efforts. According to temp leaders, in-house outsourcing was the perfect way for business owners to save money by eliminating workers who did not contribute to the bottom line. For instance, Sam Sacco, then executive vice president of the National Association of Temporary Services, argued that this kind of outsourcing allowed a company to focus on "its primary tasks while the chores are handled elsewhere." Business owners, Sacco continued, should

> [relieve] themselves of what have become burdens—functions that have little to do with the primary product or service of the company. Therefore, the challenge to business is to identify functions and processes that could be accomplished and managed more efficiently by outside "experts." For some functions, local temporary-help companies can be one of the experts. For added profitability and efficiency, explore those possibilities.[15]

Thus, Sacco and other industry leaders argued, the employees who handled the mail, cleaned the offices, and answered the phones were costly "burdens" to be eliminated, liabilities to the bottom line. Employers should focus solely on their "primary" product—making cars, developing software, selling insurance, or, perhaps, just making a profit—and let temp industry "experts" handle the rest.

In-house outsourcing splintered the employer–employee relationship at both an individual and a workplace level.[16] At an individual level, each temporary worker's employment relationship was fractured between the temp agency (the de jure employer) and the worksite employer. Although the workers were technically the employees of a temp agency, they showed up for work every day at a different company. At a workplace level, a company's workforce would be divided, potentially many times over, because temp agencies took over entire departments within the company. The employees in the mailroom might work for a different employer than those in the billing department, who might work for a different employer than those in marketing, and so on.

Because of the strength of the liability model, the temp industry's outsourcing strategy found a receptive audience in the business world of the 1990s. Early in the decade, the frontrunners of the U.S. temp industry—Kelly, Western, Olsten, and Manpower—created separate divisions dedicated to providing outsourcing services to their corporate clients. In short order, outsourcing became a key part of their bottom line. By the mid-1990s, for example, outsourcing already accounted for 15 percent of Western's profits.[17]

The proliferation of call centers at this time exemplified both the growing prevalence of outsourcing and the temp industry's role in facilitating it. Before call centers, companies typically had a number of employees who took care of customer service issues—either in a separate department or across various departments. But that changed with the development of call centers. Customer service representatives of a particular company no longer worked on-site, employed by the company they represented. At call centers, workers were both physically and economically separated from the business they served; they were not legally employees of the company. Thus, hundreds of customer service agents might work in a warehouse-like office, taking one phone call after the next, often representing numerous companies at a time. The warehouses were typically continents away from the companies they served. They were located in India, the Philippines, Malaysia—wherever labor costs were lowest. Although outsourcing customer service positions did not always involve the temp industry, a number of temp leaders capitalized on the trend. For example, Manpower created a partnership with Ameritech to facilitate call-center outsourcing: Manpower supplied the workers, Ameritech supplied the technology. As a result, corporate executives were able to easily "relieve themselves of the burden" of customer service positions—positions that, in a different model of work, might have been the first rung of the promotion ladder. Customer service workers were partitioned off, not only precluded from climbing career ladders but also from the better pay and benefits earned by the regular employees of the companies they represented.[18]

The third way industry executives extended their reach into firms' business practices was by establishing "master vendor" contracts in which their agency became a company's primary supplier of temporary workers. In the case of large corporations, this meant that one temp agency would provide them with temps on a national or even global level. As Manpower's Mitchell Fromstein told the *Wall Street Journal* in 1996, "We like to be a preferred supplier, and if it's on a global scale, we have the horses out there."[19]

Not surprisingly, the largest temp agencies were best able to offer— and profit from—master vendor agreements. For example, in the mid-1990s, Manpower became the sole supplier of temps to Hewlett-Packard, and the computer company stopped using some sixty different agencies for temps.[20] Manpower also became the "preferred supplier" for Master-Card and Northern Telecom Ltd. In the latter case, the temp agency sent two thousand workers a day to Northern's offices across the United States, Canada, and Mexico.[21] Likewise, Kelly became the master vendor for Johnson & Johnson, as Olsten did for both Lexmark and Chase Manhattan; and Interim Services (later known as Spherion) became the only agency to supply temps to Dell Computer.[22]

Taken altogether, vendor-on-premise arrangements, in-house outsourcing, and master vendor agreements linked temp agencies ever more closely to their corporate clients. They became intimately involved in the everyday affairs of these companies. As one corporate executive said of his company's temp agency managers, "I like it when they finish my sentences—then I know that they have a good sense of the problems we're experiencing here."[23] According to another business executive, her company's temp agency was like her "neighbor." The temp managers, she went on, "take us out to lunch, bring birthday gifts, and remember us on Valentine's Day."[24]

In addition to the above-mentioned strategies for penetrating deeper into firms' business practices, temp industry leaders of the 1990s continued to expand across the labor market. In particular, they pushed even higher into the upper echelons of white-collar jobs—in law, medicine, science, and finance—which typically offered higher profit margins. The best evidence for this trend was the dramatic increase in specialization within temp agencies, often fueled by the acquisition of smaller niche agencies. Kelly Services' fervid specialization over the last half of the decade was a prime example. In 1995, the leaders of Kelly Services formed Kelly Scientific Resources and bought the Wallace Law Registry, which they later renamed the Kelly Law Registry. A year later, they acquired the Oak Ridge Research Institute, which supplied temporary scientists to the defense and energy industries. In 1998, company leaders launched Kelly Engineering Services and went on to acquire other smaller engineering temp agencies to bolster this department. A year later, they started three new high-end departments: Kelly Healthcare Resources, Kelly Financial Resources, and Kelly IT Resources. And a few years later, company executives created Kelly FedSecure to supply the federal government and government contractors with professional temps with security clearance.[25]

Like Kelly, Manpower pushed even further into high-end professional and technical markets. In 1996, for instance, the company launched its own high-tech division, Manpower Technical. A year later, Manpower started placing scientists affiliated with the American Institute of Physics in temporary jobs. And in 1999, the agency expanded its technical division (renamed Manpower Professional) to include a broad range of white-collar workers, including those in information technology, engineering, telecommunications, finance, and scientific research.[26]

Temp leaders of the 1990s were quite successful in their efforts to expand into the ranks of highly skilled professional workers. At the start of the decade, employment in professional and technical jobs accounted for just 15 percent of temp work. Ten years later, the number of professional and technical temps had increased 250 percent, representing

37 percent of industry employment.[27] It is not surprising, then, that with the expansion of these high-profit sectors the volume of industry sales grew even more rapidly than industry employment in the 1990s. (As you may recall, while industry employment tripled, industry sales more than quadrupled over the course of the decade.)[28]

The new push into high-end work did not diminish the industry's traditional stronghold in low-wage industrial work, however.[29] Indeed, this segment of temp work increased dramatically as well. At the start of the decade, industrial jobs accounted for less than 28 percent of temporary work.[30] By the end of the 1990s, industrial work had emerged as the single largest sector in the industry, representing more than 35 percent of temporary employment.[31] Such a percentage was not trivial given the magnitude of the industry at the time. In fact, according to the 2004 annual report of the Council of Economic Advisers, if official employment statistics were adjusted by the number of temps in manufacturing (who were usually counted as service-sector rather than industrial workers), the widely noted decline in manufacturing employment during the 1990s would be nonexistent—an astonishing prospect.[32]

The profitable partnership between Nike and Norrell Services illustrated the industry's expansion downward into low-wage industrial work. Nike executives owned a distribution center in Memphis, Tennessee, where workers packaged and shipped shoes (largely made abroad) to retail outlets around the country. At the facility, Nike employed about 120 workers who earned at least $13 an hour plus benefits. The company also employed between 60 and 225 temps supplied by Norrell, who earned just $6.50 an hour without benefits for doing the same work.[33] Norrell, in the lucrative position of being the company's primary supplier of temps, went to extraordinary lengths to keep the Nike facility stocked with skilled temporary workers. For instance, Norrell built a 4,000-square-foot training center outfitted with the same equipment found in the Nike warehouse where temps were trained to repackage shoes. And Norrell's investment paid off for both the temp agency and Nike. According to *Fortune* magazine, while Nike's permanent employees packed an average of 210 pairs of athletic shoes an hour, their temps could pack 267 an hour.[34] This was a remarkable difference: The temps were 27 percent more productive at half the cost (not including benefits) of Nike's regular employees. These results demonstrate, once again, how the temp industry quite actively facilitated the institutionalization of the liability model of work. As employers such as Nike came to embrace the view of workers as liabilities—a view that the temp industry had been promoting for decades—agencies such as Norrell were ready with a seemingly limitless supply of trained, inexpensive, and obligation-free workers.[35]

Temp executives argued that their workers were helping to save American jobs. Industry leaders claimed that without the option to use temps, employers would have to outsource production abroad. Bruce Steinberg, a spokesperson for the National Association of Temporary Services, told the *New York Times* in 1993 that "temps, in effect, are earning wages that are competitive with worker pay in other countries." If manufacturers did not have access to these workers, he continued, "then a significant part of manufacturing might be transferred outside our borders."[36] Steinberg may have been right. But the temp industry was not a passive beneficiary of this global economic change; it was, as we have seen, an active player in creating the cultural and institutional frameworks that made it legitimate—and easy, and even necessary—to use temps or to outsource production abroad.

A prime example of the downward thrust of temp work in the 1990s was the rapid ascendance of a new division of the industry: day labor. Agencies such as Labor Ready, Labor Connection, Labor Finders International, Able Body Labor, and many others suddenly mushroomed across the country, especially in inner-city and immigrant neighborhoods.[37] These agencies typically supplied workers to industrial and construction work sites. Labor Ready, founded in 1989, quickly became the leader of this new segment of the temp industry. In fact, within a decade, it had become the nation's seventh-fastest-growing company. However, as Labor Ready and its many competitors flourished, they were increasingly accused of abuses that evoked those of the padrones early in the twentieth century: charging workers excessive fees; failing to pay workers' wages; exposing workers to hazardous conditions; and generally exploiting the most vulnerable populations, particularly immigrants.[38] In response, many activists organized in opposition to day labor agencies and their abuses. For their part, however, industry leaders maintained that day labor agencies simply employed the otherwise "unemployable." "If they weren't working with us," Labor Ready CEO Joseph Sambataro told *Business Week* in 2003, "they'd be on welfare or loitering around, causing trouble."[39]

The third and final force behind the temp industry's growth in the 1990s was its expansion across the globe. While the first two expansionary strategies—moving deeper into firms' business practices and across occupational sectors—drove much of the industry's growth in the United States, it was the temp industry's massive expansion abroad that made it a new global powerhouse. This global expansion was fueled by two major industry developments: the merging of already well-established multinational temp agencies, and the opening up of "virgin" countries previously closed to the temp industry.[40]

The brief but action-packed history of Adecco, which emerged at the turn of the twenty-first century as the largest temp agency in the world, was a perfect example of how mergers and acquisitions drove the industry's global expansion. In 1996, two major European temp agencies, the Swiss company Adia (then second-largest in the world) and the French company Ecco (third-largest), merged to form Adecco. Within a year, Adecco purchased TAD Resources International, a temp agency with a stronghold in the American northeast, which moved it from fifth to second place in the U.S. market. Then, in 2000, Adecco merged with Olsten Temporary Services, one of the largest and oldest temp agencies in the United States. This expanded the company's offices by another third and revenues by another 46 percent.[41] By 2004, Adecco had become the largest temp agency in the world, with more than 5,800 offices in sixty-seven countries.[42]

Such mergers and acquisitions were routine in the newly globalized temp industry of the 1990s. In 1996 alone, the Staffing Industry Report cited 306 mergers and acquisitions, an increase of nearly 70 percent over the previous year. The result, not surprisingly, was the emergence of a small number of massive, multinational corporations that dominated the temp industry on a global scale. One *Wall Street Journal* reporter described the situation as "Goliath vs. Goliath."[43]

The second development fueling the industry's global expansion was its aggressive political campaigns to expand temp work in countries that had previously restricted or banned it. One industry analyst dubbed such countries "virgin territory."[44] Their efforts to expand were highly successful. Industry leaders secured the legalization of temporary work in Sweden in 1993; Spain and Finland in 1994; Italy in 1997; and Japan and Greece in 1999. Meanwhile, in other industrialized countries such as Denmark, Germany, Belgium, and the Netherlands, temp leaders succeeded in removing many regulations that had long kept the industry in check. As a result, the new "Goliath" temp agencies spread their operations across the globe and became ever more powerful.[45] A telling indicator of their success was Manpower's role in the 1998 World Cup in France: Manpower staffed and managed the entire event, hiring and training more than twelve thousand workers.[46]

Ironically, however, as Peck and Theodore have observed, the same forces that drove the temp industry's expansion in the 1990s also imposed limits on the industry.[47] First, because the number of temp agencies in United States mushroomed in the 1990s—growing 50 percent in the second half of the decade alone—competition within the industry increased dramatically, driving down profits for individual agencies.[48] Moreover, the founders and long-standing leaders of the temp industry—Manpower, Kelly, and Olsten—were for the first time challenged by a growing number of overseas rivals. Manpower, for example, which had led the industry since its founding in the late 1940s, lost its first-place position, dropping to second in both the United States and abroad. Meanwhile, Kelly plummeted from second to sixth place in the United States, and, by the end of the decade, Olsten no longer existed, having been bought by Adecco.[49]

Along with heightened competition, a number of other factors threatened temp industry profits. The rapid growth of low-wage industrial temp work, for example, with its high turnover and low profit margins, increased the strain on earnings for many temp agencies.[50] Even new upscale services, such as vendor-on-premise arrangements, which were intended to give agencies a competitive edge and boost profits in the newly competitive environment, ultimately proved counterproductive. By the end of the decade, business owners had come to expect on-site managers as simply part and parcel of doing business with temp agencies. Agencies that did not provide such services lost clients.[51]

Such internal limits, along with tightening labor markets, led to a "flattening" of the temp industry's growth around the middle of the decade. In the first half of the 1990s, the industry grew at a remarkable pace: 17 percent annually. In the second half of the decade, however, the industry's growth rate dropped by half to a still respectable (but no longer astonishing) 8 percent a year.[52]

While temp leaders of the 1990s faced heightened competition and decreased profit margins, they also faced another challenge that did not come from economic forces. It came from people: temps who sued their companies for wages and benefits equal to their full-time counterparts; community activists who campaigned to protect full-time jobs and to improve temporary ones; union leaders who fought against hiring temps or sought to include them in their bargaining units; politicians who introduced legislation to diminish the exploitation of temps; and government officials who overturned long-standing policy in order to protect workers' interests. To paraphrase one industry observer, these people were seeking to "box in the temp industry" after nearly fifty years of virtually unlimited growth.[53] We now turn to their efforts.

Boxing In the Temp Industry

Given the power of the temp industry in the 1990s, "boxing in" the industry was no easy task. While there were some successes, there were still more failures, and even the best successes were qualified or "contingent." All of them, however, offered concrete plans for limiting the damage of the liability model for workers. They did so in two sometimes overlapping ways: by revising the definition of employment, and by improving temporary work. The next sections address each of these in turn.

Redefining the Employment Relationship

One of the two major challenges to the temp industry's model of work was a movement to redefine the meaning of temporary employment. In the 1950s and 1960s, as mentioned earlier, industry leaders engaged in a costly legal and marketing campaign to be considered the employers of their temporary workers.[54] In the course of this ultimately successful campaign, temp leaders argued that the employment relationship was defined by remuneration: The entity that paid wages and payroll taxes for temporary workers was the employer. Thus, according to the temp industry's definition, when a company hired permanent employees along with temp workers from a local agency, only the permanent workers were the company's employees because only they received a paycheck from the company. Even if temps worked full-time for years alongside their permanent counterparts, they were considered employees of the temp agency because it was the agency that paid their wages.

In the 1990s, however, legislators, judges, community activists, and workers began to question the temp industry's definition of employer status. Instead of defining the employment relationship by remuneration, they took into account issues such as where the work was done, how long it lasted, and who controlled it. Taking these more complicated workplace issues into account, temp industry reformers maintained, made it clear that temp agencies were not always temps' sole employers; the companies in which they worked also bore some responsibility. In some cases, they claimed, workplace employers should be held fully accountable for temporary workers. They argued that if temps did similar work alongside permanent employees, especially over long periods of time and under the supervision of the company's managers, then the temps should be considered employees of that company. In other cases, even those involving short-term temps, challengers of the temp industry maintained that the company and temp agency should be considered "co-employers" of temporary workers and, as such, should both be held responsible for fulfilling employer obligations.

One case led the way in the campaign to redefine the meaning of employment in the 1990s. In this case, the long-term temporary workers and independent contractors who worked for the Microsoft Corporation sued the computer software giant for the same benefits that their permanent counterparts received.[55] The case sent shockwaves through the business community. The president of the Information Technology Association of America called it "a threat to the whole idea of the flexible work force."[56] And, in a way, it was. Although the so-called "perma-temps" who filed suit against Microsoft did not seek to eliminate short-term hires, they did question the company's use of long-term temps, a practice that had become virtually synonymous with "flexibility" in the high-tech industry.

The Microsoft saga began in the 1980s—a time when the software giant fully embraced the temp industry's liability model. Microsoft employed a "core" of regular permanent employees surrounded by a thick ring of nonstandard workers, primarily independent contractors and temps. These "permatemps" were essentially indistinguishable from Microsoft's "real" employees: They did the same work, on a full-time basis, often for years at a time.

At that time, Microsoft had classified most of these workers as "independent contractors"—self-employed workers who were supposed to be hired for short-term projects and maintain control over their work. In 1989, the IRS became suspicious of this arrangement and launched an investigation of Microsoft's staffing practices. Ultimately, the IRS ruled that six hundred of Microsoft's independent contractors should have been classified as regular employees, because their work was fully controlled by the company. Microsoft was held liable for paying retroactive payroll, unemployment, and Social Security taxes for all six hundred workers.[57]

In response to the ruling, Microsoft hired a small number of its independent contractors as permanent employees. But it required the vast majority of them to sign up with a local temp agency. And that was not all: Microsoft required hundreds of other workers who were not directly affected by the IRS ruling to sign up with the temp agency as well. Those workers who refused to be "converted" to temps were fired. According to court documents, although the temp agencies officially "payrolled" the workers—that is, issued their paychecks—"in other respects the workers' relationship with Microsoft remained essentially unchanged."[58] They continued to work exclusively for the computer company, usually full-time and for years at a time, doing the same work that Microsoft's permanent employees did.[59]

Microsoft's actions shed a fascinating light on how the temp industry had become both a crucial tool for implementing the liability model of work and a major beneficiary of its success. In short, temp work had become a way for businesses such as Microsoft to increase profits by paying workers less. At the time, converting more and more workers to temps seemed like the perfect solution, and over the course of the decade Microsoft's use of temps skyrocketed. In the late 1980s, the computer company used 440 temps at its headquarters outside of Seattle. By the end of the 1990s, Microsoft employed some six thousand temps, who accounted for nearly a third of the company's regional workforce.[60]

The *Vizcaino v. Microsoft* case that ultimately upended this strategy began in 1992, when a number of permatemps filed a class action lawsuit against Microsoft. In the suit, the workers claimed that they were really "common-law" employees of the computer company, contrary to their classification as "temporary" workers, "independent contractors," and "freelancers." As such, they argued, they were entitled to the full package of employee benefits that regular Microsoft workers received, including health coverage, paid vacation, and pension benefits.

Throughout the dispute, Microsoft executives maintained that the temporary workers were the employees of temp agencies, not Microsoft, and they put considerable effort into distinguishing the rapidly growing number of temps from their permanent employees. For example, Microsoft's temps were required to wear different-colored badges; they had different e-mail addresses; they could not drive their cars to work; they were not allowed to buy discounted Microsoft products at the company store; and they had no access to the many amenities offered to regular employees, including the company's sports and recreation facilities, company parties, and social clubs. In fact, Microsoft temps were not even allowed to participate in activities such as Take Our Daughters to Work day. And, of course, they did not receive the same pay and benefits.[61]

As Microsoft spokesperson Dan Leach insisted in the *Washington Post*, "The employees of temporary staffing agencies are employees of temporary staffing agencies."[62] Temp executives agreed. A 1999 "friend of the court" brief filed by the National Association of Temporary and Staffing Services along with a number of other business associations asserted that "it is the temporary staffing firm—and not the client business—which is the ultimate and sole employer."[63]

Initially, the court agreed with Microsoft's claims that the temps were not real employees and, as a result, should be excluded from the class action suit. In 1998, at the behest of Microsoft's lawyers, a district judge restricted the case to only the relatively small number of independent contractors and removed temporary workers from the suit. This drastically reduced the size and muscle of the plaintiffs. A year later, however, the decision was overturned and the original class—which by then included thousands of temps—was restored.[64] In response, Microsoft's director of contingent staffing, Sharon Decker, incredulously told *Business Week*, "If you really look at what's going on, it appears as if they're saying there's no good reason to have temporary workers at all."[65]

This was a telling remark. If the main purpose of hiring temps was to avoid employer obligations, the courts had indeed decided that there was "no good reason to have temporary workers." Taking into account a variety of factors—including who recruited and trained the workers, whether Microsoft had the right to assign additional work, whether the company controlled the relationship between the temps and their agencies, and the duration of the temps' work at Microsoft—the courts found that the permatemps were employees of Microsoft, not the temp agencies that issued their paychecks.[66]

As we will see, the outcome of the case was complicated, but to some degree it was quite simple: The workers won their case, and the temp industry's model of work received its first significant setback. The protracted efforts of Microsoft's workers, their lawyers, and the courts had expanded the definition of temporary employment to include far more than just remuneration. Signing paychecks did not automatically make one the employer; place, time, control, and autonomy mattered. As one industry observer noted, "You are what you are, the courts decided. Signing a waiver saying that you're a temp doesn't make you a temp—not if you've been doing the work of a full-time employee all along."[67]

The *Microsoft* case energized widespread resistance to employers' use of permatemps and the temp industry's definition of employment. Following in the steps of Microsoft's workers, long-term temporary workers across the country sued their companies for benefits, often with considerable success. For example, in 2000, hundreds of temps working for King County, Washington, successfully argued that they were actually common-law employees and won $18.6 million in benefits and retirement funds in addition to accrued vacation and sick leave.[68] In 2004, nearly thirteen hundred Kelly temps were deemed common-law employees of the SmithKline Beecham Corporation, winning $5.2 million from the pharmaceutical giant.[69] Other lawsuits involved temporary workers employed by the cities of Seattle, Pasadena, and Fresno; temps working for the counties of San Bernardino and Los Angeles; "limited term employees" at the University of Wisconsin, Madison; and "independent contractors" at Time Warner and Hewlett-Packard. These and other cases led to numerous media pronouncements of the "Revenge of the Temps," the "Rise of the Permatemp," and the " 'Permatemp' Wars."[70]

One should not overstate the consequences of the *Microsoft* ruling, however. Due to federal employment laws already in place, its impact was far more limited than it might have been. Even as it offered an expanded definition of the temporary employment relationship, the *Microsoft* ruling left room for companies to find new ways to evade their obligations to workers. For instance, federal law gave employers considerable flexibility in determining the pay, vacation, and health care benefits of their workers; as a result, two employees of the same company could receive markedly different wages and benefits packages for doing the same work. And although federal law generally mandated that a company's pension benefits be uniform for all employees—including "common-law" employees—some workers could be excluded from benefits if the exclusion was explicit in the company's plan.[71]

Microsoft's pension plan (a stock purchase plan) did not explicitly exclude the temps and independent contractors who were found to be common-law employees of the company. Accordingly, the courts ruled that these workers were eligible to participate in the stock purchase plan retroactively, "even though they had been told when hired that they were ineligible for such benefits and had signed contracts disclaiming them."[72] Thanks to the boom in Microsoft's stock since the 1980s, winning back-dated stock options was no small victory for the company's temps. In 1987, Microsoft employees would have been able to buy 20 shares of company stock for just $818; in 1998, those 20 shares would have multiplied to 720 shares worth $107,280.[73] Thus, the courts calculated that the 8,588 members of the class action suit were entitled to almost $97 million in compensation.[74]

In the *Microsoft* decision, however, the judge conceded that had the company's stock purchase plan specifically excluded some portion of its employees—for instance, temporary workers paid by agencies—those workers would have been ineligible for any compensation from the company.[75] Temp industry leaders pounced on this distinction and embarked on an aggressive campaign to educate businesses of this loophole.[76] In books, newsletters, and literature distributed to corporate executives, temp leaders used the *Microsoft* case as a lesson on how to avoid such legal troubles. "Ironically," wrote lawyers for the American Staffing Association, "the Microsoft case provides guidance for addressing the issue of when a staffing firm customer may be considered the employer of staffing firm employees claiming benefits under the customer's plans."[77] As demonstrated by the *Microsoft* ruling, temp leaders explained, if companies amended their benefits plans to "clearly and explicitly exclude staffing firm employees," temps would not be eligible for benefits "even if they are determined to be . . . common-law employees" of the company.[78] Temp executives even provided businesses with "suggested language, developed by expert benefits counsel" that they could use "to exclude staffing firm workers from participating in the customer's benefits plans."[79]

Once again, such "educational" campaigns highlighted the temp industry's role in expanding and institutionalizing the liability model of work—a role that was embraced enthusiastically by businesses in the 1990s. Employers across the country altered their benefits plans to exclude temporary and other nonstandard workers.[80] For instance, in a lesser-known permatemp case against Verizon Communications, the judge ruled that although the company's temps were "indistinguishable" from Verizon's other employees, they were not eligible for benefits because the company's plan explicitly excluded all workers not "paid directly" by Verizon.[81] Likewise, the long-term temps who worked for McGraw-Hill were denied compensation because the company's benefits plan specifically covered only those employees on McGraw-Hill's payroll.[82] Thus, because federal employment laws did not require employers to treat all of their employees equally with respect to wages and benefits, temp executives and their corporate clients easily found a way around Microsoft's predicament.

Yet despite the loopholes that weakened the ruling, the *Microsoft* case should still be considered a victory for those who challenged the temp industry's definition of employment in the 1990s. Microsoft's temps, who received their paychecks from a temp agency, were found to be employees of Microsoft, not their agencies. The radical potential of this finding cannot be overstated. It not only undermined the legitimacy of a founding principle of the temp industry—that temps were legal employees of temp agencies alone—but also called into question its model of work. The ruling was clear: Temps should not be treated as second-class, full-time employees.

What's more, the ruling gave activists a target: revising employment law so that workers could not be exploited as Microsoft's permatemps had been. A number of legislators and political activists sought to amend federal and state laws so that employers could not treat temps differently than permanent employees with respect to pension benefits, health insurance, and wages. For example, in three consecutive sessions (2003, 2005, and 2007), Congress considered the Employee Benefits Protection Act, which would have required employers to treat all employees equally with respect to pension benefits. The language of this bill directly addressed the ambiguity raised in the *Microsoft* case, seeking to "ensure that employees are not improperly excluded from participation in employee benefit plans as a result of mislabeling or reclassifying their employment status."[83] Under this law, all workers deemed to be "common-law" employees of the company, even those classified as temps, would have been eligible for the company's benefits. But the bill never made it out of committee.

The New Jersey Senate tackled a similar problem related to health insurance. In 2006, it debated the Responsible Employer Act, which would have required all companies with at least one thousand employees to contribute a minimum amount to workers' health care benefits. According to the bill, "employees" were defined as any workers—including temps and most other contingent employees—who worked at least thirteen hours a week.[84] As of December 2009, the bill had passed the Senate Labor Committee but still needed to be approved by the Budget and Appropriations Committee and the New Jersey Senate.

Politicians and community activists also sought equal treatment for temps with respect to wages. In Greenville County, South Carolina, for example, leaders of the Carolina Alliance for Fair Employment (CAFE) successfully pressured the local government to pay temps the same wages it paid permanent employees.[85] Other efforts on this front met with less success, however. In 1999, the Illinois House of Representatives rejected the Equity for Temporary Workers Act, which—had it passed—would have prevented both temp agencies and their corporate clients from paying long-term temporary workers less than their permanent counterparts for the same work.[86] A number of failed bills in Rhode Island and New Mexico would have gone even further, defining business owners as the legal employers of their temps for the purposes of all employment laws.[87]

Temp leaders, for their part, sought to preserve their status as the sole employers of temps. And so, once again, they found themselves fighting legal and political battles over the definition of temporary employment.

In 1997, industry leaders lobbied on Capitol Hill for the Staffing Firm Worker Benefits Act. The bill's purpose was to "codify the employer status of staffing firms with respect to their workers for purposes of employment taxes and for employee benefit purposes."[88] Although the bill did not pass, industry leaders kept up the fight, working to block any bills that challenged their status as the legal employers of temps.[89]

On this front, however, the temp industry was fighting an uphill battle. Although little headway was made in amending employment law to ensure equity between temps and regular workers, by the end of the decade the temp industry's claim to employer status had been considerably weakened. This was largely because the courts and various arms of the federal government, which had long relied on broader definitions of employment, began extending these definitions to temp work, as evidenced in the *Microsoft* case. These definitions had been developed earlier in the century, primarily by the U.S. federal court system, to determine whether a company was the legal employer of its workers.[90] Although the courts' formulas for defining employment relationships varied, all were much broader than the temp industry's formula. Whereas the temp industry defined an employer as a company that issues a paycheck, the courts' definitions resembled the understanding of employment submitted by the courts in the *Microsoft* case.

Likewise, government agencies such as the Equal Employment Opportunity Commission (EEOC), the Occupational Safety and Health Administration (OSHA), and the National Labor Relations Board (NLRB) all used broad as opposed to narrow tests to define employment. The formulas they used to determine which party should be held liable in disputes over discrimination or workplace safety hazards, for example, were remarkably complex. EEOC officials examined whether the company had the right to control when, where, and how the worker performed the job; whether it had the right to assign additional projects; whether the firm could discharge the worker; who set the hours of work and the duration of the job; where the work was performed; if there was a continuing relationship between worker and firm; and whether the company and the worker believed that they were creating an employer–employee relationship.[91] And these were only a few of the factors considered. The courts repeatedly ruled that there was no "shorthand formula or magic phrase" that defined the employment relationship. "All incidents of the relationship must be assessed with no one factor being decisive."[92]

In the 1990s, government officials began to apply these more complicated definitions of employment to temps. For example, in 1997, the EEOC issued a report explaining that its broader definition of employment would hold both temp agencies and work site employers responsible for complying with a variety of worker protections, including Title VII of the Civil Rights Act of 1964, the Age Discrimination in Employment Act, the Americans with Disabilities Act, and the Equal Pay Act.[93] And in 1994, OSHA issued a standard interpretation letter, which emphasized that work site employers—not temp agencies—were primarily responsible for protecting temps from workplace hazards.[94]

As a result, even as temp executives continued to counsel their clients on how to avoid employer obligations to temps, they were forced to revise their definition of temporary employment. Indeed, by the end of the decade, the industry had largely moved away from its long-standing claim to employer status and instead emphasized "co-employment," the shared responsibility for temps by temp agencies and work site employers. "Co-employment," wrote American Staffing Association lawyers in 2000, "is an *inherent* aspect of the relationship between the staffing firm and its customers."[95]

The industry adopted co-employment language remarkably quickly. The subject of co-employment first emerged in temp industry literature in 1992 when industry leaders published a slim, fourteen-page pamphlet on the topic. By 2000, the pamphlet had become a full-length book—*Co-employment: Employer Liability Issues in Third-Party Staffing Arrangements*—which was already in its fourth printing. Over the next several years, as the laws surrounding the temporary employment relationship continued to change, industry leaders published several more editions of the book to interpret this increasingly complicated area of employment law for their corporate clients.[96]

The change in the definition of temporary employment was a real victory for the many people who sought to revise the meaning of work in the 1990s. By the end of the decade, the temp industry's model was no longer the governing paradigm among lawmakers. The revised definition that emerged was much more complicated, taking into consideration "all of the circumstances" in the employment relationship.[97] Yet this complexity captured real workplace dynamics. Someone who worked for a company day in and day out under the direction of that company's supervisors would most likely be considered an employee of the company, whether or not a temp agency issued the worker's paycheck. Short-term temps would still be considered employees of the temp agency, but both the agency and the work site employer could be held accountable for protecting the workers' rights. As a result, although employers could continue to pay temps less in terms of wages and benefits, they could no longer use temps to avoid liability for worker protections. They could no longer expect to get away with discrimination against temps or unsafe working conditions. In essence, the expanded definition of temporary employment weakened the temp industry's liability model of work, which held that employees were costly headaches to be relieved by temps. Government officials had ruled that employers could not dispense with their legal obligations simply by signing a contract for temporary workers.

The movement to revise the meaning of employment thus sought to improve the temp industry's model of work by retaining its advantages—flexibility in employment—while eliminating the exploitation of workers that had been incorporated into that flexibility. In doing so, the campaign addressed more than just the plight of temps. It took on issues of fairness and equality for all workers. However, although these efforts to redefine temp work made some headway—particularly in the "permatemp wars" and the industry's new emphasis on co-employment—significant reform of the employment relationship had not been achieved. Most importantly, employers could still pay workers different wages and benefits for the same work. Recall the example of Nike, whose temps were more productive at less than half the cost of regular workers. For many employers, the two-tiered workforce continued to characterize the employment relationship, regardless of whether temps were considered employees.

Improving Temporary Work

If the 1990s saw a movement to revise the meaning of temporary employment, it also saw a second kind of effort to make temping a decent job in its own right. Much like the efforts described above, this campaign would preserve the benefits of temporary work while diminishing its exploitation. However, instead of focusing on the legal obligations of work site employers, this effort was directed at temp agencies, pushing them to become good employers of temps. Under the temp industry's liability model of work, employees were essentially generic; even skilled employees were easily replaced with temps. Labor was a commodity, and, as such, the lowest-priced goods would prevail. By contrast, those who sought to upgrade temporary work argued that temps—and workers more generally—should not be treated as the "lowest-priced goods." Rather, they should be valued as employees (if not key assets) who were entitled to decent wages, benefits, and working conditions.

A variety of activists, including politicians, union leaders, and community organizers, worked to make temping a good job. In general, they set about this problem in three different ways. First, some focused on directly boosting temps' wages, benefits, and working conditions. Second, some activists sought to improve temp work indirectly by promoting unions for temporary workers. Finally, some worked to restrict temping to truly temporary jobs, insisting on an end to the permatemp phenomenon. There were plenty of successes among these efforts to improve temporary work, but there were even more failures. More important than their immediate success or failure, however, were their innovative ideas for solving the ongoing problems of equality and fairness in the workplace.

Politicians and labor activists first sought to improve temporary work by boosting temps' wages, benefits, and working conditions. This was no easy task. As we will see, legislating such improvements proved to be nearly impossible. And although community activists encountered somewhat greater success on a much smaller scale, they too faced numerous obstacles.

The most obvious way to improve temp work was to increase its wages and benefits. Yet this proved to be the most difficult goal to achieve. Lawmakers in a variety of states, including Illinois, Massachusetts, New Jersey, Rhode Island, and Tennessee, introduced legislation that would require agencies to give temps the same wages and/or benefits that their permanent counterparts received.[98] But such legislation met with almost unqualified failure. Community organizers encountered only slightly more success in this effort. In 1999, labor activists in Silicon Valley launched

Working Partnerships Staffing Services, a nonprofit temp agency that promised to offer temps a minimum of ten dollars an hour, inexpensive health care, and access to training. With this ambitious project, the founders hoped to "transform employment practices by marrying a placement agency to an advocacy strategy that in time will raise the wage floor, allow access to benefits, and affect overall hiring practices."[99] In short, they wanted to push the temp industry onto the "high road," integrating the best aspects of the liability model with an updated asset model of work. Despite early signs of modest success, however, the agency struggled to survive. The need to provide continuous, multilevel training for workers, as well as the persistent search for employers willing to pay top dollar for temps, ultimately proved too great an undertaking; Working Partnerships closed its doors just five years later.[100]

In another innovative strategy, the union Communications Workers of America (CWA) established its own temp agencies for workers in the telecommunications industry. The goal of CWA's "employment centers" was to provide workers with union jobs offering good wages, portable benefits, and ongoing training. Like Working Partnerships, however, the union's employment centers faced plenty of barriers. For instance, there were debates within the union about whether or not the employment centers should even exist. The union had fought for so long against employers subcontracting work; now, suddenly, CWA's own employment centers were vying to become the contractors of choice for those very same employers. The success of the employment centers, moreover, required the close collaboration of the union and the business owners, who were time-honored adversaries. Ultimately, only two employment centers in California and Ohio were able to overcome these obstacles; the rest were shut down.[101]

In Tucson, Arizona, the Primavera Foundation, a nonprofit organization that served the homeless, established perhaps the most successful nonprofit temp agency. Founded in 1996, Primavera Works connected residents of the foundation's homeless shelter to jobs, guaranteeing the workers $5.75 an hour (by 2009, it had increased to $7.00 an hour). Primavera also offered the workers a wide range of support services, including free bus passes, meals, clothing, work equipment, training, and case managers to help them find and keep jobs. This was clearly more than a typical temp agency would offer. And it resulted in more than the typical temp success stories: By 2005, nearly half of Primavera's workers had found full-time, permanent work, and, as a result, 285 formerly homeless men had left the shelter.[102] Here was an unsurprising irony: The most successful attempt to create an asset model temp agency was one that found permanent rather than temporary jobs for its workers. But this success was limited: The jobs were still at the low end of the pay scale, suggesting that the workers were only one paycheck away from critical hardship. Although such jobs certainly were a vast improvement over unemployment and homelessness, they could only help workers who were facing the most difficult situations.

While mandatory raises and benefits often seemed unattainable, activists encountered more success in improving working conditions for temps. Their efforts focused on a number of problems that characterized many day labor agencies, including hefty fees for check cashing and transportation, chronic uncertainty about the length and quality of assignments, and hazardous working conditions.

The fees that temp agencies charged workers became a popular target for advocates of temp industry reform in the 1990s. For example, it had become common practice among low-end temp agencies, most notably Labor Ready, to provide cash machines so that temps could cash their paychecks at the end of the day. In fact, "Work today, paid today" was the company's slogan. Although the cash machines were likely a valuable resource for those workers without bank accounts, the agency charged more than a dollar for each transaction, making a considerable profit off the workers' already meager earnings. Indeed, in 2000, the cash machines generated $8.3 million in revenue for the company.[103] What's more, many temp agencies charged workers for transportation to and from the work site as well as for job equipment. Altogether, these fees often lowered workers' wages well below the minimum wage. In fact, according to a 2002 study by the U.S. General Accounting Office, many day laborers earned only two dollars an hour as a result of these fees and other wage deductions.[104]

A variety of reformers sought to curb these abuses. In 2002, for example, the state of Arizona under Attorney General Janet Napolitano filed suit against Labor Ready for charging workers unreasonable fees in their check-cashing machines. In a settlement reached two years later, Labor Ready was required to refund $150,000 to workers and, at least in

Arizona, was prohibited from charging such fees in the future.[105] Likewise, in Buffalo, New York, the State Department of Labor found Labor Ready guilty of unlawful deductions from workers' wages for transportation, equipment, and check-cashing fees. In a settlement agreement, the agency was required to pay more than $38,000 to cover illegal charges for transportation and equipment. The parties could not settle the issue of the check-cashing fees, however, and left it for the courts to decide. In November 2006, the New York Court of Appeals found the fees to be "excessive" and in violation of labor law.[106]

Meanwhile, politicians in California, Florida, Illinois, Rhode Island, and Wisconsin introduced legislation that would restrict these kinds of fees.[107] For example, Illinois passed a law in 2005 that prohibited companies from charging temps for transportation and, furthermore, mandated that agency fees could not push workers' earnings below the minimum wage.[108] At about the same time, Florida and Rhode Island capped transportation fees to three dollars.[109] In other states, however, the temp industry successfully blocked similar bills.

Another target of activists' efforts was reducing the chronic uncertainty surrounding temp work. Temporary workers—particularly in the day labor segment of the industry—often did not know how long an assignment would last, what its wage rate was, or even what kind of work it would entail. Thus, workers could not make plans from one day to the next, nor could they know what kind of work they would be required to do or what equipment they would have to use. Such ambiguity about the terms of employment could lead to higher rates of worker injury if work site employers required untrained workers to use complicated equipment. It also meant that the temp agency could deny any responsibility for the worker's injuries because—as they repeatedly argued in court—they had not authorized the use of such equipment or, more generally, they did not have sufficient control over the workplace to be held responsible.[110]

A number of states sought to reduce such uncertainty by requiring temp agencies to provide workers with written terms and conditions of their employment, including the exact nature of the work and its wages, the duration of the assignment, and any workplace safety issues. Such disclosure would not only allow temps to know what their jobs would entail; it would also give them legal recourse if they were injured at the work site. Legislators in Rhode Island were successful in this effort, passing the Temporary Employee Protection Act, which required agencies to provide temps with formal disclosure of the terms and conditions of their employment.[111] Similar efforts in other states failed, however.

In some cases, lawmakers sought to include many of the above protections in a single all-encompassing statute. In New York, Massachusetts, and California, for example, state legislatures considered a comprehensive "bill of rights" for temps, which included minimum wages and benefits, restrictions of fees charged to workers, and full disclosure of the terms of employment.[112] Each of these bills failed to pass, however. As the leaders of the American Staffing Association boasted, "Thanks to the efforts of ASA and its chapters, these bills have been defeated. The New York bill saw no action and died when the legislature adjourned in June. The Mass. bill is also dead, and the California bill has stalled."[113]

Union leaders and community organizations met with somewhat more success in recruiting temp agencies to voluntarily commit to a "code of conduct" that covered a range of worker protections. The New Jersey Temp Workers Alliance, for example, successfully enlisted thirty-two temp agencies to endorse its "Principles for Fair Conduct for Temporary Employment Agencies," which mandated written job descriptions for temps, adequate training, and fair treatment for workers filing for unemployment benefits.[114] In South Carolina, the leaders of CAFE took a two-pronged approach to improve worker protections: They urged temp agencies to sign their code of conduct and, at the same time, they pressured the state government to use only those agencies that had signed on.[115] These movements represented remarkable victories and were a crucial first step in moving away from the temp industry's liability model of work, but ultimately they had only a limited impact on the temp industry as a whole. In New Jersey, for instance, the thirty-two agencies that committed to the code of conduct represented only 6 percent of the state's temp industry, and in South Carolina the employment practices of the state government had little influence on the private sector.

Yet despite the many obstacles these efforts faced, campaigns to improve temporary work accomplished a great deal. They laid the groundwork for future efforts to improve temping not only by identifying the aspects of temp work that needed improvement but also by devising strategies to make such changes happen. Their campaigns offered a glimpse of a new model of work—an updated asset model based on equality and fairness rather than treating workers as expensive liabilities.

The second strategy for improving temp work was to unionize temporary workers.[116] Labor leaders proceeded in two ways: First, they worked to organize unions for temporary workers and, second, they tried to make it possible for temps to join the unions of regular employees. As with other strategies, however, their efforts met considerable obstacles. In the first place, temps were extraordinarily difficult to organize. Although temp agencies might employ thousands of temps, few of these temps actually worked together. Most hopped from workplace to workplace, isolated from both their temporary and permanent counterparts. And even if they did work for a prolonged time at a single work site, few temps could risk engaging in union activities: Not only could they be fired from the work site but they could also be removed from the temp agency's roster altogether. In the second place, unions were not always eager to embrace temporary workers. After all, employers had regularly used temps as strikebreakers.[117] And finally, labor law itself posed a significant barrier to organizing temps by making it nearly impossible for them to join the unions of permanent employees.[118] Despite these difficulties, however, labor leaders increasingly worked to unionize temps in the 1990s. "Organizing temporary workers is a big part of the American labor movement's strategy for organizing new workers," Gerald McEntee, president of the American Federation of State, County, and Municipal Employees (AFSCME), told the *Wall Street Journal* in 2000.[119]

The first way they went about organizing temps was to target work sites that employed large numbers of temporary workers. For example, in New Orleans, Local 100 of the Service Employees International Union (SEIU) organized the city's temporary garbage collectors with impressive results. Years before, in the 1980s, New Orleans had privatized its garbage collection and contracted virtually all the city's garbage collectors to temp agencies. The upshot was that 250 public sector workers suddenly became temps earning minimum wage and no benefits. But then SEIU Local 100 started organizing the workers and planned a devastating work stoppage. In the middle of a hot summer in the mid-1990s, the temps simply stopped collecting the city's garbage. As the garbage piled up on the streets, the temp agencies had to bargain with the workers or risk losing their contracts with the city. As a result, the temps won wage increases across the board.[120] "Too many people have bought the notion that temporary workers are unorganizable," said SEIU's Wade Rathke.[121]

Another effort to organize temporary workers came out of the *Microsoft* case. In 1998, in what was reportedly the first attempt to organize the sprawling population of temps in the high-tech sector, several of Microsoft's former permatemps founded WashTech, the Washington Alliance of Technology Workers.[122] In subsequent years, WashTech made some headway in bringing together high-tech temps and providing them with inexpensive training. Indicative of the difficulty in organizing temps, however, the union's first major victory did not involve temporary workers at all but rather call center workers. In 2005, WashTech organized nine hundred Cingular Wireless customer service workers in Bothell, Washington, securing guaranteed pay raises and inexpensive health care as well as increased job security and opportunities to move up the ladder.[123] Although this victory had little to do with temps, in the future WashTech might be able to leverage its success to secure such gains for temporary workers.

While labor leaders at WashTech and SEIU sought to create a temp workers' union, other labor activists worked to include temps in regular workers' unions. But long-standing labor law made this nearly impossible. Maintaining that temps and permanent workers had two distinct employers—the temp agency and the work site employer, respectively—labor law regarded a union of the two as a "multi-employer" unit, which required the consent of both employers.[124]

In the 1990s, labor leaders disputed this statute in a number of cases before the NLRB.[125] For example, in 1993 at a nursing home in Brooklyn, New York, Local 1199 of the Drug, Hospital, and Health Care Employees Union sought to include temporary nurses in the permanent health care workers' bargaining unit.[126] A year later, the United Paperworkers International Union fought to include twenty-three temps in the permanent employees' bargaining unit at a paper packaging plant in Kalamazoo, Michigan.[127] And in 2000, Teamsters Local 89 campaigned to include thirty temporary workers in the regular employees' bargaining unit at Jeffboat, a large shipbuilder on the Ohio River in Jefferson, Indiana.[128]

In the first two of these cases, involving the nurses and paperworkers, union leaders were unsuccessful. In each case, the NLRB adhered to precedent, ruling that temps could not join the unions of permanent workers without the consent of all employers involved. In the Jeffboat case, however, labor leaders met with resounding—and highly controversial—success.

In the 2000 ruling for Jeffboat, commonly known as the *Sturgis* case, the new Clinton-appointed majority of the NLRB ruled that temps should be able to join the unions of permanent employees without employer consent as long as two conditions are met. First, the temps had to share a "community of interest" with the regular employees by, for example, doing similar work at the same workplace. Second, they had to be "jointly employed" by both the temp agency and the company, meaning that both businesses determined the terms and conditions of employment.[129] Thus, for example, if a company supervised temps on a day-to-day basis, disciplined them, and dismissed them (if necessary), the temps were most likely considered to be "jointly employed." In most cases, temp workers easily met these two conditions. The *Sturgis* decision thus opened the door for temps to join permanent employees' unions. This amounted to a major union victory.

Not surprisingly, the *Sturgis* ruling elicited strong reactions from both its opponents and its supporters. For instance, both the National Association of Temporary and Staffing Services (NATSS) and the AFL-CIO filed amicus curiae briefs presenting their opposing positions in the case. Temp executives maintained that the decision unfairly favored the interests of union leaders, giving "unions the power to force temporary employees into bargaining units with a customer's regular employees."[130] What's more, they argued, the ruling could depress the economy by creating a "significant chilling effect on the use of temporary workers."[131] On the other hand, AFL-CIO president John Sweeney applauded the decision as an "important step in addressing the rights of contingent . . . employees, who have too often been relegated second-class status and rights—if any."[132]

Despite the ruling, however, the government proved an unreliable ally for union efforts to organize temps. As the National Labor Relations Board shifted from a Clinton- to a Bush-appointed majority in the early 2000s, it overturned a number of rulings from the previous era, including the *Sturgis* decision. In its 2004 *Oakwood Care Center* decision, the NLRB once again ruled that temps and their permanent counterparts were legally employed by two different employers. The ruling declared that bargaining units consisting of temps were "multi-employer" units that required the consent of each employer.[133] The reversal of the 2000 ruling was welcomed with enthusiasm by the business community, especially the temp industry. Leaders of the American Staffing Association wrote that even though they had expected the new Bush-appointed board to reconsider previous decisions, "the completeness of the repudiation of the prior board's reasoning in *Sturgis* comes as something of a surprise, albeit a welcome one from the standpoint of the staffing industry and its customers."[134]

Thus, like the campaign to mandate better wages, benefits, and working conditions for temps, union efforts to organize temporary workers ran into tremendous difficulty. Nonetheless, their work was not a total loss. Their efforts proved that no one was "unorganizable." By working to organize day laborers, high-tech contractors, and temps of all stripes, union leaders laid the groundwork for a powerful new labor movement for the twenty-first century and, even more so, a revised asset model of work that incorporated rather than excluded temps.

The third campaign to improve temporary work was somewhat different from the previous two. Instead of trying to make temp work better, this campaign sought to ensure that temp jobs did not replace permanent ones. Reformers tackled this issue in two ways. First, they sought to proscribe long-term temporary work. Second, they devised creative strategies to transform temp jobs into permanent, secure positions. With their renewed emphasis on asset model "careers" rather than "no strings attached" liability work, these efforts offered a promising alternative to the temp industry's model of work.

The movement to circumscribe long-term temporary work was spearheaded by a major reversal of policy at the Office of Personnel Management (OPM) in 1994. As described in Chapter 3, in the mid-1980s, the government drastically expanded its use of direct-hire temporary workers—short-term employees hired directly by federal agencies. At that time, Reagan-appointed officials increased the maximum length of "temporary" assignments in the federal government from two to four years. In 1994, however, Jim King, the Clinton-appointed director of the Office of Personnel Management, reversed that ruling and reinstated the two-year limit on temps.[135] "The use of temporary employees in the federal government must be restricted to jobs which are truly temporary," King declared. "There is a legitimate role for a temporary work force in government, although, abuse of the temporary hiring authority flies in the face of fairness."[136]

The decision to restrict public-sector temp work was prompted by a series of investigations that revealed endemic misuse of temporary workers by federal agencies. As the inquiries revealed, the government was inappropriately hiring temporary workers for long periods of time—up to ten years or more—without providing them with the benefits or security that civil service employment guaranteed. The investigations highlighted the tragic case of James Hudson, who had worked for the National Park Service in an ongoing series of temporary appointments over the course of eight years. In 1993, Hudson died of a heart attack after working three shifts over a two-day weekend. Because he was a temporary worker, his family was not eligible for pension or life insurance benefits. However, as part of the Department of Interior and Related Agencies Appropriations Act of 1994, Congress gave Hudson's family $38,400, equivalent to what they would have received in life insurance benefits had he been a permanent employee.[137]

In truth, the federal government employed many permatemps like James Hudson. According to a 1992 OPM study, in some federal agencies up to 20 percent of temporary workers were "making a career" out of temp work.[138] In these agencies, government officials observed, temporary work "has expanded to become quasi-permanent employment for many. In contravention of OPM rules, temporary employees are being utilized to perform ongoing work."[139]

The disclosure of such practices provoked considerable consternation. After hearing the testimonies of numerous temps who had worked for years in federal jobs, U.S. Representative Frank McClosky declared, "The fact that a temporary worker has been employed for 20 years without any rights is heinous and must not be allowed to continue."[140] The resulting limits on long-term temporary assignments seemed to indicate that federal employment policy had changed direction, backing away from its former embrace of the temp industry's liability model of work.

Ultimately, however, this proved not to be the case. First and foremost, the impact of the 1994 policy was severely limited. It suffered from two significant problems, one of which was lack of oversight. Although the ten federal agencies that employed the vast majority of temps dutifully imposed the new time limits on temporary assignments, they did not monitor workers' total years of continuous temporary employment, and neither did the Office of Personnel Management. According to government employment data, six years after the policy was implemented, sixteen thousand temporary workers—or 11 percent of the government's temporary workforce—already had five or more years of federal service, well above the two-year limit.[141]

The second problem with the government's policy was its loopholes that allowed federal agencies to hire long-term temps. Even though two years arguably exceeded a reasonable length of time for a "temporary" assignment, the policy permitted extensions on the already generous limit. For instance, federal agencies could repeatedly re-appoint or convert temporary workers to new appointments without violating the policy's guidelines. They could also sidestep the two-year limit if temporary employees worked less than six months a year. OPM officials found that, as a result, thousands of park rangers were hired in temporary appointments at one park for the summer season and at another park for the winter season, year after year, on a "quasipermanent" basis. Because the Office of Personnel Management considered each park a separate employer, this long-term, essentially full-time employment of "temporary" workers in federal jobs could continue unchecked. Federal agencies could also exceed the two-year limit by obtaining approval from OPM officials. According to the U.S. General Accounting Office, such approval was increasingly forthcoming. In 1998, OPM officials approved 110 requests for extensions of temporary assignments that affected 332 employees. The following year, they authorized 50 percent more extensions, involving 426 temporary workers. And in 2000, the numbers continued to rise.[142]

But the most significant challenge to the government's 1994 restrictions on public sector temporary workers came just two years later, as OPM officials expanded federal agencies' ability to use temps from private-sector companies such as Manpower and Kelly.[143] As described in

Chapter 3, the government first authorized the use of private-sector temps in federal agencies in 1989. Their use, however, was severely limited. Under the 1989 policy, government agencies could not use any one temp for more than forty-five work days (about two months), nor could they staff any one federal job with temps for more than 120 calendar days (about four months).[144] In 1996, however, OPM officials did away with these relatively strict limits. Under the new regulations, federal agencies could use private-sector temps for up to 240 work days.[145] Given that there are 260 federal work days in a year, the revised policy meant that temps from Manpower and Kelly could work full-time for nearly a year in government jobs. Although this time limit was still about half that of direct-hire temps, the move to expand rather than contract temp work indicated that the government had not really changed direction at all. In fact, even in the face of significant pushback, the liability model continued to make inroads into this last redoubt of asset model work.

In addition to seeking to proscribe long-term temporary work, activists sought to create permanent, secure positions out of temporary ones. Relying on a combination of collective power and innovation, labor leaders in a variety of sectors sought to satisfy employers' need for flexibility while at the same time providing "good" jobs to workers. The Communications Workers of America (CWA), for example, negotiated with AT&T to create a team of full-time, unionized clerical workers who would rotate across temporary jobs in the company's various departments, effectively eliminating the need for temps.[146] Similarly, the American Federation of State, County, and Municipal Employees (AFSCME) successfully bargained with the state of Pennsylvania to reduce its reliance on temps by creating an internal pool of unionized temporary workers who would be given priority for permanent job openings.[147] Finally, the Labor Pool Workers Union in Atlanta, Georgia, pressured Emory University to give its temporary construction workers full-time, living wage jobs.[148]

Despite numerous challenges, activists and reformers mounted significant opposition to the temp industry in the 1990s. At a glance, their campaigns could hardly be called a success: Even their greatest triumphs were severely limited in scope. This was, in part, because the temp industry was expanding and gaining strength like never before, as was the liability model of work. But it was also because resistance efforts (perhaps necessarily) challenged only the temp industry's more extreme abuses rather than the liability model itself.

Yet even though their efforts did not result in systematic reform of the employment relationship, they laid the foundation necessary for such change. Their campaigns proved that using the temp industry's model of work was not the only way to organize work and make a profit. They showed that employers could gain flexibility without exploiting workers. And, most of all, they made it possible to imagine a new model of work—one that takes the best aspects of the temp industry and incorporates them into a revised asset model of work for the twenty-first century.

CONCLUSION

A Model of Work for the Twenty-First Century

Despite the emergence of organized opposition to the temp industry, the history of the industry has been, by and large, a tremendous success story. At the start of the twenty-first century, the temp industry's triumph seemed nearly complete: The industry employed some three million workers a day, and 90 percent of employers used temp industry services. Moreover, the liability model of work had not experienced so much power since before World War II. Given the scope and scale of this victory, the success of the temp industry's model of work might seem inevitable—almost a force of nature. But a closer look indicates that this success was far from predetermined. It was, instead, the result of active efforts by the industry to change the way employers—and all Americans—thought about the meaning of work.

As we have seen, the temp industry's purposeful march through the American economy has recently encountered challengers. These challengers have had relatively little success, but this does not mean that the industry's triumph is inexorable. Think of the temp industry's story itself: It began as a marginalized business of ill-repute with formidable enemies and became a world-renowned colossus vastly overshadowing the opposition. It is an awe-inspiring story indeed—but not just for the temp industry. Others who wish to bring about transformations in the meaning of work can take heart in the story as well. In this chapter, I draw on both temp industry innovations and reformers' challenges to outline a new version of the asset model that brings together the best of both.

To do this, we first need to take a clear-eyed look at the temp industry's success. At its core, the temp industry is a genuinely innovative idea. Many workers desire short-term work for a variety of reasons: They may be students on summer vacation, young workers testing out jobs, full-time workers hoping to earn extra money, retirees wanting to stay active, and so on. At the same time, many businesses need short-term workers when employees are out of the office, during the busy season, for projects that require outside specialists, and for other reasons.

Thus, it is not surprising that the temp industry has emerged as an important fixture in the economy. In fact, it has become a key link between workers and employers, helping them find each other in an increasingly complicated economic landscape. And at a time when employers are cutting training programs and hiring already experienced applicants, the industry has become an indispensable training provider, equipping workers with much-needed skills while furnishing businesses with qualified employees. Finally, the industry has become a major source of flexibility in an intensely competitive, fast-paced economy. In short, genuine innovation has helped make the temp industry an entrepreneurial success story.

Genuine innovation cannot explain all of the temp industry's success, however. Indeed, much of its growth has come from less benign sources. From innovative ideas metastasized an industry that mounted a comprehensive assault on worker pay and protections. Instead of selling flexibility to those who needed it, the temp industry promoted flexibility for everyone, casting permanent employees as expensive inventory that should not be kept in stock. The industry amassed profits by pushing beyond simple economies of scale; it sought to cut costs however possible and encouraged businesses to do the same. Thus, the positive aspects of the temp industry have become entangled with the exploitation of workers and the degradation of work.

This need not be the case. Building on the efforts described in the previous chapter, I propose that it is possible to create a new asset model of work that responds to (and incorporates) the temp industry's true innovations while limiting its harm for workers. To develop such a model, activists and lawmakers might consider four kinds of policy changes: First, re-link "work" and "place"; second, decouple social welfare programs from the workplace; third, make temping—and other low-wage jobs—decent, family-supporting work; and finally, take temps out of the anti-labor movement and let them into the labor movement. Taken together, these policies outline a new model of work—an asset model for the twenty-first century—that would strengthen the positive aspects of the temp industry while mitigating its destructive consequences for workers.

The first step in developing a revised model of work is to re-link "work" and "place." In the temp industry's model of employment, the workplace is an abstraction—an intangible place that is the source of temps' paychecks but not the site of their labor. As a consequence, temps have often slipped through the cracks of many employment laws that attribute employer obligations to work site employers, such as those dealing with workplace safety, workers' compensation, discrimination, wrongful discharge, and more. In the 1950s and 1960s, industry leaders inserted a wedge between "work" and "place" by creating a new category of white, middle-class work that did not have a "place" at all because, they argued, temps were not really "workers." They were wives and mothers, and their real "place" was in the home. For these women, temp work was "something nice, something extra."[1] In the 1970s, temp leaders deepened the divide between "work" and "place." They encouraged business owners to replace permanent employees with "permanent temporaries," to shift regular employees to the payrolls of temp agencies, and to outsource entire departments of permanent workers to the temp industry. Although at the time these strategies were only occasionally put to use, by the early 1990s they had become a fixture of many companies' business practices.

As we saw in Chapter 4, the growing prevalence and publicity of the permatemp phenomenon galvanized popular opposition to the temp industry. Activists argued that by using temps on a full-time, long-term basis, business owners were creating a permanent tier of second-class employees. Ultimately, although some permatemps met with success in their court battles, little changed. Employers continued to use temps as long-term full-time employees who did not receive the same pay and benefits that permanent workers received. It is thus necessary to re-link "work" and "place" by clearly defining to what place workers belong and by requiring the equitable treatment of all workers at that place. In the case of permatemps, their "place" of work is clear: It is the site and beneficiary of their labor.

A greater emphasis on the connection between "work" and "place" would affect not only permatemps but all temporary workers. As described in the previous chapter, both work site employers and temp agencies have exploited the complexities of the triangular employment relationship to avoid responsibility for workers. In the case of worker injuries, for example, temp agencies regularly disputed liability because they did not have sufficient control over the workplace, while businesses disputed liability because they were not the legal employers of temps. The result was an absurd standoff that could only be solved in the courts; meanwhile, the injured worker waited or, worse, paid legal fees.

But there was some progress in the area of worker protections. In the 1990s, the courts and federal agencies increasingly began to hold work site employers—in addition to temp agencies—accountable for a range of worker protections. The rules for establishing accountability have been developed in a piecemeal fashion, however; they vary from agency to agency and are incredibly complex, often requiring court hearings for resolution. New policies are needed to establish clear-cut, uniform regulations that hold temp agencies and work site employers jointly liable for a range of employer obligations, including workplace safety, freedom from discrimination, compliance with labor laws, and lawful hiring and firing decisions. Such policies would prevent temps from slipping through the cracks of employment laws that attribute worker protections to a single "place."

Policies re-linking "work" and "place" would have a mixed impact on the temp industry. On one hand, by reducing the incentive for businesses to use permatemps while strengthening agencies' obligations toward temp workers, such policies would undoubtedly increase costs for the industry. On the other hand, by requiring work site employers to share the expense of protecting temps, the policies may actually lessen the industry's burden (although they might also reduce employers' eagerness to use temps in some circumstances). The outcome for workers would be less ambiguous. Employers could no longer treat temps as second-class employees, nor could they evade liability for inadequate working conditions. In short, policies that re-link "work" and "place" would allow the temp industry to thrive, but the industry would no longer be able to redraw the lines of the labor market so that exploitation of workers would be a viable way to boost profits.

The second objective of the revised asset model of work is to decouple social welfare programs—such as health care benefits—from the employment relationship. In the 1950s and 1960s, early industry leaders established a new sphere of white, middle-class work that was exempt from the obligation to provide social protections to workers. The industry was able to do this because temps were portrayed as housewives working for pin money rather than as breadwinners supporting families. In the 1970s, even as industry leaders expanded beyond their original niche in the secondary labor market, they retained this distinction. In fact, avoiding "fringe benefit nonsense" became a major selling point.[2] Industry leaders repeatedly warned businesses of the high and growing costs of worker benefits such as health insurance ("30% of every payroll dollar").[3] And many employers took the bait. As described in Chapter 3, avoiding the cost of health insurance was a major reason for the government's drastic increase in federal temporary workers in 1985. And as we saw in Chapter 4, by the 1990s the disparity between temps' and regular workers' access to health insurance and other fringe benefits had become an area of intense conflict leading to the *Microsoft* case and many other court battles.

Indeed, a number of recent studies have found that avoiding health insurance costs remains one of the primary motivations for using temps.[4] Not surprisingly, the consequences for workers have been dramatic. Only 7 percent of temps (compared with 61 percent of traditional workers) receive health benefits from their employers, and this is not because they typically get insurance coverage from other sources. According to the research, fewer than half of all temporary workers are insured, compared with 83 percent of the regular workforce.[5]

Taking health care benefits out of the employment relationship would correct this imbalance. Many activists and scholars have pointed to the need for a single-payer, universal health care system.[6] Such a policy would have a mixed effect on the temp industry. By diminishing the incentive to use temps simply to avoid health care costs, it could lower temp industry employment. But a universal health care system could also be a great boon for the industry. Without having to worry about health insurance, workers could more freely choose temp work over permanent employment.

If the effects of such a policy on the industry would be mixed, the consequences for workers would be clear. They would have equal and unimpeded access to health care, regardless of their occupation and employment status. In addition, as others have noted, universal health care would provide a range of other social benefits, including lower health care costs and decreased social inequality. In short, decoupling social welfare programs from the workplace would preserve a place in the economy for those who specialize in personnel management, but it would not allow employers to increase profits by not adequately protecting workers. What's more, it would eliminate a major downside of temporary employment for workers.

The third step in developing a revised model of work is to make temping—along with other low-wage jobs—decent, family-supporting work. The simplest way to do this would be to raise the minimum wage to a "living wage." As we saw in Chapter 1, early industry leaders sold temp work as a way for housewives to earn some extra spending money. Industry executives maintained that these were secondary jobs for secondary workers, not family-supporting jobs. In the 1970s, as industry leaders rebuilt the model of temp work to include male breadwinners, they continued to market temping as a source of "supplemental income"; alternately, they argued that temps were willing to trade greater flexibility for lower wages. As shown in Chapter 3, this portrayal of temps continued into the 1980s; industry leaders described temps as wanting a "more entrepreneurial life," with greater freedom, autonomy, and leisure time—and they were willing to give up wages to get it. As evidenced by the rash of permatemp cases in the 1990s, however, many temps worked full-time year round—in other words, without flexibility—while earning lower wages and benefits than their permanent counterparts.

In fact, according to labor market scholars, temps earn significantly lower wages than permanent employees, even when controlling for differences between workers.[7] Not surprisingly, the majority of temps would choose full-time, permanent work over the so-called "entrepreneurial life" of temping.[8] And the temp industry's low wages have affected not only temps; a number of researchers have argued that the industry's low wages exert a downward pressure on wages for all workers.[9]

As many activists have acknowledged, one way to stop such a downward spiral would be to make temping a decent job in its own right. However, instead of developing complicated laws that would equalize the wages of temps and permanent workers, a simpler and more far-reaching approach would be to boost wages across the board by making the federal minimum wage a "living wage." This is hardly a unique proposition. As the real value of the minimum wage has declined over the past thirty years, many scholars have argued for the need to increase the minimum wage; this would help the growing population of people who are poor despite the fact that they are working full-time and holding down several jobs at once.[10]

Increasing the minimum wage would not undermine the temp industry's positive impact on the labor market, including its role in connecting workers to jobs, providing workers with much-needed training and labor market information, and increasing flexibility for employers. It would, however, diminish the industry's profits derived from paying workers substandard wages. Yet by not forcing workers to choose between family-supporting jobs and employment flexibility, such a policy might actually increase the ranks of temporary workers.

The fourth component in a revised model of work has two parts: First, take temps out of the anti-labor movement and, second, let them into the labor movement. As we saw in Chapter 1, early temp industry leaders strategically marketed temp work as women's work in order to avoid opposition from powerful unions in the (male) manufacturing sector. This was a clever strategy given the labor movement's long-term exclusion of women workers, and, for the most part, industry leaders escaped union antagonism. Even when the temp industry expanded into male breadwinning jobs in the 1970s, temp executives continued to show great deference for union power (even if it was not always upheld), particularly during labor disputes.

This changed in the 1980s, however. As described in Chapter 3, two key rulings by Reagan-appointed officials in 1985 turned temporary workers into powerful weapons against unions. By allowing employers to replace union workers with temps during both strikes and lockouts, the rulings significantly contributed to the already shifting balance of power between labor and management. This shift was furthered by temp leaders who launched agencies expressly to supply strikebreakers to businesses involved in labor disputes. Yet even as labor law shifted in favor of management in the 1980s, quite a few employers exceeded the bounds of the newly expansive laws in using temps to quash unions. In the cases of Middle Earth Graphics and M.P.C. Plating, for example, employers illegally forced their permanent employees onto the payrolls of temp agencies in order to thwart union organization. These were not isolated incidents, nor were they unique to the 1980s: Employers have continued to use temps illegally in order to defeat labor unions.[11]

It is necessary to level the labor-management playing field by prohibiting such practices. During labor disputes, workers and their employers are supposed to have reasonably equivalent incentives to reach a compromise. Locked out or striking workers lose much-needed wages, while their employers lose production and business. However, as long as employers are easily able to replace workers, their incentive for compromise is greatly reduced.

It is not enough, however, to take temps out of the anti-labor movement. A revised model of work requires that they be allowed to enter the labor movement. In the postwar era, the women's work that the temp industry advertised was far removed from labor unions; this was, in part, a result of unions' exclusionary practices, but it was also because, at that time, temps were truly short-term, interim workers. In the 1970s and 1980s, union leaders were consumed with the struggle to hold on to their industrial base, so organizing a new population of workers, especially a population as difficult to organize as temps, seemed a Herculean task. But as we saw in Chapter 4, union leaders have recently begun to argue that temps and other nonstandard workers are essential to a revitalized labor movement. The impressive story of SEIU Local 100 and the garbage collectors in New Orleans is a case in point. But even if more union leaders were to follow this example, only modest progress could be made without removing the undue burden on temps seeking to join unions. As described in Chapter 4, the National Labor Relations Board's *Sturgis* ruling was a decisive move in the right direction. Although its reversal four years later proved just how tenuous—and controversial—the ruling was, it also demonstrated that labor law is not irrevocable.

With a revised asset model of work, the temp industry will continue to thrive as an important link between workers and employers, a key source of information and training, and a purveyor of much-needed flexibility. It will no longer be able to profit from the exploitation of workers, but the genuine innovation of the temp industry's model of work suggests that it does not need this kind of exploitation to remain a healthy and viable industry.

The version of the asset model of work described here is undoubtedly a utopian vision. It is one in which workers can choose flexible employment without giving up decent wages, access to benefits, and basic workplace rights. In this model, all workers, including temps, have the equal and unobstructed right to organize and bargain collectively. Employers are free to adjust their staff levels to correspond with ebbs and flows in demand, but they can no longer avoid responsibility for workers, nor can they treat some workers as second-class. They also are not able to pit workers against each other in their opposition to unions. This is indeed an idyllic vision. And like all such visions, it will not be easy to achieve. But with the example of the temp industry itself before us—an industry that used a few central innovations to leverage a wide-scale transformation of work—it may not be too much to hope for.

APPENDIX

A Note on Sources

I gathered the data for this book over the course of two years. Instead of waiting until all the data were in to evaluate them, I continually made preliminary interpretations, analyzing and writing as I went. This invariably led to new questions, further research, other scholarly literatures, and revised analyses. Research for this book thus took the shape of an ever-changing series of three-dimensional concentric circles—expanding horizontally into larger, broader circles while at the same time expanding vertically into smaller, more focused ones. It was, as Howard Becker would say, a truly "iterative process."[1] The purpose of this Appendix is to give readers an overview of the data that were used in this process.

The data for this project can be divided into six categories of documents: industry publications; popular media; business publications; advertisements; court cases; and government documents. The temp industry itself was an indispensable source of data. Although few realize it today, temp executives were once prolific authors. They produced a treasure trove of would-be popular books that have thus far escaped scholarly attention. For instance, Elmer Winter, the founder and first president of Manpower, wrote six books: *A Woman's Guide to Earning a Good Living* (1961); *How to Be an Effective Secretary* (1965); *Cutting Costs through the Effective Use of Temporary and Part-Time Help* (1966); *1,015 Ways to Save Time, Trouble, and Money in the Operation of Your Business* (1967); *Women at Work: Every Women's Guide to Successful Employment* (1967); and *Your Future as a Temporary Office Worker* (1968). These and more than a dozen other books written by temp executives yielded invaluable insight into the temp industry and its rhetoric. Another source of temp publications was the industry's trade association—first called the Institute for Temporary Services, today known as the American Staffing Association. I analyzed two hundred of its documents, from "fact sheets" describing the industry to legal guides for agency managers, from inventories of the industry's legislative efforts to white papers on permatemps. These documents provided a crucial "insider's view" to the temp industry.

To examine popular media on the temp industry, I used *The Reader's Guide to Periodical Literature* to find some 550 magazine articles on the temp industry from 1946 to 2000. These articles came from a range of magazines, from *McCall's* to *Ms. Magazine*, from *Retirement Living* to *Parents* magazine (see Table A1 for a complete list). Finding these articles required some ingenuity, however, since the entry "Employees, temporary" was not indexed in the *Reader's Guide* until 1955. Thus, I searched for the names of individual temp agencies and their founders (for instance, Sam Workman, generally believed to be the founder of the first modern temp agency, debuted in the *Reader's Guide* in 1949). In addition, I searched for a wide variety of potentially related keywords, including "Employees," "Employment," "Employment agencies," "Employment management," "Office management," "Office workers," "Secretaries," "Woman, employment," "Woman, occupations," "Working girls and women," "Married women, employment," "Business and professional women," "Work," and "Industrial relations." Even after "Employees, temporary" was indexed, I continued using this expanded list of keywords to ensure a complete dataset. The articles in these magazines were quite diverse: Many were written by temp industry executives themselves, touting the benefits of the industry for workers, businesses, and the economy; others were written by industry boosters, encouraging housewives to try temping, for example, or describing the flexibility of the "free agent" lifestyle; and yet others worried over the growing industry and its downsides for workers.

In order to analyze business publications, I used the *Business Periodicals Index* (known as the *Industrial Arts Index* until 1958) to find some 820 articles on the temp industry from 1946 to 2000. These were published in a wide variety of trade journals, from *Black Enterprise* to *National Petroleum News*, from *International Management* to *Printer's Ink* (see Table A2 for a complete list). Because *Business Periodicals* did not index "Employees, temporary" until 1958, I expanded my search using the supplementary keywords described above, with the addition of

TABLE A1   POPULAR MAGAZINES

Chatelaine	*Ladies' Home Journal*	*Reader's Digest*
Collier's	*Mademoiselle*	*Redbook*
Essence	*McCall's*	*Retirement Living*
Glamour	*Ms. Magazine*	*Time*
Good Housekeeping	*Newsweek*	*U.S. News and World Report*
Independent Woman	*Parents*	*Working Woman*

a number of search terms related to the entry "Labor"—such as "Labor, cost," "Labor, supply," and "Labor, casual." Even more often than in popular media, these business articles were written by temp industry executives themselves, describing inventive ways to use temps and the advantages of doing so; others were written by business pundits, usually echoing industry rhetoric in describing the cost savings of temps.

These popular magazines and business journals also yielded another crucial source of data: temp industry advertisements. I collected nine hundred of these. The cornerstone of this dataset was the entire population of ads from 1955 to 1995 in four trade journals that were particularly favored by temp industry marketers: *The Office, Personnel Journal, Personnel Administrator*, and *Administrative Journal*. At times, temp ads in these journals were nearly ubiquitous. Throughout the 1970s, for example, Manpower published a full-page advertisement in virtually every volume of *The Office* and the *Personnel Journal*. And in the early 1980s, the readers of *Personnel Administrator* could not miss the full-page ads of the top three temp agencies that appeared in every issue: Manpower on page 1, Olsten Services on page 3, and Kelly Services on the back cover. Indeed, it was not only the content but the sheer volume of such advertisements that helped shape my argument about the importance of the temp industry's role in articulating and circulating the liability model of work.

National newspapers provided an additional source of both advertisements and popular media coverage of the temp industry. I analyzed four hundred classified ads from the temp industry in the *New York Times*, the *Chicago Tribune*, and

---

TABLE A2   BUSINESS AND TRADE JOURNALS

Administrative Management	*Financial World*	*Office Administration and Automation*
Advanced Management Journal	*Forbes*	*Office Executive*
Advertising Age	*Fortune*	*Office Management*
American Business	*Harvard Business Review*	*Office Solutions*
Barron's Weekly	*Industry Week*	*Office Systems*
Black Enterprise	*International Management*	*Personnel Administrator*
Burroughs Clearing House	*Management Accounting*	*Personnel Journal*
Business Abroad	*Management Review*	*Personnel Management*
Business Marketing	*Management Today*	*Physics Today*
Business Week	*Management World*	*Printer's Ink*
Commercial and Financial Chronicle	*Managing Office Technology*	*Purchasing*
Credit and Financial Management	*Media Decisions*	*Sales Management*
Dun's Review	*Modern Office Technology*	*Steel*
Editor and Publisher	*National Petroleum News*	*Taxes*
Financial Times	*Nation's Business*	*Training*
	The Office	*Workforce*
		Workforce Management

the *Los Angeles Times* from 1946 to 2000. At times, the industry's advertising efforts in these newspapers were truly astounding. In the 1950s and 1960s, for instance, the leading temp agencies—Manpower, Kelly Girl, Workman Service, Employers Overload, and Western Girl—published more than six thousand ads in the *New York Times* alone. These newspapers also yielded a host of useful articles related to the temp industry, from profiles of early Kelly Girls to reports on the "downsizing of America."

Finally, I examined tens of thousands of pages of court cases and government documents related to the temp industry. These included 250 state and federal court cases, 50 pieces of legislation, 40 National Labor Relations Board cases, 32 reports by the U.S. Government Accountability Office (formerly the U.S. General Accounting Office), 24 congressional hearings, 12 reports by the Office of Personnel Management, and an assortment of other government documents, including reports by the Equal Employment Opportunity Commission and the Federal Trade Commission.

NOTES

FOREWORD

1. Nelson Lichtenstein, *The Retail Revolution: How Wal-Mart Created a Brave New World of Business* (New York: Metropolitan Books, 2009).
2. Tobias Higbie, *Indispensable Outcasts: Hobo Workers and Community in the American Midwest, 1880–1930* (Urbana: University of Illinois Press, 2003), 8.
3. See in particular Sanford Jacoby, *Modern Manors: Welfare Capitalism since the New Deal* (Princeton, NJ: Princeton University Press, 1997); and Jennifer Klein, *For All These Rights: Business, Labor, and the Shaping of America's Public-Private Welfare State* (Princeton, NJ: Princeton University Press, 2003).

PREFACE

1. John Pawasarat, "The Employer Perspective: Jobs Held by the Milwaukee County AFDC Single Parent Population, January 1996–March1997," University of Wisconsin-Milwaukee, Employment and Training Institute, 1999.
2. Richard Dunham, "Clinton's Welfare-to-Work CEOs," *BusinessWeek Online*, 9 January 1997, available at http://www.businessweek.com/bwdaily/dnflash/january/new0109a.htm (accessed 1 October 2009).
3. There are many examples of this. For example, see Richard Yamarone, *The Trader's Guide to Key Economic Indicators* (New York: Bloomberg Press, 2004); and U.S. Congress, *Economic Report of the President*, 108th Cong., 2nd Sess., 2004, pp. 94–95.

INTRODUCTION

1. "The Downsizing of America," *New York Times*, 3–9 March 1996, p. A1.

2. Arne Kalleberg, Barbara Reskin, and Ken Hudson, "Bad Jobs in America: Standard and Nonstandard Employment Relations and Job Quality in the United States," *American Sociological Review* 65, no. 2 (2000): 256–279.

3. Jamie Peck and Nikolas Theodore, "The Business of Contingent Work: Growth and Restructuring in Chicago's Temporary Employment Industry," *Work, Employment and Society* 12, no. 4 (1998): 655–674; Jamie Peck and Nik Theodore, "Contingent Chicago: Restructuring the Spaces of Temporary Labor," *International Journal of Urban and Regional Research* 25, no. 3 (September 2001): 471–496; Jamie Peck and Nikolas Theodore, "Temped Out? Industry Rhetoric, Labor Regulation, and Economic Restructuring in the Temporary Staffing Business," *Economic and Industrial Democracy* 23, no. 2 (2002): 143–175; Jamie Peck and Nik Theodore, "Flexible Recession: The Temporary Staffing Industry and Mediated Work in the United States," presented at the Annual Meeting of the Society for the Study of Social Problems (24 November 2004); Jamie Peck and Nik Theodore, "Temporary Downturn? Temporary Staffing in the Recession and the Jobless Recovery," *Focus* 23, no. 3 (2005): 35–41; also see George Gonos, "The Contest over 'Employer' Status in the Post-War United States: The Case of Temporary Help Firms," *Law Society Review* 31, no. 1 (1997): 81–110; George Gonos, "The Interaction between Market Incentives and Government Actions," in *Contingent Work: American Employment Relations in Transition*, ed. Kathleen Barker and Kathleen Christensen (Ithaca, NY: Cornell University Press, 1998), 170–191; George Gonos, "Fee-Splitting Revisited: Concealing Surplus Value in the Temporary Employment Relationship," *Politics and Society* 29, no. 4 (2001): 589–611; Nikolas Theodore and Jamie Peck, "The Temporary Staffing Industry: Growth Imperatives and Limits to Contingency," *Economic Geography* 78, no. 4 (2002); Nikolas Theodore, "Political Economies of Day Labour: Regulation and Restructuring of Chicago's Contingent Labour Markets," *Urban Studies* 40 (2003): 1811–1828; and Jamie Peck, Nik Theodore, and Kevin Ward, "Constructing Markets for Temporary Labour: Employment Liberalization and the Internationalization of the Staffing Industry," *Global Networks* 5, no. 1 (2005): 3–26.

4. Timothy Brogan, *Scaling New Heights: ASA's Annual Analysis of the Staffing Industry* (Alexandria, VA: American Staffing Association, 2001); and Steven Berchem, *Staffing Success* (Alexandria, VA: American Staffing Association, 2008). For more numbers on the temp industry, see Theodore and Peck, "The Temporary Staffing Industry," 463–493; Peck and Theodore, "Temporary Downturn?" 35–41; and American Staffing Association, *Staffing Facts* (Alexandria, VA: American Staffing Association, 2007).

5. Lance Morrow, "The Temping of America," *Time*, 29 March 1993, pp. 40–42; Janice Castro, "Disposable Workers," *Time*, 29 March 1993, pp. 43–47; also see U.S. Senate Committee on Labor and Human Resources, *Toward a Disposable*

Workforce: The Increasing Use of "Contingent" Labor, 103rd Cong., 1st Sess., 1993; and "The Contingency Work Force," *Fortune,* 24 January 1994, pp. 30–36.

6. J. Bradford DeLong, "The Jobless Recovery Has Begun," 20 July 2009, available at http://delong.typepad.com/sdj/2009/07/we-are-live-at-the-week-with-the-jobless-recovery-has-begun.html (accessed 29 July 2009).

7. Peter Drucker, "They're Not Employees, They're People," *Harvard Business Review* (February 2002): 5.

8. James Surowiecki, "It's the Workforce, Stupid!" *New Yorker,* 30 April 2007, p. 32.

9. Louis Uchitelle, "Pink Slip? Now, It's All in a Day's Work," *New York Times,* 5 August 2001, p. BU1. For more on the changing nature of employment, see Peter Cappelli, Laurie Bassi, Harry Katz, David Knoke, Paul Osterman, and Michael Useem, *Change at Work* (New York: Oxford University Press, 1997); and Paul Osterman, *Securing Prosperity: The American Labor Market: How It Has Changed and What to Do about It* (Princeton, NJ: Princeton University Press, 1999).

10. "Former Scott Paper Chief Named to Top Position at Sunbeam," *New York Times,* 19 July 1996, p. D5.

11. Glenn Collins, "Sunbeam to Halve Work Force of 12,000 and Sell Some Units," *New York Times,* 13 November 1996, p. D1; and Dana Canedy, "Amid Big Losses, Sunbeam Plans to Cut 6,400 Jobs and 8 Plants," *New York Times,* 12 May 1998, p. D1.

12. Floyd Norris, "S.E.C. Accuses Former Sunbeam Official of Fraud," *New York Times,* 16 May 2001, p. A1.

13. Albert Dunlap and Bob Andelman, *Mean Business: How I Save Bad Companies and Make Good Companies Great* (New York: Times Books, 1996).

14. Vicki Smith, "New Forms of Work Organization," *Annual Review of Sociology* 23 (1997): 315–339; and Paul Osterman, *Securing Prosperity.*

15. Brian Hassett, *The Temp Survival Guide: How to Prosper as an Economic Nomad of the Nineties* (Secaucus, NJ: Citadel Press, 1996); also see Peggy O'Connell Justice, *The Temp Track: Make One of the Hottest Job Trends of the 90s Work for You* (Princeton, NJ: Peterson's, 1993).

16. For example, see the extensive work of Joel Rogers and Laura Dresser at the Center on Wisconsin Strategy (COWS) at the University of Wisconsin, Madison, available at http://cows.org/ (accessed 13 November 2009).

17. The liability and asset models of work, as I conceive them, roughly parallel other categorizations that scholars have made. For instance, in the 1940s economic historian Karl Polanyi identified a "double movement" between the desire for a free market on the one hand, and, on the other hand, the struggle for worker protections (*The Great Transformation* [New York: Octagon Books, 1944]). Arne Kalleberg recently reframed Polanyi's "double movement" as a pendulum that has swung between employment flexibility and job security ("Precarious Work, Insecure Workers: Employment Relations in Transition," *American Sociological*

Review 74 [February 2009]: 1–22). And, finally, Stephen Barley and Gideon Kunda examined the periodic alternation of rational and normative approaches to managerial control ("Design and Devotion: Surges of Rational and Normative Ideologies of Control in Managerial Discourse," *Administrative Science Quarterly* 37, no. 3 [September 1992]: 363–399).

18. Again, a good example among many is the extensive work of Joel Rogers and Laura Dresser at the Center on Wisconsin Strategy (COWS) at the University of Wisconsin, Madison, available at http://cows.org/ (accessed 13 November 2009).

19. Nelson Lichtenstein, *Walter Reuther: The Most Dangerous Man in Detroit* (New York: Basic Books, 1995); and Lichtenstein, *State of the Union: A Century of American Labor* (Princeton, NJ: Princeton University Press, 2003); also see Nancy MacLean, *Freedom Is Not Enough: The Opening of the American Workplace* (Cambridge, MA: Harvard University Press, 2006).

20. Lichtenstein, *Walter Reuther*; and Lichtenstein, *State of the Union*.

21. Osterman, *Securing Prosperity*.

22. For example, one Sunbeam executive told the *New York Times* in 1996, "We wouldn't have blamed [Dunlap] if he fired us all" (Glen Collins, "For a Struggling Sunbeam, Shock Therapy," New York Times, 11 August 1996, C1).

23. Bennett Harrison and Barry Bluestone, *The Great U-Turn: Corporate Restructuring and the Polarization of America* (New York: Basic Books, 1988).

24. Harrison and Bluestone, *The Great U-Turn*; Thomas Kochan, Harry Charles Katz, and Robert McKersie, *The Transformation of American Industrial Relations*, 2nd ed. (New York: Basic Books, 1994).

25. Scholars have generally not made this argument, although a number of studies have shown that it was employers' demand for temp industry services—rather than workers' preference for becoming temps—that helped drive temp industry growth (for instance, see Lonnie Golden and Eileen Appelbaum, "What Was Driving the 1982–88 Boom in Temporary Employment? Preference of Workers or Decisions and Power of Employers," *American Journal of Economics and Sociology* 51 [1992]: 473–493). The current study builds on this argument by showing how temp industry leaders created and shaped employer demand over time.

26. Samuel Sacco, "Temporary Help/Staffing Services: Still Growing, Still Evolving," *Managing Office Technology* 39, no. 5 (May 1994): A2.

27. Castro, "Disposable Workers."

28. Lisa Adler, "Discourses of Flexibility and the Rise of the Temp Industry, or How I Met the 'Kelly Girl' Commuting between Public and Private," *International Feminist Journal of Politics* 1, no. 2 (September 1999): 215 (emphasis in original).

29. Press release from Kelly Services, January 14, 1998 (quoted in Adler, "Discourses of Flexibility"); also see Martha Finney and Deborah Dasch, *A Heritage of Service: The History of Temporary Help in America* (Alexandria, VA: National Association of Temporary Services, 1991), 82.

30. Roland Marchand, *Advertising the American Dream: Making a Way for Modernity, 1920–1940* (Berkeley: University of California Press, 1985); and James Twitchell, *Twenty Ads That Shook the World: The Century's Most Groundbreaking Advertising and How It Changed Us All* (New York: Three Rivers Press, 2000); also see Susan Strasser, *Satisfaction Guaranteed: The Making of the American Mass Market* (New York: Pantheon Books, 1989).

31. Pierre Bourdieu, "La précarité est aujourd'hui partout," in *Contre-feux* (Paris: Liber-Raison d'agir, 1998), 95–101; also see Kalleberg, "Precarious Work, Insecure Workers."

32. For a complete discussion of these definitions, see Arne Kalleberg, Edith Rasell, Naomi Cassirer, Barbara Reskin, Ken Hudson, David Webster, Eileen Appelbaum, and Roberta Spalter-Roth, *Nonstandard Work, Substandard Jobs: Flexible Work Arrangements in the United States* (Washington, DC: Economic Policy Institute, 1997); and Kalleberg et al., "Bad Jobs in America."

33. Gonos, "The Interaction between Market Incentives and Government Actions"; also see Efren Cordova, "From Full-Time Wage Employment to Atypical Employment: A Major Shift in the Evolution of Labour Relations?" *International Labour Review* 125 (1986): 641–657; Robert Moberly, "Temporary, Part-Time, and Other Atypical Employment Relationships in the U.S.," *Labor Law Journal* 16 (1987): 620–634; and Heidi Gottfried, "In the Margins: Flexibility as a Mode of Regulation in the Temporary Service Industry," *Work, Employment, and Society* 6, no. 3 (1992): 443–460.

34. It should be noted, however, that the temp industry's claim to employer status was highly contentious and hard won, as George Gonos has shown. For more, see George Gonos, "A Sociology of the Temporary Employment Relationship" (Ph.D. diss., Rutgers University, 1994); Gonos, "The Contest over 'Employer' Status"; and Gonos, "The Interaction between Market Incentives and Government Actions."

35. The majority of American workers—standard and nonstandard alike—are employed under the doctrine of "at-will employment," meaning that employers can fire workers for any reason. But over the last half of the twentieth century, employers' ability to fire workers became increasingly limited, and, as a result, some groups of workers gained protections from "wrongful discharge." Temps, however, were not among them. In reality, businesses can terminate temps for any reason, including discrimination that is otherwise illegal, because they are not temps' legal employer. For more, see David Autor, "Outsourcing at Will: Unjust Dismissal Doctrine and the Growth of Temporary Help Employment," NBER Working Paper No. 7959 (February 2000); and "Outsourcing at Will: The Contribution of Unjust Dismissal Doctrine to the Growth of Employment Outsourcing," *Journal of Labor Economics* 21, no. 1 (January 2003): 1–42.

36. For a few examples of the many court cases in which industry leaders disputed temp workers' compensation and unemployment benefits claims, see *Cooke v. Kelly Services and CNA Insurance*, 591 So. 2d 1041 (Fla. App. 1991); *Vejdani v.*

Western Temporary Services, 486 N.W. 2d 461 (Minn. App. 1992); *Olsten Temporary Services v. State of Wyoming*, 870 P. 2d 360 (Wyo. 1994); *Donald v. Manpower and Unemployment Insurance Appeal Board*, No. 93A-10-006 (Del. Super. 1995); *Harris v. Western Temporary Services*, C9-95-1426 (Minn. App. 1995); *Andrews v. Manpower, Inc.*, C7-98-158 (Minn. App. 1998); *Ess v. Olsten Staffing Services*, CX-99-939 (Minn. App. 1999); and *Kelly Temporary Services v. Workers' Compensation Appeals Board*, Unpub. (Cal. App. 2004). In some cases, temp industry leaders even backpedaled on their own claim to be the legal employer of temps, supposedly responsible for all the typical legal obligations to workers, by arguing that they should not be held liable because they did not control the workplace. For example, see *Bilotta v. Labor Pool*, 321 N.W.2d 888 (Minn. Sup. Court 1982); *Colwell and the State Compensation Insurance Fund v. Perry Oatman and Labor Pool of Colorado, Inc.*, 510 P.2d 464 (Colo. App. 1973); and *Henderson v. Manpower*, 319 S.E.2d 690 (N.C. App. 1984).

37. National Employment Law Project, "Temp Work and Unemployment Insurance—Helping Employees at Temporary Staffing and Employee Leasing Agencies: When May an Employee Be Denied Unemployment Benefits between Jobs?" Report published by NELP, New York, August 2001; also see Nikolas Theodore and Chirag Mehta, *Contingent Work and the Staffing Industry: A Review of Worker-Centered Policy and Practice* (Chicago: Center for Urban Economic Development, University of Illinois at Chicago, 1999); and, for a specific example, see *Manpower, Inc. v. State of Kansas*, 11 Kan. App.2d 382, 724 P.2d 690 (Kan. App. 1986).

38. Kathleen Barker and Kathleen Christensen, eds., *Contingent Work: American Employment Relations in Transition* (Ithaca, NY: Cornell University Press, 1998); Rebecca Blank, "Contingent Work in a Changing Labor Market," in *Generating Jobs*, ed. Richard Freeman and Peter Gottschalk (New York: Russell Sage Foundation, 1998), 258–294; Sharon Cohany, "Workers in Alternative Employment Arrangements: A Second Look," *Monthly Labor Review* 121, no. 11 (1998): 3–22; Marcello Estevão and Saul Lach, "The Evolution of the Demand for Temporary Help Supply Employment in the United States," NBER Working Paper 7427 (Cambridge, MA: National Bureau of Economic Research, 1999); Brogan, *Scaling New Heights*; Berchem, *Staffing Success*; and Susan Houseman, Arne Kalleberg, and George Erickcek, "The Role of Temporary Agency Employment in Tight Labor Markets," *Industrial and Labor Relations Review* 57, no. 1 (2003).

39. Matt Vidal and Leann Tigges, "Temporary Employment and Strategic Staffing in the Manufacturing Sector," *Industrial Relations* 48, no. 1 (January 2009): 55–72; Theodore and Peck, "The Temporary Staffing Industry: Growth Imperatives and Limits to Contingency."

40. Theodore and Peck, "The Temporary Staffing Industry: Growth Imperatives and Limits to Contingency"; also see Lewis Segal and Daniel Sullivan, "The Temporary Labor Force," *Economic Perspectives* 19, no. 2 (1995): 2–19; Cohany, "Workers in Alternative Employment Arrangements"; Estevão and Lach, "The

Evolution of the Demand for Temporary Help Supply Employment in the United States"; and Peck and Theodore, "Temporary Downturn."

41. Peck and Theodore, "The Business of Contingent Work."

42. Theodore and Peck, "The Temporary Staffing Industry: Growth Imperatives and Limits to Contingency"; Kevin Ward, "Going Global? Internationalization and Diversification in the Temporary Staffing Industry," *Journal of Economic Geography* 4, no. 3 (June 2004): 251–273; Chris Forde, " 'You Know We Are Not an Employment Agency': Manpower, Government and the Development of the Temporary Help Industry in Britain," *Enterprise and Society* 9, no. 2 (2008): 337–365; and, Peck, Theodore, and Ward, "Constructing Markets for Temporary Labour."

43. Lawrence Katz and Alan Krueger, "The High Pressure U.S. Labor Market of the 1990s," *Brookings Papers on Economic Activity* 1, no. 1 (1999): 1–65; Theodore and Peck, "The Temporary Staffing Industry: Growth Imperatives and Limits to Contingency"; and Peck and Theodore, "Temporary Downturn."

44. Peck and Theodore, "The Business of Contingent Work"; Peck and Theodore, "Contingent Chicago"; Peck and Theodore, "Temped Out"; Peck and Theodore, "Flexible Recession"; Peck and Theodore, "Temporary Downturn"; also see Gonos, "The Contest over 'Employer' Status"; Gonos, "The Interaction between Market Incentives and Government Actions"; Gonos, "Fee-Splitting Revisited"; Theodore and Peck, "The Temporary Staffing Industry: Growth Imperatives and Limits to Contingency"; Theodore, "Political Economies of Day Labour"; and, Peck, Theodore, and Ward, "Constructing Markets for Temporary Labour."

45. David Gordon, *Fat and Mean: The Corporate Squeeze of Working Americans and the Myth of Managerial "Downsizing"* (New York: Martin Kessler, 1996); Peck and Theodore, "The Business of Contingent Work"; Kalleberg et al., *Nonstandard Work, Substandard Jobs*; Roberta Spalter-Roth and Heidi Hartmann, "Gauging the Consequences for Gender Relations, Pay Equity, and the Public Purse," in *Contingent Work: American Employment Relations in Transition*, ed. Kathleen Barker and Kathleen Christensen (Ithaca, NY: Cornell University Press, 1998), 69–102; Annette Bernhardt and Thomas Bailey, "Improving Worker Welfare in the Age of Flexibility," *Challenge* 41, no. 5 (September/October 1998): 16–45; Martina Morris, "Inequality in Earnings at the Close of the Twentieth Century," *Annual Review of Sociology* 25 (1999): 623–657; Leah Vosko, *Temporary Work: The Gendered Rise of a Precarious Employment Relationship* (Toronto: University of Toronto Press, 2000); Annette Bernhardt, Martina Morris, Mark Handcock, and Marc Scott, *Divergent Paths: Economic Mobility in the New American Labor Market* (New York: Russell Sage Foundation, 2001); Peck and Theodore, "Contingent Chicago"; Paul Osterman, "Employers in the Low-Wage/Low-Skill Labor Market," in *Low-Wage Workers in the New Economy*, ed. Richard Kazis and Marc Miller (Washington, DC: Urban Institute, 2001), 67–87; Heidi Gottfried, "Temp(t)ing Bodies: Shaping Gender at Work in Japan," *Sociology: The Journal of the British Sociological Association* 37, no. 2 (2003): 257–276; and Daniel Kerr and Christopher Dole,

"Cracking the Temp Trap: Day Laborer's Grievances and Strategies for Change in Cleveland, Ohio," *Labor Studies Journal* 29, no. 4 (2005): 87–108.

46. Gonos, "The Contest over 'Employer' Status"; Gonos, "The Interaction between Market Incentives and Government Actions"; Gonos, "Fee-Splitting Revisited"; also see Anthony Carnevale, Lynn Jennings, and James Eisenmann, "Contingent Workers and Employment Law," in *Contingent Work: American Employment Relations in Transition*, ed. Kathleen Barker and Kathleen Christensen (Ithaca, NY: Cornell University Press, 1998), 281–305; Vosko, *Temporary Work*; Peck and Theodore, "Temped Out"; and Peck, Theodore, and Ward, "Constructing Markets for Temporary Labour."

47. Adler, "Discourses of Flexibility."

48. Vosko, *Temporary Work*.

49. Blank, "Contingent Work in a Changing Labor Market"; Cohany, "Workers in Alternative Employment Arrangements"; Anne Polivka, Sharon Cohany, and Steven Hipple, "Definition, Composition, and Economic Consequences of the Nonstandard Workforce," in *Nonstandard Work: The Nature and Challenges of Changing Employment Arrangements*, ed. Françoise Carré, Marianne Ferber, Lonnie Golden, and Stephen Herzenberg (Champaign-Urbana: University of Illinois, Champaign-Urbana, Industrial Relations Research Association Series, 2000), 41–94; and Marisa DiNatale, "Characteristics of and Preference for Alternative Work Arrangements, 1999," *Monthly Labor Review* (March 2001): 28–49.

50. Kalleberg et al., "Bad Jobs in America"; also see Maureen Martella, *"Just a Temp": Expectations and Experiences of Women Clerical Temporary Workers* (Darby, PA: Diane Publishing, 1991); Yinon Cohen and Yitchak Haberfeld, "Temporary Help Service Workers: Employment Characteristics and Wage Determination," *Industrial Relations* 32, no. 2 (1993): 272–287; Robert Parker, *Flesh Peddlers and Warm Bodies: The Temporary Help Industry and Its Workers* (New Brunswick, NJ: Rutgers University Press, 1994); Segal and Sullivan, "The Temporary Labor Force"; Kevin Henson, *Just a Temp* (Philadelphia: Temple University Press, 1996); Stanley Nollen, "Negative Aspects of Temporary Employment," *Journal of Labor Research* 17, no. 4 (1996): 567–581; Susan Houseman, "Flexible Staffing Arrangements in the U.S.," *Worklife Report* 10, no. 4 (1997): 6; Lewis Segal and Daniel Sullivan, "The Growth of Temporary Services Work," *Journal of Economic Perspectives* 11, no. 2 (1997): 117–136; Blank, "Contingent Work in a Changing Labor Market"; Cohany, "Workers in Alternative Employment Arrangements"; Jean McAllister, "Sisyphus at Work in the Warehouse: Temporary Employment in Greenville, SC," in *Contingent Work: American Employment Relations in Transition*, ed. Kathleen Barker and Kathleen Christensen (Ithaca, NY: Cornell University Press, 1998); Jackie Krasas Rogers, *Temps: The Many Faces of the Changing Workplace* (Ithaca, NY: Cornell University Press, 2000); Ken Hudson, "The Disposable Worker," *Monthly Review* 52, no. 11 (April 2001): 43–56; Kerr and Dole, "Cracking the Temp Trap."

51. David Autor and Susan Houseman, "Do Temporary Help Jobs Improve Labor Market Outcomes for Low-Skilled Workers? Evidence from 'Work First'" *American Economic Journal: Applied Economics* (forthcoming); David Autor and Susan Houseman, "The Role of Temporary Employment Agencies in Welfare to Work: Part of the Problem or Part of the Solution?" *Focus* 22, no. 1 (2002): 63–70; Julia Lane, Kelly Mikelson, Pat Sharkey, and Douglas Wissoker, "Pathways to Work for Low-Income Workers: The Effect of Work in the Temporary Help Industry," *Journal of Policy Analysis and Management* 22, no. 4 (2003): 581–598; David Autor, "Labor Market Intermediation: What It Is, Why It Is Growing, and Where It Is Going," *NBER Reporter* (Fall 2004): 7–10; Fredrik Andersson, Harry Holzer, and Julia Lane, *Moving Up or Moving On: Who Advances in the Low-Wage Labor Market?* (New York: Russell Sage Foundation, 2005); Carolyn Heinrich, "Temporary Employment Experiences of Women on Welfare," *Journal of Labor Research* 26, no. 2 (2005): 335–350; Carolyn Heinrich, Peter Mueser, Kenneth Troske, "Welfare to Temporary Work: Implications for Labor Market Outcomes," *Review of Economics and Statistics* 87, no. 1 (2005): 154–174; and Smith and Neuwirth, *The Good Temp.*

52. Parker, *Flesh Peddlers and Warm Bodies*; Donna Rothstein, "Entry Into and Consequences of Nonstandard Work Arrangements," *Monthly Labor Review* 119, no. 10 (1996): 75; Barker and Christensen, *Contingent Work*; Blank, "Contingent Work in a Changing Labor Market"; Françoise Carré and Chris Tilly, "Part-Time and Temporary Work: Flexibility for Whom?" *Dollars and Sense* 215 (January/February 1998): 22–26; Cohany, "Workers in Alternative Employment Arrangements"; Spalter-Roth and Hartmann, "Gauging the Consequences"; Michael Morris and Alexander Vekker, "An Alternative Look at Temporary Workers, Their Choices, and the Growth in Temporary Employment," *Journal of Labor Research* 22, no. 2 (2001): 373–391; and Barbara Wiens-Tuers and Elizabeth Hill, "How Did We Get Here from There? Movement into Temporary Employment," *Journal of Economic Issues* 2, no. 36 (2002): 303.

53. Peck and Theodore, "The Business of Contingent Work"; Peck and Theodore, "Contingent Chicago"; Peck and Theodore, "Temped Out"; Theodore and Peck, "The Temporary Staffing Industry: Growth Imperatives and Limits to Contingency"; Peck and Theodore, "Flexible Recession"; Peck, Theodore, and Ward, "Constructing Markets for Temporary Labour"; and Cynthia Ofstead, "Temporary Help Firms as Entrepreneurial Actors," *Sociological Forum* 14, no. 2 (1999): 273–294.

54. Peck and Theodore, "Contingent Chicago."

55. Gonos, "The Contest over 'Employer' Status"; Gonos, "The Interaction between Market Incentives and Government Actions"; and Gonos, "Fee-Splitting Revisited."

56. Vicki Smith and Esther Neuwirth, *The Good Temp* (Ithaca, NY: Cornell ILR Press, 2008).

CHAPTER 1

1. Quoted in Nan Robertson, "Homemakers Take Jobs to Stave Off Boredom," *New York Times*, 22 January 1958, p. 20.

2. Richard Cooper, "The Kelly Girls Are Two Men," *New York Times*, 14 April 1963, p. 133.

3. Despite industry leaders' claims otherwise, however, George Gonos and Leah Vosko have argued that the modern temp industry was not new at all, but emerged directly from the private employment industry that flourished in the first half of the twentieth century. George Gonos, "A Sociology of the Temporary Employment Relationship" (Ph.D. diss., Rutgers University, 1994); George Gonos, "The Interaction Between Market Incentives and Government Actions," in *Contingent Work: American Employment Relations in Transition*, ed. Kathleen Barker and Kathleen Christensen (Ithaca, NY: Cornell University Press, 1998), 170–191; and Leah Vosko, *Temporary Work: The Gendered Rise of a Precarious Employment Relationship* (Toronto: University of Toronto Press, 2000).

4. "Manpower, Inc.," *The Commercial and Financial Chronicle*, 7 December 1961, p. 2501(5). For more on the advertising efforts of the early temp industry, see Mack Moore, "The Role of Temporary Help Services in the Clerical Labor Market" (Ph.D. diss., University of Wisconsin, Madison, 1963); Martin Gannon, "An Analysis of the Temporary Help Industry," in *Labor Market Intermediaries* (Washington, DC: National Commission for Manpower Policy, 1978), 195–225; *Chicago Daily Tribune*, 26 January 1960, p. C8; and, Louise Hodgson, *Elmer L. Winter: The Manpower Man* (Minneapolis, MN: T. S. Denison, 1969). For more on the promotional efforts of specific temp agencies, such as American Girl and Kelly Girl, see "Temporary Help Firms Growing Ad Source," *Editor and Publisher*, 6 June 1964, p. 22; and "Dailies Both Stock and Sell Kelly Girls," *Editor and Publisher*, 4 December 1965, p. 18.

5. For more on this gendered strategy among industry leaders in Canada, see Vosko, *Temporary Work*.

6. As clerical work became feminized in the early twentieth century, there was a great deal of cultural work needed to normalize the female office worker in American popular culture. For more on this, see Lisa Fine, *Souls of the Skyscraper: Female Clerical Workers in Chicago, 1870–1930* (Philadelphia: Temple University Press, 1990); also see Angel Kwolek-Folland, *Engendering Business: Men and Women in the Corporate Office, 1870–1930* (Baltimore, MD: Johns Hopkins University Press, 1998).

7. *New York Times*, 4 November 1962, p. F11; for an advertisement for "Kelly Girl Fashions by Henry Rosenfeld," see *Chicago Tribune*, 26 August 1962, p. C18.

8. Sharon Bredeson, "The Temporary Help Industry—New Dimension in Its Third Generation," *Management World* (June 1981): 1–7.

9. Gunther Peck, *Reinventing Free Labor: Padrones and Immigrant Workers in the North American West, 1880–1930* (Cambridge: Cambridge University Press,

2000); also see Tomás Martinez, *The Human Marketplace: An Examination of Private Employment Agencies* (New Brunswick, NJ: Transaction, 1976).

10. Alice Kessler-Harris, *Out to Work: A History of Wage-Earning Women in the United States* (New York: Oxford University Press, 1982); and Ruth Milkman, *Gender at Work: The Dynamics of Job Segregation by Sex during World War II* (Champaign: University of Illinois Press, 1987).

11. Kathleen Barry, *Femininity in Flight: A History of Flight Attendants* (Durham, NC, and London: Duke University Press, 2007), 3; see also William Henry Chafe, *The American Woman: Her Changing Social, Economic, and Political Roles, 1920–1970* (New York: Oxford University Press, 1972).

12. "Extra Money for Extra Work for Extra Women," *Good Housekeeping* 143 (November 1956): 49–50.

13. Barry, *Femininity in Flight*, 51.

14. Richard Cooper, "The Kelly Girls Are Two Men," *New York Times*, 14 April 1963, p. 133.

15. For more on the unionization of flight attendants and their fight against age and gender discrimination, see Barry, *Femininity in Flight*; and Dorothy Sue Cobble, *The Other Women's Movement: Workplace Justice and Social Rights in Modern America* (Princeton, NJ: Princeton University Press, 2004).

16. It is also true, however, that before the early 1970s the temp industry could be better characterized as a cluster of businesses, dominated by Manpower and Kelly Girl, rather than a unified industry. Only after 1973 did the temp industry take its "greatest spurt forward" to become the global industry that we know today (Gonos, "The Interaction between Market Incentives and Government Actions," 185).

17. Ibid.

18. For industry employment in 1961, see "Manpower, Inc.," *The Commercial and Financial Chronicle*, 7 December 1961, p. 2501(5). For industry growth during the 1960s, see Gonos, "The Interaction between Market Incentives and Government Actions"; also see Martha Finney and Deborah Dasch, *A Heritage of Service: The History of Temporary Help in America* (Alexandria, VA: National Association of Temporary Services, 1991); and Charles Deale, "How to Choose a Temporary Help Service: A Guide to Quality Supplemental Staffing," *Personnel Administrator* (December 1980): 55–57.

19. Bredeson, "The Temporary Help Industry."

20. Samuel Sacco, "Temporary Help Industry: Its Impact on Business," *The Office* (September 1985): 138, and "Efficient Use of Temporaries May Be Key to Future Office Staffing," *The Office* (December 1972): 39–43; Gonos, "The Interaction between Market Incentives and Government Actions."

21. Moore, "The Role of Temporary Help Services in the Clerical Labor Market"; and Mack Moore, "The Temporary Help Service Industry: Historical Development, Operation, and Scope," *Industrial and Labor Relations Review* 18 (1965): 554–569.

22. Norris Willatt, "The Business Front: Manpower Abroad," *Barron's National Business and Financial Weekly* 45, no. 1 (1965): 11.

23. "Manpower, Inc.," *Fortune* (November 1956): 280.

24. Moore, "The Role of Temporary Help Services in the Clerical Labor Market"; Moore, "The Temporary Help Service Industry"; and *New York Times*, 8 January 1968, p. 111.

25. Willatt, "The Business Front," 11.

26. "Temporaries Win Permanent Role," *Business Week*, 23 December 1967, pp. 64–66.

27. "Renting Workers to Industry," *Fortune* (September 1960): 254; also see "Temporary Hiring Climbs up the Ladder," *Business Week*, 15 July 1961.

28. "Temporaries Win Permanent Role."

29. In 1971 the Institute for Temporary Services was renamed the National Association of Temporary Services (NATS), which would remain the association's name until the 1990s. Today it is called the American Staffing Association. For more on the formation of the Institute for Temporary Services, see Finney and Dasch, *A Heritage of Service*, 65–66.

30. William Olsten, "Temporary Personnel Services Gain Recognition Abroad," *Administrative Management* 28 (August 1967): 58–59.

31. Willatt, "The Business Front," 11.

32. Marion Whalen, "Renting People Is Good Business," *Credit and Financial Management* (February 1965): 27.

33. Bennett Harrison and Barry Bluestone, *The Great U-Turn: Corporate Restructuring and the Polarizing of America* (New York: Basic Books, 1988).

34. David Halberstam, *The Reckoning* (New York: Morrow, 1986): 363, quoted in Harrison and Bluestone, *The Great U-Turn*, 4.

35. Peck, *Reinventing Free Labor*; and, Vosko, *Temporary Work*.

36. Peck, *Reinventing Free Labor*, 229; see also: Moore, "The Role of Temporary Help Services in the Clerical Labor Market"; and *Florida Industrial Commission v. Manpower, Inc. of Miami*, 91 So. 2d 197 (Fla. 1956).

37. Quoted in Henry Guzda, "The U.S. Employment Service at 50: It Too Had to Wait Its Return," *Monthly Labor Review* (June 1983): 13.

38. Quoted in Ibid.

39. George Gonos, "The Contest over 'Employer' Status in the Post-war United States: The Case of Temporary Help Firms," *Law Society Review* 31, no. 1 (1997): 81–110; and Moore "The Role of Temporary Help Services in the Clerical Labor Market."

40. Moore, "The Role of Temporary Help Services in the Clerical Labor Market," 187; and Gonos, "A Sociology of the Temporary Employment Relationship."

41. *State of Nebraska v. Manpower of Omaha*, 161 Neb. 387 (1955).

42. *Florida Industrial Commission v. Manpower*.

43. Gonos, "The Interaction between Market Incentives and Government Actions"; Gonos, "The Contest"; and Gonos, "A Sociology of the Temporary Employment Relationship."

44. *Florida Industrial Commission v. Manpower.*

45. Moore, "The Role of Temporary Help Services in the Clerical Labor Market," 2–3.

46. *Florida Industrial Commission v. Manpower*; see also Gonos, "The Contest."

47. George Gonos, "Fee-Splitting Revisited: Concealing Surplus Value in the Temporary Employment Relationship," *Politics and Society* 29, no. 4 (2001): 589; see also Gonos, "The Interaction"; Gonos, "The Contest"; and Gonos, "A Sociology of the Temporary Employment Relationship."

48. Nelson Lichtenstein, *State of the Union: A Century of American Labor* (Princeton, NJ: Princeton University Press, 2002).

49. Ibid.; and Gonos, "The Interaction."

50. Moore, "The Role of Temporary Help Services in the Clerical Labor Market."

51. Quoted in G. W. Nordman, "Temporary Help Services Industry—Wave of the Future?" (Master's thesis, Rollins College, 1967), 32–33; see also "Labor-for-Rent War," *Business Week*, 5 November 1966, p. 160.

52. OEIU, "White Collar: Official Organ of the Office Employees International Union," AFL-CIO (April 1962): 4, quoted in Moore, "The Role of Temporary Help Services in the Clerical Labor Market," 184–185.

53. In fact, it was not until the late 1980s and 1990s that unions began to organize around this issue. For example, as noted in a 1988 report by Eileen Appelbaum and Judith Gregory, in the late 1980s unions had "only recently" begun to address temp work ("Union Responses to Contingent Work: Are Win-Win Outcomes Possible?" in *Proceedings of the Conference on the Contingent Workplace: New Directions for Work in the Year 2000* [Washington, DC: Women's Bureau, U.S. Department of Labor, 1988]: 69).

54. "Manpower, Inc.," *Fortune* (November 1956): 280; see also "Now Manpower Inc. Goes in for Steady Jobs," *Business Week*, 23 August 1976, p. 41.

55. As described in Chapter 3, the Federal Trade Commission would later file a formal complaint against the industry's ban on supplying strikebreakers (Bureau of National Affairs, *The Changing Workplace: New Directions in Staffing and Scheduling* (Washington, DC: Bureau of National Affairs, 1986); David Nye, *Alternative Staffing Strategies* (Washington, DC: Bureau of National Affairs, 1988); and U.S. Federal Trade Commission, *1985 Annual Report* (Washington, DC: U.S. Government Printing Office, 1985), available at http://www.ftc.gov/os/annualreports/ar1985.pdf (accessed 30 March 2007).

56. "How Temporary Employees Pay Off," *Steel*, 13 February 1961, pp. 66–67.

57. Cobble, *The Other Women's Movement*.

58. There has been a substantial body of recent literature, however, that has examined some postwar industrial unions' support for women workers, notably Ruth Milkman's *Gender at Work: The Dynamics of Job Segregation by Sex during World War II* (Chicago: University of Illinois Press, 1987). Nonetheless, the dramatically different unionization rates of men and women in the postwar era, as well as a long history of many industrial unions seeking to exclude women from their rank and file, contributed to this prevalent cultural assumption that women's work was beyond the purview of the powerful postwar labor unions.

59. Barry, *Femininity in Flight*.

60. Olsten, "Temporary Personnel Services Gain Recognition Abroad."

61. There is an important parallel, however, between the immigrant workers recruited by padrones in the early twentieth century and the white, middle-class women recruited by temp agencies half a century later. As Leah Vosko has observed, the success of both padrones and temp agencies relied on the assumption that these two groups of workers did not provide for their own social reproduction. Just as immigrant workers' costs were assumed to be borne largely by the sending country, middle-class women were assumed to be only secondary wage earners (*Temporary Work*).

62. The labor force participation rate of white, married women grew 44 percent in the 1950s, more than twice that of women in general (19 percent) (Claudia Goldin, *Understanding the Gender Gap: An Economic History of American Women* (New York: Oxford University Press, 1990). For more on cultural pressure on women not to work (and some women's ambivalence about doing so), see Elaine Tyler May, *Homeward Bound: American Families in the Cold War Era* (New York: Basic Books, 1990); Julia Kirk Blackwelder, *Now Hiring: The Feminization of Work in the United States, 1900–1995* (College Station: Texas A&M University Press, 1997); and Chafe, *The American Woman*. For more on the many exceptions to the "June Cleaver" ideal, see Joanne Meyerowitz, ed., *Not June Cleaver: Women and Gender in Postwar America, 1945–1960* (Philadelphia: Temple University Press, 1994); Cobble, *The Other Women's Movement*; Nancy Gabin, *Feminism in the Labor Movement: Women and the United Auto Workers, 1935–1975* (Ithaca, NY: Cornell University Press, 1990); and Leila Rupp and Verta Taylor, *Survival in the Doldrums: The American Women's Rights Movement, 1945 to the 1960s* (New York: Oxford University Press, 1987).

63. W. Keith, "Married Women, You're Fools to Take a Job," *Chatelaine* (January 1960): 148, quoted in Vosko, *Temporary Work*, 103–104.

64. Blackwelder, *Now Hiring*; and Meyerowitz, *Not June Cleaver*.

65. Manpower executives were explicit about the goal of their White Glove Girl campaign. As described by James Scheinfeld, Manpower's vice president of advertising, the White Glove Girl campaign was created "to counteract the inherent masculinity of the corporate name" ("'Respectable Sex Symbol' Builds Solid Image," *Printer's Ink*, 27 July 1962, p. 36; see also "Manpower Inc. Promotes 'White Gloves' Theme," *Advertising Age*, 9 April 1962, p. 119).

66. Moore, "The Temporary Help Service Industry"; and Willatt, "The Business Front," 11.

67. Moore, "The Temporary Help Service Industry."

68. Quoted in Moore, "The Role of Temporary Help Services in the Clerical Labor Market," 29 (emphasis in original).

69. "Respectable Sex Symbol," 38; "Manpower Inc. Promotes 'White Gloves' Theme," 119.

70. *Chicago Daily Tribune*, 22 June 1960, p. C6.

71. *New York Times*, 20 September 1962, p. 44.

72. *U.S. News and World Report*, 20 May 1963, p. 88.

73. "Respectable Sex Symbol," 36–37. A year earlier, in fact, real-life Kelly Girl Jean Kent had won the title of "Pin-Up Girl" in the *Chicago Tribune* ("Office Pin-Up," *Chicago Daily Tribune*, 16 July 1961, p. B29).

74. "Employment: Part Time Full Blast," *Time*, 4 August 1967, p. 75.

75. Author's analysis of industry advertisements in newspapers, popular magazines, and trade journals.

76. *Newsweek*, 19 July 1965, p. 4.

77. "Manpower, Inc., Stresses Brawn," *New York Times*, 20 September 1962, p. 44.

78. *Newsweek*, 25 May 1964, p. 119.

79. Author's analysis of industry advertisements in newspapers, popular magazines, and trade journals.

80. Elmer Winter, *Your Future as a Temporary Office Worker* (New York: Richard Rosen Press, 1968), 36.

81. For example, see *Chicago Tribune*, 15 April 1964, p. E1; *Personnel Journal* (December 1964): inside front cover; and a Manpower brochure inserted in the *Personnel Journal* (September 1964): 432.

82. For example, see a Manpower brochure inserted in the *Personnel Journal* (July–August 1964): 37.

83. *Chicago Daily Tribune*, 22 June 1960, p. C6.

84. *U.S. News and World Report*, 16 December 1963, p. 104.

85. For example, see *Personnel Journal* (May 1963): inside back cover; *Personnel Journal* (June 1964): inside back cover; and *Newsweek*, 18 May 1964, p. 11.

86. *Advertising Age* 35 (16 March 1964): 2.

87. *Chicago Tribune*, 15 April 1964, p. E1 (emphasis in original).

88. *Personnel Journal* (December 1964): inside front cover. These highly publicized manuals included "An Introduction to Manpower and Temporary Office Work"; "Adapting Quickly to New Office Routine and Advanced Telephone Technique"; "Tips and Shortcuts in Typing, Dictation, Filing and Office Procedure"; and "The White Glove Girls Book of Beauty, Wardrobe and Personal Grooming" (Manpower Brochure, *Personnel Journal* [July–August 1964]: 37). The latter, for example, much like the guides for flight attendants described in Barry's *Femininity in Flight*, offered many "beauty tips" for temporary workers

that would be considered highly inappropriate by today's standards. For an exhaustive list, see Elmer Winter, *How to Be an Effective Secretary* (New York: Pocket Books, 1965), 46–58.

89. *Advertising Age* 35 (16 March 1964): 2.

90. *Personnel Journal* 43 (1964): 439 (emphasis in original).

91. Robertson, "Homemakers Take Jobs," 20.

92. Elmer Winter, *A Woman's Guide to Earning a Good Living* (New York: Simon and Schuster, 1961), 16.

93. "Extra Money for Extra Work for Extra Women," 49–50.

94. *Manpower, Inc.: The Inside Story of Temporary Help* (Milwaukee, WI: Manpower, 1957), 14.

95. Elmer Winter, "Money and Part-Time Jobs for Women," *McCall's* 88 (April 1961): 68–69.

96. "Women at Your Beck and Call," *Forbes*, 15 July 1967, p. 44.

97. *New York Times*, 2 July 1961, p. W4.

98. Barry, *Femininity in Flight*; and Lizabeth Cohen, *A Consumers' Republic: The Politics of Mass Consumption in Postwar America* (New York: Vintage Books, 2003).

99. Moore, "The Role of Temporary Help Services in the Clerical Labor Market," 96–98.

100. Sarah Evans, *Tidal Wave: How Women Changed America at Century's End* (New York: Free Press, 2003); Cohen, *A Consumers' Republic*; and Chafe, *The American Woman*.

101. Keith, "Married Women, You're Fools to Take a Job."

102. Goldin, *Understanding the Gender Gap*.

103. Barry, *Femininity in Flight*; Kessler-Harris, *Out to Work*; Blackwelder, *Now Hiring*; Goldin, *Understanding the Gender Gap*; and Susan Rimby Leighow, *Nurses' Questions/Women's Questions: The Impact of the Demographic Revolution and Feminism on United States Working Women, 1946–1986* (New York: Peter Lang, 1996).

104. Keith, "Married Women, You're Fools to Take a Job."

105. Susan Rimby Leighow, "An 'Obligation to Participate': Married Nurses' Labor Force Participation in the 1950s," in Meyerowitz, *Not June Cleaver: Women and Gender in Postwar America, 1945–1960*, 37–56.

106. "Renting Workers to Industry."

107. *Chicago Tribune*, 19 August 1965, p. A12 (emphasis in original).

108. Winter, *A Woman's Guide*, x–xi.

109. Ibid., 22.

110. Ibid., 19–20.

111. Ibid., 90–91.

112. Ibid., 19–20.

113. For more about other promised cures for this "disease," see David Herzberg, *Happy Pills in America: From Miltown to Prozac* (Baltimore, MD: Johns Hopkins University Press, 2008).

114. Winter, *A Woman's Guide*, 12–13.
115. William Russell Kelly and Richard Kelly, *Work Smartly* (New York: Charles Scribner's Sons, 1963), 10.
116. For example, see Herzberg, *Happy Pills*.
117. May, *Homeward Bound*; Ruth Feldstein, *Motherhood in Black and White: Race and Sex in American Liberalism, 1930–1965* (Ithaca, NY: Cornell University Press, 2000); and Nancy Walker, *Shaping Our Mothers' World: American Women's Magazines* (Jackson: University Press of Mississippi, 2000).
118. Eva Moskowitz, *In Therapy We Trust: America's Obsession with Self-Fulfillment* (Baltimore, MD: Johns Hopkins University Press, 2001); and Barbara Ehrenreich and Deirdre English, *For Her Own Good: Two Centuries of the Experts' Advice to Women*, 2nd ed. (New York: Anchor Books, 2005).
119. Joanne Meyerowitz, "Beyond the Feminine Mystique," in Meyerowitz, *Not June Cleaver*, 242.
120. Winter, *A Woman's Guide*, 58–59.
121. Kelly and Kelly, *Work Smartly*, 79.
122. Keith, "Married Women, You're Fools to Take a Job."
123. *Chicago Tribune*, 2 September 1965, p. B3.
124. *New York Times*, 12 May 1965, p. 86.
125. Moore, "The Role of Temporary Help Services in the Clerical Labor Market," 158–159 (emphasis in original).
126. "Temporaries Win Permanent Role," *Business Week*, 23 December 1967, pp. 64–66.

CHAPTER 2

1. *Personnel Journal* (April 1972): 225 (emphasis in original).
2. Ibid.
3. *The Office* (January 1971): 19.
4. For an example of industry leaders offering flexibility to the "nth degree," see *Personnel Journal* (April 1972): 225. For an example of industry executives urging businesses to focus exclusively on profits, see James Scheinfeld, "Helping Management to Take Care of Business," *The Office* (January 1976): 90–92.
5. Bennett Harrison and Barry Bluestone, *The Great U-Turn: Corporate Restructuring and the Polarization of America* (New York: Basic Books, 1988).
6. This literature is far too vast to be adequately synthesized here. For a more complete analysis, see Harrison and Bluestone, *The Great U-Turn*. Also see Barry Bluestone and Bennett Harrison, *The Deindustrialization of America: Plant Closings, Community Abandonment, and the Dismantling of Basic Industry* (New York: Basic Books, 1982); John Kenneth Galbraith, "Inequality and Unemployment," *Research on Economic Inequality* 8 (1998): 121–154; and William Julius Wilson, *When Work Disappears: The World of the New Urban Poor* (New York: Vintage Books, 1996).

7. For example, see Paul Osterman, *Securing Prosperity: How the American Labor Market Has Changed and What to Do about It* (Princeton, NJ: Princeton University Press, 1999); and Annette Bernhardt, Martina Morris, Mark Handcock, and Marc Scott, *Divergent Paths: Economic Mobility in the New American Labor Market* (New York: Russell Sage Foundation, 2001).

8. Harrison and Bluestone, *The Great U-Turn*, 22.

9. Harrison and Bluestone, *The Great U-Turn*; Thomas Kochan, Harry Charles Katz, and Robert McKersie, *The Transformation of American Industrial Relations*, 2nd ed. (New York: Basic Books, 1994).

10. Robert Townsend, *Up the Organization: How to Stop the Organization from Stifling People and Strangling Profits* (Robbinsdale, MN: Fawcett, 1970), 23.

11. Eric Pace, "Robert Townsend, 77, Dies; Wrote 'Up the Organization,'" *New York Times*, 14 January 1998, available at http://www.nytimes.com/1998/01/14/business/robert-townsend-77-dies-wrote-up-the-organization.html (accessed 4 September 2009).

12. Charles Babbage, *On the Economy of Machine and Manufactures* (London: Charles Knight, 1832).

13. *Newsweek*, 9 May 1966; and *U.S. News and World Report* (May 1966): 60 (emphasis in original).

14. Author's analysis of historical documents.

15. Author's analysis of historical documents.

16. *Administrative Management* (September 1967): 14.

17. *The Office* (February 1974): 40.

18. Kelly Services, "The Rise of Free Agents," *Issues and Trends: A Kelly Services Report* (2005).

19. "Temporary Help Is Now a Permanent Necessity," *The Office* (May 1979): 164; "Temporary Help Service—Here and Overseas," *Personnel Journal* (October 1974): 777; Howard Scott, "The Development of the Temporary Help Industry," *The Office* (December 1974): 20–21; Elmer Winter, *Your Future as a Temporary Office Worker* (New York: Richard Rosen Press, Inc., 1968); Damon Stetson, "For Many Concerns: An Inadvertent 4-Day Week," *New York Times*, 14 May 1972, p. F3; and "A Big Boost for the 'Temps,'" *BusinessWeek*, 6 October 1980, p. 98.

20. Quoted in Kenneth Ross, "Inflation Benefits Manpower, Inc.," *Chicago Tribune*, 3 June 1974, p. C9; also see Stetson, "For Many Concerns."

21. *Personnel Journal* (March 1976): back cover.

22. *The Office* (December 1974): 30.

23. Kelly Services, "Celebrating 50 Years: A Kelly Services Timeline," Kelly Services 1996 Annual Report, available at http://media.corporate-ir.net/media_files/NSD/KELYA/reports/annual96/timeline.html (accessed 23 July 2009); Irwin Ross, "For Rent: Secretaries, Salesmen, Physicists, and Human Guinea Pigs," *Fortune* (October 1968): 164; and author's analysis of historical documents.

24. Author's analysis of historical documents.

25. For the "obvious sexual teases" in airline advertisements of the 1970s, see Kathleen Barry, *Femininity in Flight: A History of Flight Attendants* (Durham, NC: Duke University Press, 2007), 100–101.

26. *New York Times*, 12 July 1971, p. 42.

27. *The Office* (September 1968): 20.

28. As a number of scholars have noted, the temp industry's growth in the 1970s and 1980s was driven by employer demand rather than worker preference. See Lonnie Golden and Eileen Appelbaum, "What Was Driving the 1982–88 Boom in Temporary Employment? Preference of Workers or Decisions and Power of Employers," *American Journal of Economics and Sociology* 51 (1992): 473–493; and Nikolas Theodore and Jamie Peck, "The Temporary Staffing Industry: Growth Imperatives and Limits to Contingency," *Economic Geography* 78, no. 4 (2002): 463–493. This chapter explains how temp industry leaders created employer demand for their products.

29. Samuel Sacco, "Temporary Help Industry: Its Impact on Business," *The Office* (September 1985): 138.

30. George Gonos, "The Interaction Between Market Incentives and Government Actions," in *Contingent Work: American Employment Relations in Transition*, ed. Kathleen Barker and Kathleen Christensen (Ithaca, NY: Cornell University Press, 1998), 170–191; Sharon Bredeson, "The Temporary Help Industry—New Dimension in Its Third Generation," *Management World* (June 1981): 1–7; and Garth Mangum, Donald Mayall, and Kristin Nelson, "One Person's Job Security Is Another's Insecurity—But 'Help' Is on the Way," *Personnel Administrator* (March 1985): 93–101.

31. Katherine Abraham, "Restructuring the Employment Relationship: The Growth of Market-Mediated Work Arrangements," in *New Developments in the Labor Market: Toward a New Institutional Paradigm*, ed. Katherine Abraham and Robert McKersie (Cambridge, MA: MIT Press, 1990), 85–120; also see Leah Vosko, *Temporary Work: The Gendered Rise of a Precarious Employment Relationship* (Toronto: University of Toronto Press, 2000), 127–128.

32. *Personnel Journal* (June 1964): inside front cover.

33. This was a very common theme in industry advertisements. For example, see Scheinfeld, "Helping Management to Take Care of Business," 90–92; Elmer Winter, "Planned Staffing for Profit," *The Office* (November 1967): 152–155; *Personnel Journal* (March 1971): back cover; *Personnel Journal* (March 1976): back cover; and *The Office* (January 1979): 9.

34. *Personnel Journal* (September 1969): 671.

35. Michael Notaro, "Advantages of Temporary Help During a Business Slowdown," *The Office* (March 1970): 78–163. This was very a common theme in temp industry publications. For example, see *The Office* (January 1971): 41; *Personnel Journal* (September 1969): 671; *Personnel Journal* (July 1969): 489; "Instant Help," *Financial World* 124 (8 December 1965): 10–11; Elmer Winter, "Program Your Optimum Staff Needs," *Administrative Management* 31 (November 1970):

24–27; and "Raps State of Office Personnel," *Chicago Tribune*, 19 January 1970, p. C6.

36. "Instant Help," *Financial World* 124 (8 December 1965): 10.

37. For example, see *Personnel Journal* (October 1968): 693.

38. *Personnel Journal* (September 1966): 462.

39. *Personnel Journal* (September 1969): 671; and Notaro, "Advantages of Temporary Help."

40. For example, see Margaret Pacey, "The Business Front: Providers of Temporary Help Are Working to Regain It," *Barron's National Business and Financial Weekly* 48, no. 10 (4 March 1968): 23; *Administrative Management* (June 1965): 12; and *Personnel Journal* (February 1970): 83.

41. *Administrative Management* (June 1965): 12. Remarkably, there are as many references to "machines" as there are sentences in this advertisement.

42. *Personnel Journal* (February 1970): 83.

43. For example, see Winter, "Planned Staffing for Profit"; Deborah Wise, "Part-Time Workers: Rising Numbers, Rising Discord," *BusinessWeek*, 1 April 1985, p. 62; Thomas Low, "Temporary Help for Restructured Workload," *The Office* (August 1976): 32; and *Personnel Journal* (March 1972): 188–189.

44. Notaro, "Advantages of Temporary Help."

45. This was a prevalent theme in both industry advertisements and articles. For examples, see *BusinessWeek*, 31 May 1969, p. 95; *Personnel Journal* (April 1968): 220; *Personnel Journal* (March 1970): 273; William Olsten, "Lean on Temps to Reduce 'Fat,' " *The Office* (January 1970): 79–80; *Personnel Journal* (October 1971): inside front cover; *The Office* (November 1974): 53; Richard Essey, "Temporary Help Services Save the Employers' Money," *The Office* (January 1974): 67; Scott, "The Development of the Temporary Help Industry"; *Personnel Journal* (February 1975): 74; *Personnel Journal* (March 1976): back cover; *Personnel Journal* (June 1978): back cover; *Personnel Journal* (March 1969): 164; *Personnel Journal* (July 1969): 489; and Dwayne Meisner, "The New Economics of Temporary Personnel," *Administrative Management* 35 (May 1974): 20–21.

46. The early era of this management philosophy—lasting from the 1920s to the 1950s—is generally referred to as the Human Relations movement. Later adherents to this philosophy are variously referred to as behaviorists, behavioral scientists, human behaviorists, or organizational behaviorists. For simplicity's sake, however, I will categorize this entire management philosophy as the Human Relations school of thought.

47. Daniel Wren, *The Evolution of Management Thought*, 4th ed. (New York: John Wiley and Sons, 1994).

48. Although Mayo is widely considered the founder of the Human Relations movement, he was not the first to point out that taking care of workers would have a positive effect on productivity. For instance, see Kyle Bruce, "Henry S. Dennison, Elton Mayo, and Human Relations Historiography," *Management and Organizational History* 1, no. 2 (May 2006): 177–199.

49. Manfred Moldaschl and Wolfgang Weber, "The 'Three Waves' of Industrial Group Work: Historical Reflections on Current Research on Group Work," *Human Relations* 51, no. 3 (March 1998): 347–389.

50. Elton Mayo, *The Human Problems of an Industrial Civilization* (New York: Macmillan, 1933); Elton Mayo, *The Social Problems of an Industrial Civilization* (Boston: Harvard Graduate School of Business Administration, 1946).

51. For a summary of the debate surrounding the Hawthorne Studies, see Jeffrey Sonnenfeld, "Shedding Light on the Hawthorne Studies," *Journal of Occupational Behaviour* 6, no. 2 (April 1985): 111–130.

52. Thomas O'Connor, "Human Relations Management," 25 May 2008, available at http://www.apsu.edu/oconnort/4000/4000lect02a.htm (accessed 9 July 2009). For more on Elton Mayo and the Human Relations movement, see Ellen O'Connor, "The Politics of Management Thought: A Case Study of Harvard Business School and the Human Relations School," *Academy of Management Review* 24, no. 1 (1999): 117–131; Ellen O'Connor, "Minding the Workers: The Meaning of 'Human' and 'Human Relations' in Elton Mayo," *Organization* 6, no. 2 (1999): 223–246; John Cunningham Wood and Michael C. Wood, eds., *George Elton Mayo: Critical Evaluations in Business and Management* (New York: Routledge, 2004); Richard Trahair, *Elton Mayo: The Humanist Temper*, 2nd ed. (New Brunswick, NJ: Transaction, 2005); and Wren, *The Evolution of Management Thought.*

53. Sanford Jacoby, *Modern Manors: Welfare Capitalism since the New Deal* (Princeton, NJ: Princeton University Press, 1997); Osterman, *Securing Prosperity*; and Mauro Guillén, *Models of Management: Work, Authority, and Organization in a Comparative Perspective* (Chicago: University of Chicago Press, 1994).

54. Sanford Jacoby quoted in Sheri Caudron, "It's Taken 75 Years to Say. . . . Here's to You!" *Workforce* 76, no. 1 (January 1997): 77.

55. Douglas McGregor, *The Human Side of Enterprise* (New York: McGraw-Hill, 1960); and Wren, *The Evolution of Management Thought.*

56. Townsend, *Up the Organization.*

57. Frederick Herzberg, *The Motivation to Work* (New York: John Wiley and Sons, 1959); Frederick Herzberg, "One More Time: How Do You Motivate Employees?" *Harvard Business Review* 65, no. 5 (September/October 1987): 109–120; and Wren, *The Evolution of Management Thought.*

58. Henri Fayol, *General and Industrial Management*, trans. Constance Storrs (London: Sir Isaac Pirman and Sons, 1949), 37. For more on Fayol and the Administrative school of personnel management, see Gareth Jones and Jennifer George, *Contemporary Management*, 5th ed. (New York: McGraw-Hill/Irwin, 2008), 43; and Wren, *The Evolution of Management Thought.*

59. In truth, there was some opposition to the temp industry in the 1970s. For instance, in 1971, there was a congressional hearing on the need to protect day laborers (House Committee on Education and Labor, *Day Labor Protection Act of 1971*, 92nd Cong., 1st Sess., 1971, pp. 70–125). And throughout the decade, there were periodic exposés in newspapers about temp industry practices (George Gonos,

"A Sociology of the Temporary Employment Relationship" [Ph.D. diss., Rutgers University, 1994]). The industry even faced accusations from NOW (the National Organization of Women), that it was confining women to low-wage, marginal employment (Martha Finney and Deborah Dasch, *A Heritage of Service: The History of Temporary Help in America* (Alexandria, VA: National Association of Temporary Services, 1991). But these resistance efforts were both piecemeal and sporadic, and they posed little threat to the temp industry, which was by then well established and rapidly gaining power.

60. For instance, see *The Office* (September 1974): 129; *Personnel Journal* (September 1979): 587; and *Personnel Journal* (March 1971): back cover.

61. For example, see *Personnel Journal* (October 1968): 693.

62. For more on industry leaders' depiction of businesses' "complicated workforce problems," see W. Robert Stover, "The Third-Generation Use of Temporary Services," *Management Review* 63 (December 1974): 22.

63. *Administrative Management* (June 1965): 14 (emphasis in original).

64. *Personnel Journal* (September 1968): inside front cover.

65. Ibid.

66. For example, see "Efficient Use of Temporaries May Be Key to Future Office Staffing," *The Office* (December 1972): 39–43; S. A. Russo Jr., "Temps Pretrained for the Job," *The Office* (December 1970): 48; and Finney and Dasch, *A Heritage of Service.*

67. For examples of Olsten's "money-saving booklet," see *The Office* (January 1970): 8; *Personnel Journal* (September 1969): inside back cover; and *Personnel Journal* (April 1968): 220. For an example of Manpower's brochure that offered to explain how "The Manpower Idea" could help "control costs and protect profits," see *The Office* (May 1970): 133. For an example of the "Staff Builders' Guide," which offered business owners the "tips you need more than ever now, with permanent payroll costs heading sky high," see: *Personnel Journal* (March 1978): 119. For an example of the "free fringe benefit cost calculator" from AGS, see *Personnel Journal* (April 1968): 229. And for Dot Temporaries' "profit slide rule that shows what it really costs to hire and maintain permanent employees," see *Personnel Journal* (November 1972): 791.

68. Sam Bellotto Jr., "Male Temps: Clerks to Controllers," *Administrative Management* 32 (1971): 80.

69. Thomas Rohan, "New Style Temporary Help Arrives," *Industry Week* 173 (10 April 1972): 33.

70. For example, see Sam Bellotto Jr., "3 Ways to Budget for Temps," *Administrative Management* 33 (March 1972): 32–33; Bellotto, "Male Temps"; *Personnel Journal* (November 1972): 797; *Personnel Journal* (September 1979): 587; *Personnel Journal* (January 1970): 81; and Finney and Dasch, *A Heritage of Service.*

71. *Personnel Journal* (May 1971): 345.

72. *Administrative Management* (August 1967): 22.

73. *Personnel Journal* (April 1970): 275 (emphasis in original).

74. Senate Select Committee on Small Business, *The Impact of Franchising on Small Business*, 91st Cong., 2nd Sess., 1970, pp. 695–704; Senate Committee on Labor and Public Welfare, *Manpower Development and Training Legislation, 1970*, 91st Cong., 1st and 2nd Sess., 1970, pp. 2327–2343; House Committee on Education and Labor, *Day Labor Protection Act of 1971*, 92nd Cong., 1st Sess., 1971, pp. 70–125; House Committee on Education and Labor, *Equal Opportunity and Full Employment*, 94th Cong., 1st Sess., 1975, pp. 56–77; House Committee on Education and Labor, *Oversight Hearings on the Comprehensive Employment and Training Act*, 94th Cong., 2nd Sess., 1976; House Select Committee on Aging, *Alternatives to Retirement*, 95th Cong., 1st Sess., 1977, pp. 133–137; Senate Committee on Human Resources, *Full Employment and Balanced Growth Act of 1978*, 95th Cong., 2nd Sess., 1978, pp. 203–206; House Committee on Ways and Means, *Independent Contractors*, 96th Cong., 1st Sess., 1979, pp. 528–532; and House Select Committee on Aging, *National Policy Proposals Affecting Midlife Women*, 96th Cong., 1st Sess., 1979, pp. 19–24, 105–107.

75. For an example of an advertisement for Franchisepower, see *Chicago Tribune*, 25 January 1972, p. C9.

76. There are many examples. For a few examples, see "Job Mart Gaining, but Not Booming," *Chicago Tribune*, 27 May 1973, p. S_A31; Leonard Wiener, "New Survey Released: Uncertain Job Outlook Here," *Chicago Tribune*, 4 January 1975, p. H7; "Manpower Study: U.S. Employment Outlook Improving, Survey Finds," *Chicago Tribune*, 1 April 1976, p. C9; "Better Job Outlook Is Found in Survey," *New York Times*, 28 March 1977, p. 43; Agis Salpukas, "Outlook for Hiring Better around U.S.," *New York Times*, 4 July 1977, p. 26; Elizabeth Fowler, "Careers: Job-Outlook Lead Held by South," *New York Times*, 3 January 1979, p. D14; "Firms Intend to Increase Hiring, Survey Reveals," *Los Angeles Times*, 7 April 1977, p. D13; Mary Lou Wiles, "National and Local Job Market Expands as Economy Improves," *Los Angeles Times*, 17 October 1977, p. G2; and Alexander Auerbach, "Job Market Expected to Improve Sharply," *Los Angeles Times*, 3 April 1978, p. D10.

77. Rohan, "New Style Temporary Help Arrives," 30; also see *Personnel Journal* (September 1968): inside front cover; *The Office* (January 1971): 56; and Stover, "The Third-Generation Use of Temporary Services."

78. *Personnel Journal* (September 1969): inside back cover.

79. *Personnel Journal* (October 1968): 693.

80. *Personnel Journal* (March 1970): 273 (emphasis in original).

81. *Personnel Journal* (July 1969): 489.

82. Rohan, "New Style Temporary Help Arrives," 30.

83. For example, see Low, "Temporary Help for Restructured Workload"; *The Office* (May 1970): 133; *Personnel Journal* (September 1970): back cover; *Personnel Journal* (April 1970): 275; and Elmer Winter, "How Temporary Help Can Cut Your Payroll Costs," *The Office* (December 1974): 56–57.

84. This was a very common theme in temp industry publications. For example, see "Efficient Use of Temporaries May Be Key"; Stover, "The Third-Generation

Use of Temporary Services"; Low, "Temporary Help for Restructured Workload"; Notaro, "Advantages of Temporary Help"; *Personnel Journal* (September 1974): back cover; "Temporary Help in Business Today," *The Office* (August 1975): 18–28; and Mitchell Fromstein, "The Socio-economic Roles of the Temporary Help Service in the United States Labor Market," in *Labor Market Intermediaries: A Special Report of the National Commission for Manpower Policy, Report #22* (Washington, DC: Government Printing Office, 1978), 227–254.

85. For example, see Winter, "How Temporary Help Can Cut Your Payroll Costs"; Stover, "The Third-Generation Use of Temporary Services"; Scott, "The Development of the Temporary Help Industry"; William Olsten, "Pointers on Using Temporary Help Services," in *U.S. Small Business Administration: Management Assistance Support Services Section* (Washington, DC: Government Printing Office, 1981); and "Efficient Use of Temporaries May Be Key."

86. *Personnel Journal* (February 1971): 177 (emphasis in original).

87. Michael Notaro, "Effective Use of Temporary Help," *Personnel Journal* (June 1971): 462.

88. *Personnel Journal* (January 1971): 44–45.

89. *The Office* (January 1971): 56 (emphasis in original).

90. Rohan, "New Style Temporary Help Arrives."

91. Scheinfeld, "Helping Management to Take Care of Business."

92. Robert Parker, *Flesh Peddlers and Warm Bodies: The Temporary Help Industry and Its Workers* (New Brunswick, NJ: Rutgers University Press, 1994), 143–144; also see Andrew Pollack, "No. 2 Motorola Closes the Gap," *New York Times*, 13 April 1982, p. D1; "Making It in Today's Markets," *Chicago Tribune*, 19 February 1984, p. D2; and "Job Security Wings Support as Sound Business Policy," *Chicago Tribune*, 27 January 1985, p. F1.

93. *Personnel Journal* (March 1962): inside back cover.

94. For instance, see *Personnel Journal* (March 1964): 117.

95. For example, see Howard Scott, "Reinforce with Temporaries," *The Office* (January 1972): 82. Temp industry publications provide many other examples. See "How Companies Are Using Leased Manpower," *Management Review* 51 (December 1962): 51–53; *Personnel Journal* (March 1962): inside back cover; Allen Trueman, "How Companies Are Using Temporary Workers," *Management Review* 53 (September 1964): 47–50; *Personnel Journal* (March 1964): 117; "Women at Your Beck and Call," *Forbes*, 15 July 1967, p. 44; Winter, "Program Your Optimum Staff Needs"; "Efficient Use of Temporaries May Be Key"; Bellotto, "Male Temps"; Bellotto, "3 Ways to Budget for Temps"; Scheinfeld, "Helping Management to Take Care of Business"; and Jan Paul, "People Leasing: How to Add Special Skills to Your Staff without Bloating Your Payroll," *Black Enterprise* (April 1979): 59.

96. *Nation's Business* 56 (1968): S-38.

97. "People for Rent: More Companies Use Temporary Office Help Provided by Agencies," *Wall Street Journal*, 12 December 1963, p. 1.

98. "A Boost for Temporary Help," *BusinessWeek*, 3 August 1974, pp. 60–62. For more examples of companies' use of "permanent temporaries" in this time period, see Elmer Winter, *1,015 Ways to Save Time, Trouble, and Money in the Operation of Your Business* (Englewood Cliffs, NJ: Prentice-Hall, 1967); Finney and Dasch, *A Heritage of Service*; *Personnel Journal* (September 1969): inside front cover; *Personnel Journal* (October 1969): 753; *Personnel Journal* (October 1972): back cover; Harold Dickhut, "Temporary Help," *The Office* (September 1962): 297; and Scheinfeld, "Helping Management to Take Care of Business."

99. For other examples of industry leaders marketing payrolling, see Marion Whalen, "Renting People Is Good Business," *Credit and Financial Management* (February 1965): 12–15; Scott, "The Development of the Temporary Help Industry"; *Personnel Journal* (October 1971): inside front cover; and "Temporary Help in Business Today," *The Office* (August 1975): 18–28.

100. Stover, "The Third-Generation Use of Temporary Services," 19.

101. *Personnel Journal* (October 1971): inside front cover.

102. Whalen, "Renting People Is Good Business," 15.

103. Stover, "The Third-Generation Use of Temporary Services," 19; also see Whalen, "Renting People Is Good Business"; Meisner, "The New Economics of Temporary Personnel"; "Temporary Help in Business Today," *The Office* (August 1975): 18–28; and Victor Lederer, "Office Temps: New Strategies, New Benefits," *Administrative Management* 38 (May 1977): 42–44.

104. Lederer, "Office Temps: New Strategies, New Benefits," 44.

105. Stover, "The Third-Generation Use of Temporary Services," 18–19.

106. Ibid., 18–20. Other temp industry leaders agreed that the "transfer of personnel" could benefit workers. For example, see Scott, "The Development of the Temporary Help Industry"; and Meisner, "The New Economics of Temporary Personnel."

107. *Personnel Journal* (October 1971): inside front cover (emphasis in original); also see Stover, "The Third-Generation Use of Temporary Services."

108. "Temporary Help in Business Today," *The Office* (August 1975): 20, 28; also see Bellotto, "3 Ways to Budget for Temps."

109. Winter, "Planned Staffing for Profit," 155; also see Stover, "The Third-Generation Use of Temporary Services."

110. Stover, "The Third-Generation Use of Temporary Services," 22.

111. *Personnel Journal* (March 1971): back cover; also see Essey, "Temporary Help Services Save the Employers' Money"; and "Efficient Use of Temporaries May Be Key."

112. *Personnel Journal* (March 1976): back cover.

113. Ibid.

114. *Personnel Journal* (March 1971): back cover (emphasis in original).

115. See Essey, "Temporary Help Services Save the Employers' Money."

116. Quoted in "Now Manpower Inc. Goes in for Steady Jobs," *Business-Week*, 23 August 1976, p. 41. The earliest evidence of industry leaders' success in

selling this kind of outsourcing can be found in Mack Moore's 1963 study of the temp industry, in which he described Northwest Mutual Insurance Company contracting a supervised team of keypunch operators from Manpower for a period of two years (Mack Moore, "The Role of Temporary Help Services in the Clerical Labor Market" [Ph.D. diss., University of Wisconsin, Madison, 1963], 44).

117. For examples of industry analysts portraying the strategies as products of the 1990s, see "From Temporaries to Outsourcing," *Purchasing* 17 (March 1994): 62–64; Samuel Sacco, "Today's Temporary-Help Employees Are Essential to Business," *Office Systems* 9, no. 10 (October 1992): 52–55; and Charles Lincoln, "Temporary Services and the Global Economy," *The Office* 117, no. 1 (January 1993): 48.

118. Samuel Sacco, "Temps Rising," *Office Systems* 10, no. 10 (October 1993): 56–58.

CHAPTER 3

1. Thomas O'Boyle, *At Any Cost: Jack Welch, General Electric, and the Pursuit of Profit* (New York: Knopf, 1998), 71.

2. Quoted in "Neutron Jack: Monster or Mentor?" PersonnelToday.com, 1 February 2002, available at http://www.personneltoday.com/articles/2002/02/01/13783/neutron-jack-monster-or-mentor.html (accessed 5 August 2009).

3. Geoffrey Colvin, "The Ultimate Manager," *Fortune*, 22 November 1989, p. 185; Tim Smart, "Jack Welch's Encore," *BusinessWeek*, October 28, 1996, p. 154.

4. "For Whom Bell Tolls," *Newsweek*, 15 January 1996, available at http://www.newsweek.com/id/101252 (accessed 5 August 2009).

5. As President Reagan himself famously proclaimed, "You can't be for big government, big taxes, and big bureaucracy, and still be for the little guy," quoted in James Humes, *The Wit and Wisdom of Ronald Reagan* (Washington, DC: Regnery Publishing, 2007), p. 13.

6. Quoted in Steven Greenhouse, "Labor Board Stirs Up a Storm," *New York Times*, 5 February 1984, p. F4.

7. For example, *Newsweek* called Welch "a shining corporate hero" (Jolie Solomon and Daniel McGinn, "Scratches in the Teflon: GE's Jack Welch Is America's Most Venerated Executive. Has He Lost His Midas Touch?" *Newsweek*, 3 October 1994, available at http://www.newsweek.com/id/108447/page/1 (accessed 13 August 2009).

8. Robert Half, "Managing Your Career: 'Should I Look for a Part-Time Job?'" *Management Accounting* (February 1990): 12.

9. Anne H. Nelson, "Temporary Help Is Becoming a Permanent Solution," Flexible Workstyles: A Look at Contingent Labor: Conference Summary (Washington, DC: Women's Bureau, 1988), 50.

10. The campaigns were not entirely lackluster. Industry executives continued their efforts to legitimize temporary work for male breadwinners, and they

adopted the increasingly popular core-periphery rhetoric as their own, urging companies to use temps to "protect" permanent employees from layoffs. Such ideas were not new to the temp industry, however, and the main focus of their efforts—and the story of change and transformation—no longer lay in their marketing campaigns.

11. U.S. General Accounting Office, "Workers in Contingent Employment Lack Insurance, Other Benefits," GAO/HRD-91-56 (Washington, DC: U.S. Government Printing Office, 1991).

12. "If there was a national fear index," Richard Belous, chief economist for the National Planning Association in Washington, told *Time* magazine in 1993, "it would be directly related to the growth of contingent work" (Janice Castro, "Disposable Workers," *Time,* 29 March 1993, pp. 43–47).

13. Michael A. Urquhart and Marillyn A. Hewson, "Unemployment Continued to Rise in 1982 as Recession Deepened," *Monthly Labor Review* 106, no. 2 (February 1983): 3–12.

14. Nik Theodore and Jamie Peck, "The Temporary Staffing Industry: Growth Imperatives and Limits to Contingency," *Economic Geography* 78, no. 4 (2002): 470 (emphasis in original); also see Jamie Peck and Nikolas Theodore, "Temped Out? Industry Rhetoric, Labor Regulation and Economic Restructuring in the Temporary Staffing Business," *Economic and Industrial Democracy* 23, no. 2 (2002): 143–175.

15. Cherlyn Granrose and Eileen Appelbaum, "The Efficiency of Temporary and Part-Time Employment," *Personnel Administrator* (January 1986): 71–83.

16. Virginia duRivage, *Working at the Margins: Part-Time and Temporary Workers in the United States* (Cleveland: 9 to 5, National Association of Working Women, 1986), 11; also see Joseph Duncan, "How Business Holds Down Hiring: Large Companies Are Turning to Temporary Services, According to a Dunn & Bradstreet Survey," *Dun's Business Month* (March 1985): 41; and Max Carey and Kim Hazelbaker, "Employment Growth in the Temporary Help Industry," *Monthly Labor Review* (April 1986): 37–44.

17. Theodore and Peck, "The Temporary Staffing Industry," 463–493.

18. Theodore and Peck, "The Temporary Staffing Industry"; Virginia duRivage, ed., *New Policies for the Part-Time and Contingent Workforce,* Economic Policy Institute Series (Armonk, NY: M. E. Sharpe, 1992); Dorie Seavey and Richard Kazis, *Skills Assessment, Job Placement, and Training: What Can Be Learned from the Temporary Help/Staffing Industry? An Overview of the Industry and a Case Study of Manpower, Inc.* (Boston: Jobs for the Future, 1994); and Richard Belous, *The Contingent Economy: Growth of the Temporary, Part-Time, and Subcontracted Labor Force* (Washington, DC: National Planning Association, 1989).

19. Charles Deale, "How to Choose a Temporary Help Service: A Guide to Quality Supplemental Staffing," *Personnel Administrator* (December 1980): 55–57; Garth Mangum, Donald Mayall, and Kristin Nelson, "One Person's Job Security Is Another's Insecurity—But 'Help' Is on the Way," *Personnel Administrator*

(March 1985): 93–101; Patricia Fernberg, "Enjoying Impressive Growth and Diversity," *Modern Office Technology* (January 1989): 116; and Susan McHenry, "The Agency Route—Is It Better?" *Ms.* (March 1989): 94.

20. McHenry, "The Agency Route"; also see Fernberg, "Enjoying Impressive Growth." Among the top U.S. temp agencies, Adia was the only relative newcomer, but, in fact, Adia was a well-established temp agency in its own right, founded in Switzerland in 1957. Today, Adia is known as Adecco, having merged with the French temp agency Ecco in 1996. For more information, see Adecco Company History, available at http://www.adecco.com/AboutAdecco/Pages/History.aspx (accessed 15 June 2010).

21. Belous, *The Contingent Economy*.

22. Ibid.

23. "Why and How Business Uses Temporary Help," *The Office* (June 1980): 97–102.

24. "The Office Reader Survey Report: Temporary Help," *The Office* (May 1986): 91–96; and "The Office Reader Survey Report: Temporary Help Firms Are Doing Their Jobs," *The Office* (August 1988): 39–42. Although the results of these surveys were not necessarily representative or even accurate, they were reasonable markers of change in companies' use of temps over the course of the decade. Also see Bureau of National Affairs, *The Changing Workplace: New Directions in Staffing and Scheduling* (Washington, DC: Bureau of National Affairs, 1986); Belous, *The Contingent Economy*; Lonnie Golden and Eileen Appelbaum, "What Was Driving the 1982–88 Boom in Temporary Employment?" *American Journal of Economics and Sociology* 51, no. 4 (October 1992): 473–493; and Morton Grossman and Margaret Magnus, "Temporary Services: A Permanent Way of Life," *Personnel Journal* (January 1989): 38–40.

25. "Why and How Business Uses Temporary Help."

26. "The Office Reader Survey Report."

27. See Theodore and Peck, "The Temporary Staffing Industry."

28. As early as 1982, the federal government made legislative note of the increasing use of long-term temps. The Tax Equity and Fiscal Responsibility Act of 1982 (TEFRA) required employers to extend their regular pension plans to temps who worked at their companies "substantially full time" (about twenty-nine hours a week) for a year, unless they already received pension benefits from the temp agency (Tax Equity and Fiscal Responsibility Act, Public Law No. 97-248, 96 Stat. 324 [September 3, 1982]). The temp industry argued strongly against this provision, which, they said, "limited the length of temporary assignments and perhaps even the use of temporary employees" (Daniel Struve, "Demand for Temporaries Spurs Opportunities," *The Office* [September 1985]: 143; also see Walter Macauley, "Developing Trends in the Temporary Services Industry," *Personnel Administrator* (January 1986): 61–68; House Subcommittee of the Committee on Government Operations, *Rising Use of Part-Time and Temporary*

Workers: Who Benefits and Who Loses? 100th Congress, 2nd Sess., 19 May 1988; duRivage, *Working at the Margins*; and Bureau of National Affairs, *The Changing Workplace*.

29. Patricia Fernberg, "Forging a Continuing Relationship," *Modern Office Technology* (February 1990): 40–43. The trend has continued unabated. By 2006, in fact, the average length of "temporary" assignments was a whopping 12.5 weeks, an increase of more than 600 percent since 1990, and many reports indicated that as much as one-third of temporary assignments lasted more than a year (American Staffing Association, "Fact Sheet: Staffing Employee Turnover Declined Substantially in 2005, Increasing Average Tenure to 12.5 Weeks," available at http://www.americanstaffing.net/statistics/pdf/04-Turnover%20rates.pdf [accessed 7 March 2006]; also see Steven Greenhouse, *The Big Squeeze: Tough Times for the American Worker* [New York: Knopf, 2008]).

30. Quoted in "Need a Pro? Try Temporary Help," *Office Administration and Automation* (August 1984): 49–50; also see Granrose and Appelbaum, "The Efficiency of Temporary and Part-Time Employment."

31. "Need a Pro? Try Temporary Help."

32. Theodore and Peck, "The Temporary Staffing Industry."

33. "A Challenging Kind of Guy," *Business Marketing* (August 1989): 10–12.

34. Robert Hurtado, "Acquisition by Olsten May Gain It Some Respect on Wall Street," *New York Times*, 20 July 1993, p. D8.

35. Theodore and Peck, "The Temporary Staffing Industry"; and Julie Froud, L. Johal, and K. Williams, "The U.S. Staffing Industry: The Business Model and the Paradoxes of Extension," Working Paper No. 1 (Chicago: Center for Urban Economic Development, University of Illinois at Chicago, 2001).

36. *Personnel Administrator* (July 1981): 73.

37. *Personal Administrator* (July 1983): 32; also see *Personal Administrator* (August 1984): 90.

38. Leah Vosko, *Temporary Work: The Gendered Rise of a Precarious Employment Relationship* (Toronto: University of Toronto Press, 2000).

39. *New York Times*, 9 July 1986, p. A14.

40. Mitchell Fromstein, "What Makes Temporaries a Permanency," *Management Today* (May 1982): 95; Martha Finney and Deborah Dasch, *A Heritage of Service: The History of Temporary Help in America* (Alexandria, VA: National Association of Temporary Services, 1991); and William Lewis and Nancy Schuman, *The Temp Worker's Handbook: How to Make Temporary Employment Work for You* (New York: American Management Association, 1988).

41. Lewis and Schuman, *The Temp Worker's Handbook*, 1–4.

42. For examples, see Susan Lee and Stuart Flack, "Hi Ho, Silver," *Forbes*, 9 March 1987, pp. 90–98; James Miller, "Employer–Employee Interests Aided by Temporary Services," *The Office* (October 1985): 152; Barbara Johnson, *Working*

Whenever You Want: All about Temporary Employment (Englewood Cliffs, NJ: Prentice-Hall, 1983); and Finney and Dasch, *A Heritage of Service*; also see Robert Half, "Managing Your Career: 'Should I Look for a Part-Time Job?'" *Management Accounting* (February 1990): 12.

43. Half, "Managing Your Career."

44. For more examples, see "And Now, 'Temp' Managers," *Newsweek*, 26 September 1988, p. 52; and "Behind Hiring of More Temporary Employees," *U.S. News and World Report*, 25 February 1985, pp. 76–79.

45. Lee and Flack, "Hi Ho, Silver."

46. "And Now, 'Temp' Managers," *Newsweek*, 26 September 1988, p. 52.

47. Quoted in Beth Brophy and Mary Lord, "The 'Just in Time' Worker," *U.S. News and World Report*, 23 November 1987, pp. 45–46.

48. Quoted in Bureau of National Affairs, *The Changing Workplace*, 26–27. It must also be noted, however, that while temping offered autonomy to some temps and insecurity to others, it also provided some workers with better job opportunities. For example, although many nonwhite workers had trouble getting interviews at predominantly white workplaces, at least a few were able to "get in the door" with the help of the New York City temp agency Clark Unlimited Personnel. Founded by Ruth Clark in 1975 with the mission to "get as many people [of color] as possible into corporate America," Clark Unlimited sought professional employment for traditionally disadvantaged workers, including African Americans, Asians, Latinos, women, seniors, gays, and even men in "non-traditional" occupations (Allan Halcrow, "We've All Been Victims: It's Time We Helped Each Other," *Personnel Journal* [January 1985]: 14).

49. Quoted in Ben Franklin, "Atom Plants Are Hiring Stand-ins to Spare Aides the Radiation Risk," *New York Times*, 16 July 1979, p. A1; also see Joy Horowitz, "Working inside a Nuclear Plant," *Los Angeles Times*, 12 October 1980, p. H1; and "Pay Lures Workers to Risks at A-Plant," *Los Angeles Times*, 8 February 1981, p. 3.

50. Not surprisingly, temp industry executives did not look favorably on companies starting their own temp agencies and, in their vocal responses, emphasized the benefits of using agency temps over in-house temps. In a 1982 article, for example, William Olsten of Olsten Temporary Services offered a strong critique of in-house temps; three years later, Sam Sacco of the National Association of Temporary Services published a nearly identical analysis (William Olsten, "The In-House Temp Option—Is It Really?" *Management World* [August 1982]: 44; and Samuel Sacco, "Are In-House Temporaries Really an Option?" *Personnel Administrator* [May 1985]: 20–22).

51. "The Contingency Work Force," *Fortune*, 24 January 1994, pp. 30–36.

52. David Nye, *Alternative Staffing Strategies* (Washington, DC: Bureau of National Affairs, 1988).

53. Today this is more commonly referred to as the "core-periphery" approach.

54. For example, see Elmer Winter, "Planned Staffing for Profit," *The Office* (November 1967): 152–155; Thomas Low, "Temporary Help for Restructured Workload," *The Office* (August 1976): 32l; and *Personnel Journal* (March 1972): 188–189.

55. Thomas Lueck, "A Boom in Temporary Work," *New York Times*, 24 October 1985, p. D8.

56. *The Office* (June 1983): 9. This was an extremely common advertisement in 1983 and 1984. For another variation of this ad, see *Personnel Administrator* (April 1983): 13.

57. *Personnel Administrator* (February 1984): 83.

58. Peter Hall, "Temporary Services: Lasting Success?" *Financial World*, 6–19 March 1985, pp. 90–91.

59. *Personnel Administrator* (February 1983): 54.

60. For more on Hewlett-Packard, see David Naguib Pellow and Lisa Sun-Hee Park, *The Silicon Valley of Dreams: Environmental Justice, Immigrant Workers, and the High-Tech Global Economy* (New York: New York University Press, 2002); "No Temporary Phenomenon," *Industry Week*, 3 April 1989, 13–18; and "Matching Temps to Industry Needs," *Personnel Management* (July 1988): 67. For more on Motorola, see Robert Parker, *Flesh Peddlers and Warm Bodies: The Temporary Help Industry and Its Workers* (New Brunswick, NJ: Rutgers University Press, 1994); Louis Uchitelle, "Temporary Workers Are on the Increase in Nation's Factories," *New York Times*, 6 July 1993, pp. A1–D2; Andrew Pollack, "No. 2 Motorola Closes the Gap," *New York Times*, 13 April 1982, p. D1; "Making It in Today's Markets," *Chicago Tribune*, 19 February 1984, p. D2; and "Job Security Wings Support as Sound Business Policy," *Chicago Tribune*, 27 January 1985, p. F1.

61. Deborah Wise, "Part-Time Workers: Rising Numbers, Rising Discord," *BusinessWeek*, 1 April 1985, p. 62.

62. Quoted in Ibid.

63. Carla Lazzareschi, "Apple Will Lay Off 75 at 2 Orange County Facilities," *Los Angeles Times*, 1 May 1985, p. F3.

64. David Kirkpatrick, "Smart New Ways to Use Temps," *Fortune*, 15 February 1988, p. 111.

65. Garth Mangum, Donald Mayall, and Kristin Nelson, "One Person's Job Security Is Another's Insecurity—But 'Help' Is on the Way," *Personnel Administrator* (March 1985): 93–101; David Beers, "Forever Temporary," *Working Woman* (June 1986): 53–54; Lee and Flack, "Hi Ho, Silver"; and Wise, "Part-Time Workers."

66. Kate Evans-Correia, "More than a Pretty Face," *Purchasing*, 17 August 1989, pp. 98–99.

67. In 1987, for example, Manpower and IBM entered into a mutually profitable partnership: Manpower trained the employees at companies that purchased IBM computers, and, in return, Manpower gained access to the latest IBM equipment

before it was released to the public. By the end of the decade, "Skillware" had been translated into nine different languages and was used to train 100,000 workers a year. By the mid-1990s, the permanent workforces of nearly 90 percent of Fortune 100 companies had been trained on the program (Joseph Oberle, "Manpower, Inc. Training Because There's No Other Way," *Training* [March 1990]: 57–62; Nye, *Alternative Staffing Strategies*; Belous, *The Contingent Economy*; Jobs for the Future, *Skills Assessment, Job Placement, and Training: What Can Be Learned from the Temporary Help/Staffing Industry? An Overview of the Industry and a Case Study of Manpower, Inc.* [Boston: Jobs for the Future, 1997]). For more on the partnership between Manpower and IBM, see "Manpower in the Training Biz." *Training* (May 1983): 12–14; "A Marriage Made in Marketing Heaven," *Training* (May 1987): 12; and "IBM, Manpower Training Pact," *The Office* (May 1987): 128.

68. Evans-Correia, "More than a Pretty Face." Another example is Johnson & Johnson; see "Need a Pro? Try Temporary Help," *Office Administration and Automation* (August 1984): 48–70.

69. Beers, "Forever Temporary."

70. Bureau of National Affairs, *The Changing Workplace*; and Nye, *Alternative Staffing Strategies*.

71. Quoted in Beers, "Forever Temporary."

72. Michael LeRoy, "Lengthening Duration of Permanent Replacement Strikes: Public Policy Implications, *Proceedings of the Forty-Ninth Annual Meeting of the Industrial Relations Research Association* 49 (1997): 219–225; Michael LeRoy, "The PATCO Strike: Myths and Realities," *Proceedings of the Forty-Ninth Annual Meeting of the Industrial Relations Research Association* 49 (1997): 15–22; Michael LeRoy, "Regulating Employer Use of Permanent Striker Replacements: Empirical Analysis of NLRA and RLA Strikes, 1935–1991," *Berkeley Journal of Employment and Labor Law* 16 (1995): 169–208; Michael LeRoy, "The Changing Character of Strikes Involving Permanent Striker Replacements, 1935–1990," *Journal of Labor Research* 16, no. 4 (1995): 423–437; Parbudyal Singh and Harish Jain, "Striker Replacement in the United States, Canada, and Mexico: A Review of the Law and Empirical Research," *Industrial Relations* (January 2001): 22–53; Joseph McCartin, "'Fire the Hell out of Them': Sanitation Workers' Struggles and the Normalization of the Striker Replacement Strategy in the 1970s," *Labor: Studies in Working-Class History of the Americas* 2, no. 3 (2005): 67–92; and U.S. Senate, Committee on Labor and Human Resources, *Workplace Fairness Act*, S. Rep. No 102–111 (1991).

73. Quoted in Bureau of National Affairs, *The Changing Workplace*; Nye, *Alternative Staffing Strategies*; and Edward Lenz, e-mail communication with the author, 4 November 2006.

74. Federal Trade Commission, *1985 Annual Report* (Washington, DC: U.S. Government Printing Office, 1985), available at http://www.ftc.gov/os/annualreports/ar1985.pdf (accessed 1 April 2007) (emphasis added).

75. National Labor Relations Board, *Harter Equipment, Inc.*, 22-CA-11527 (24 June 1986); also see National Labor Relations Board, *National Gypsum Company*, 1-CA-21122 (29 September 1986). Court documents in the *National Gypsum Company* case do not specify whether the replacement workers were agency temps or direct hires.

76. National Labor Relations Board, *Harter Equipment, Inc.*

77. Ibid.

78. National Labor Relations Board, *Marquette Company*, 3-CA-10274 (11 September 1987).

79. The NLRB found that Middle Earth executives behaved "in complete disregard of the rights of its employees" and engaged in "repeated and pervasive" violations of the National Labor Relations Act (National Labor Relations Board, *Middle Earth Graphics, Inc.*, 7-CA-24013(1), 7-CA-24019, 7-CA-24013(2), 7-CA-24914(1), 7-CA-24013(3), 7-CA-24856(2), 7-CA-24030(1), 7-CA-25033, 7-CA-24030(2), 7-CA-24030(3), 7-CA-24030(5), 7-CA-24052, and 7-CA-24921 [19 May 1987]).

80. National Labor Relations Board, *M.P.C. Plating, Inc.*, 8-CA-18513, 8-CA-18514, and 8-CA-18515 (15 June 1989).

81. Ibid.

82. For more examples, see National Labor Relations Board, *Storall Manufacturing Company*, 26-CA-10428, 26-CA-10483, 26-CA-10534, 26-CA-10595, 26-CA-10704, and 26-CA-10758 (26 April 1985); National Labor Relations Board, *National Gypsum Company*, 1-CA-21122 (29 September 1986); National Labor Relations Board, *General Portland Inc.*, 16-CA-11785 (30 April 1987); and National Labor Relations Board, *Continental Winding Company*, 7-CA-22770 and 7-CA-23067 (30 September 1991).

83. U.S. Nursing Corporation, available at http://www.usnursing.com/ (accessed 26 August 2009). Throughout the 1990s and into the 2000s, U.S. Nursing did brisk business in supplying strikebreakers to hospitals. According to the company's Web site, the company was involved in 95 percent of all health care disputes nationwide.

84. John Kohl and David Stephens, "Replacement Workers during Strikes: Strategic Options for Managers," *Personnel Journal* 65 (April 1986): 98.

85. The former two-year limit was already significantly longer than past policies allowed. In 1938, temporary employees could not work more than thirty days in federal jobs without approval of the Civil Service Commission, OPM's predecessor. In 1960, the limit on temporary appointments was extended to one year (U.S. General Accounting Office, "Federal Employees: OPM Data Do Not Identify if Temporary Employees Work for Extended Periods," GAO-02-296 [Washington, DC: U.S. Government Printing Office, 2002], 7). The 1985 temporary hiring policy also upgraded the positions to which white-collar temporary appointments could be made. Previously, temps could only be hired for low-level clerical and technical positions; the new policy allowed them to take mid-level professional jobs paying more than $40,000 a year. This did not change federal

policy on agencies' ability to make temporary appointments to blue-collar positions, which were already allowed at all grade levels. For a good overview of federal hiring policies, see U.S. General Accounting Office, "Federal Workforce: Use of Temporary Employees at Three Puget Sound Naval Installations," GAO/GGD-88-76 (Washington, DC: U.S. Government Printing Office, 1988).

86. In the first year of the new regulation, the number of temporary appointments in professional, administrative, and technical jobs increased dramatically (40 percent, 51 percent, and 34 percent, respectively), whereas temporary appointments in each of these occupational groups had declined the year before (U.S. General Accounting Office, "Federal Workforce: New Authority to Make and Extend Temporary Appointments, GAO/GGD-86-111BR [Washington, DC: U.S. Government Printing Office, 1986]).

87. U.S. General Accounting Office, "Federal Workforce: Use of Temporary Employees at Three Puget Sound Naval Installations," 8; also see U.S. General Accounting Office, "Federal Workforce: New Authority to Make and Extend Temporary Appointments."

88. U.S. Office of Personnel Management, "Federal Personnel Letter 316-21," 2 January 1985; also see Bureau of National Affairs, *The Changing Workplace*, 86; and Nye, *Alternative Staffing Strategies*.

89. Robert Pear, "Temporary Hiring by U.S. Is Pushed under New Policy," *New York Times*, 1 January 1985, p. 1; also see Bennett Harrison and Barry Bluestone, *The Great U-Turn: Corporate Restructuring and the Polarization of America* (New York: Basic Books, 1988), 103.

90. Quoted in "U.S. Agencies Told to Increase Hiring of Temporary Workers," *Los Angeles Times*, 2 January 1985, p. B2.

91. Quoted in "Federal Agencies Urged to Use Temporary Help," *Los Angeles Times*, 3 January 1985, p. B19.

92. Robert Pear, "U.S. Is Pressing Temporary Jobs in a New Policy," *New York Times*, 2 January 1985, p. B10.

93. Ibid., p. A1.

94. U.S. General Accounting Office, "Federal Workforce: Use of Temporary Employees at Three Puget Sound Naval Installations," 8; U.S. General Accounting Office, "Federal Workforce: New Authority to Make and Extend Temporary Appointments," 3; also see U.S. General Accounting Office, "Federal Workforce: Temporary Appointments and Extensions in Selected Federal Agencies," GAO/GGD-89-15 (Washington, DC: U.S. Government Printing Office, 1989); and U.S. General Accounting Office, "Federal Workforce: Selected Sites Cannot Show Fair and Open Competition for Temporary Jobs," GAO/GGD-90-106 (Washington, DC: U.S. Government Printing Office, 1990).

95. U.S. General Accounting Office, "Federal Workforce: Selected Sites Cannot Show Fair and Open Competition for Temporary Jobs"; U.S. Office of Personnel Management, Personnel Systems and Oversight Group, Agency Compliance and Evaluation, "Temporary Employment within Land Management Agencies of

the Federal Government" (Washington, DC: U.S. Government Printing Office, 1992), cited in U.S. General Accounting Office, "Federal Employees: OPM Data Do Not Identify if Temporary Employees Work for Extended Periods," 20.

96. "As We See It," *The Office* (February 1985): 164.

97. Ibid.

98. Quoted in Bureau of National Affairs, *The Changing Workplace*, 113.

99. U.S. Office of Personnel Management, "Proposed Rule: Government Use of Private Sector Temporaries," 53 Federal Register 40546 (17 October 1988).

100. U.S. Office of Personnel Management, "Final Rule: Government Use of Private Sector Temporaries," 54 Federal Register 3762 (25 January 1989).

CHAPTER 4

1. As measured by the number of W-2 forms filed each year, in 1993 Manpower outgrew GM, which had long been America's largest private-sector employer. Of course, this comparison is a bit misleading, given the difference in job tenure between GM workers and Manpower temps. Nonetheless, the fact that Manpower employed more workers than GM was more than symbolic: It represented a fundamental change in labor market norms.

2. Lance Morrow, "The Temping of America," *Time*, 29 March 1993, pp. 40–42; Janice Castro, "Disposable Workers," *Time*, 29 March 1993, 43–47; also see Senate Committee on Labor and Human Resources, *Toward a Disposable Workforce: The Increasing Use of "Contingent" Labor*, 103rd Cong., 1st Sess., 1993; and "The Contingency Work Force," *Fortune*, 24 January 1994, pp. 30–36.

3. Peggy O'Connell Justice, *The Temp Track: Make One of the Hottest Job Trends of the 90s Work for You* (Princeton, NJ: Peterson's, 1993).

4. For example, see temp industry leaders' 1997 legislative attempt to define *employer* as the entity that paid workers' wages and payroll taxes (Staffing Firm Worker Benefits Act of 1997, HR 1891, 105th Cong., 1st Sess., 1997, available at http://thomas.loc.gov/cgi-bin/query/z?c105:H.R.1891.IH: [accessed 16 April 2007]). However, as George Gonos's work has shown, the 1997 bill was only a small part of industry leaders' decades-long fight to secure their status as legal employer. See George Gonos, "The Contest over 'Employer' Status in the Post-war United States: The Case of Temporary Help Firms," *Law Society Review* 31, no. 1 (1997): 81–110; and George Gonos, "The Interaction between Market Incentives and Government Actions," in *Contingent Work: American Employment Relations in Transition*, ed. Kathleen Barker and Kathleen Christensen (Ithaca, NY: Cornell University Press, 1998), 170–191.

5. Many scholars have examined the wages, benefits, job security, and mobility of temporary and other contingent workers. For example, see Arne Kalleberg, Barbara Reskin, and Ken Hudson, "Bad Jobs in America: Standard and Nonstandard Employment Relations and Job Quality in the United States," *American Sociological Review* 65, no. 2 (2000): 256–279.

6. Susan Houseman, "The Benefits Implications of Recent Trends in Flexible Staffing Arrangements," in *Benefits for the Workplace of the Future*, ed. Olivia Mitchell, David Blitzstein, Michael Gordon, and Judith Mazo (Philadelphia: University of Pennsylvania Press, 2003), 89–109.

7. Steven Berchem, "Annual Economic Analysis: American Staffing 2006" (Alexandria, VA: American Staffing Association, 2006); American Staffing Association, "America's Staffing Companies Match Millions of People to Millions of Jobs Every Day" (7 March 2006), available at http://www.americanstaffing.net/statistics/pdf/03-Employment.pdf (accessed 17 April 2007).

8. Timothy Brogan, *Thriving in a Dwindling Pool of Available Workers: ASA's Annual Analysis of the Staffing Industry* (Washington, DC: American Staffing Association, 2000); Jamie Peck and Nikolas Theodore, "Temped Out? Industry Rhetoric, Labor Regulation, and Economic Restructuring in the Temporary Staffing Business," *Economic and Industrial Democracy* 23, no. 2 (2002): 143–175; and Berchem, "Annual Economic Analysis."

9. For more examples of VOP arrangements, see William Lewis and Nancy Molloy, *How to Choose and Use Temporary Services* (New York: American Management Association, 1991); Patricia Fernberg, "On-Site Representative Builds Service, Support, and Savings," *Modern Office Technology* 37, no. 6 (1992): 57–58; Samuel Sacco, "All Employment Relationships Are Changing," *Modern Office Technology* (May 1993): 47–48; "The Menu Expands: Full-Service Firms Offer Even More," *Modern Office Technology* (May 1993): 50–52; Robert Rose and Martin du Bois, "Temporary-Help Firms Start New Game: Going Global," *Wall Street Journal*, 16 May 1996, p. B4; and Valerie Frazee, "Vendor-on-Premise Staffing Comes of Age," *Personnel Journal* 75, no. 10 (October 1996): 21.

10. Adrienne Dortch, "Get Flexible Staffing and Benefits Cost Savings by Outsourcing Automotive Products," *Personnel Journal* (November 1993): 11.

11. Julie Cohen Mason, "A Temp-ting Staffing Strategy," *Management Review* 85, no. 2 (February 1996): 36.

12. Staffing Industry Analysts, *Staffing Industry Sourcebook: Facts and Figures for Market Research* (Los Altos, CA: Staffing Industry Analysts, 2001); and Kevin Ward, "Going Global? Internationalization and Diversification in the Temporary Staffing Industry," *Journal of Economic Geography* 4, no. 3 (June 2004): 251–273.

13. For more on how the triangular employment relationship inherent in the temp industry's model of employment severs the employer–employee relationship, see Gonos, "The Contest over 'Employer' Status."

14. Quoted in "From Temporaries to Outsourcing," *Purchasing* 17 (March 1994): 63; also see Lewis and Molloy, *How to Choose and Use Temporary Services*, 116–117; Samuel Sacco, "Temps Rising," *Office Systems* 10, no. 10 (1993): 56–57; Sacco, "All Employment Relationships Are Changing"; and "The Menu Expands: Full-Service Firms Offer Even More."

15. Sacco, "Temps Rising," 57.

16. For more on the "fractured" employment of temporary workers, see Vicki Smith, "The Fractured World of the Temporary Worker: Power, Participation, and Fragmentation in the Contemporary Workplace," *Social Problems* 45, no. 4 (November 1998).

17. "From Temporaries to Outsourcing."

18. Paul Osterman, *Securing Prosperity: The American Labor Market: How It Has Changed and What to Do about It* (Princeton, NJ: Princeton University Press, 1999); and Rosemary Batt, Larry Hunter, and Steffanie Wilk, "How and When Does Management Matter? Job Quality and Career Opportunities for Call Center Workers," in *Low-Wage America: How Employers Are Reshaping Opportunity in the Workplace*, ed. Eileen Appelbaum, Annette Bernhardt, and Richard Murnane (New York: Russell Sage Foundation, 2003), 270–316.

19. Quoted in Rose and du Bois, "Temporary-Help Firms Start New Game."

20. Silvia Sansoni, "Move Over, Manpower," *Forbes*, 7 July 1997, 74; and, Osterman, *Securing Prosperity.*

21. Rose and du Bois, "Temporary-Help Firms Start New Game."

22. Osterman, *Securing Prosperity*; and Mason, "A Temp-ting Staffing Strategy."

23. Quoted in "Temps: A Permanent Necessity," *Managing Office Technology* 39, no. 12 (December 1994): 27.

24. Quoted in Ibid.

25. Linnea Anderson, "Hoover's Coverage of Kelly Services, Inc.," available at www.hoovers.com (accessed 12 December 2005); also see Kelly Services, "Brands/Divisions," available at http://easypr.marketwire.com/easyir/bupa.do?easyirid=95BBA2C450798961 (accessed 14 December 2009).

26. Jean Kumagai, "AIP-Manpower Inc. Agreement Aims to Boost Industry's Use of Physicists," *Physics Today* 49, no. 12 (1 December 1997); Jack Gordon, Marc Hequet, and David Stamps, "Now Renting: Attorneys and Rocket Scientists," *Training* 34, no. 2 (February 1997): 10–12; and Manpower, Inc., "Manpower Historical Timeline," available at http://www.manpower.com/about/history.cfm (accessed 17 April 2007).

27. At the start of the decade, professional and technical jobs were usually combined in industry statistics, but by the end of the decade the two occupational groups were routinely disaggregated. In 2001, professional and managerial work represented 21 percent of temporary employment, while jobs in information technology and other technical fields accounted for nearly 16 percent of the temp market. See Edward Lenz, "Staffing Industry's Positive Role in the U.S. Economy," *Issue Paper for the American Staffing Association* (3 March 2006); American Staffing Association, "Temporary and Contract Employees Work in All Occupations" (22 June 2005) available from http://www.americanstaffing.net/statistics/pdf/05-Occupations.pdf, accessed 9 July 2010; and Steven Berchem, "The Staffing Solution," *Office Solutions* 22, no. 3 (May/June 2005): 32–33.

28. Berchem, "Annual Economic Analysis"; American Staffing Association, "America's Staffing Companies Match Millions of People to Millions of Jobs Every Day"; and, Brogan, *Thriving in a Dwindling Pool of Available Workers*.

29. Nik Theodore and Jamie Peck, "The Temporary Staffing Industry: Growth Imperatives and Limits to Contingency," *Economic Geography* 78, no. 4 (2002): 463–493; Jamie Peck and Nikolas Theodore, "Contingent Chicago: Restructuring the Spaces of Temporary Labor," *International Journal of Urban and Regional Research* 25, no. 3 (2001): 471–496; Marcello Estevão and Saul Lach, "The Evolution of the Demand for Temporary Help Supply Employment in the United States," *NBER Working Paper Series, No. 7427* (Cambridge, MA: National Bureau of Economic Research, 1999); and Dale Belman and Lonnie Golden, "Nonstandard and Contingent Employment: Contrasts by Job Type, Industry, and Occupation," in *Nonstandard Work: The Nature and Challenges of Changing Employment Arrangements*, ed. Françoise Carré, Marianne Ferber, Lonnie Golden, and Stephen Herzenberg (Champaign-Urbana: Industrial Relations Research Association, University of Illinois at Champaign-Urbana, 2000), 167–212.

30. Arne Kalleberg, David Knoke, Peter Marsden, and Joe Spaeth, *Organizations in America: Analyzing Their Structures and Human Resource Practices* (Thousand Oaks, CA: Sage Publications, 1996).

31. American Staffing Association, "Temporary and Contract Employees Work in All Occupations" (22 June 2005), available at http://www.americanstaffing.net/statistics/pdf/05-Occupations.pdf (accessed 17 April 2007).

32. Council of Economic Advisers, *2004 Annual Report* (H. Doc. 108-145, 108th Cong., 2nd Sess., 2004), 73; also see Louis Uchitelle, "Temporary Workers Are on the Increase in Nation's Factories," *New York Times*, 6 July 1993, pp. A1–D2.

33. Uchitelle, "Temporary Workers Are on the Increase in Nation's Factories."

34. "The Contingency Work Force."

35. According to one study, for example, among those companies that cut jobs between 1990 and 1995, nearly 60 percent reported a subsequent increase in their use of temps (Vicki Smith, "New Forms of Work Organization," *Annual Review of Sociology* 23 [1997]: 315–339).

36. Quoted in Uchitelle, "Temporary Workers Are on the Increase in Nation's Factories," D2.

37. For more on the geography of day labor agencies, see Peck and Theodore, "Contingent Chicago."

38. For more, see Abel Valenzuela, Nik Theodore, Edwin Meléndez, and Ana Luz Gonzalez, "On the Corner: Day Labor in the United States," National Day Labor Study, available at http://www.sscnet.ucla.edu/issr/csup/index.php (accessed 14 December 2009).

39. Quoted in Brian Grow, "A Day's Pay for a Day's Work—Maybe," *Business Week*, 8 December 2003, p. 100. This quote offers an interesting parallel to

Manpower president Mitchell Fromstein's query, "What would our workers be doing without us? Unemployment lines? Welfare? Suicide?" (see Introduction).

40. As noted in Chapter 1, however, the temp industry was not a new global industry. Manpower leaders led the industry's worldwide expansion earlier in the century, opening their first international branch in 1955. By the end of the 1960s, Manpower executives had offices in thirty-six countries. However, the 1990s witnessed a new kind of global expansion not previously seen in the temp industry. For more on the industry's early expansion abroad, see Chris Forde, " 'You Know We Are Not an Employment Agency': Manpower, Government and the Development of the Temporary Help Industry in Britain," *Enterprise and Society* 9, no. 2 (2008): 337–365; "Manpower, Inc.," *Fortune* (November 1956): 280; Robert Cole, "Temporary Help Gaining Abroad," *New York Times*, 14 July 1963, p. 92; Ward, "Going Global"; and Manpower, Inc., "Manpower Historical Timeline." For more on the industry's global expansion in the 1990s, see Jamie Peck, Nik Theodore, and Kevin Ward, "Constructing Markets for Temporary Labour: Employment Liberalization and the Internationalization of the Staffing Industry," *Global Networks* 5, no. 1 (2005): 3–26; and Michael Neugart and Donald Storrie, "The Emergence of Temporary Work Agencies," *Oxford Economic Papers* 58 (2006): 137–156.

41. William Hall, "Adecco Lifted by Olsten," *Financial Times*, 27 October 2000, p. 32.

42. Ward, "Going Global."

43. Timothy Schellhardt, "Temporary-Help Industry Now Features Battle of Giants—Adecco's Moves Increase Pressure on Manpower Inc. and Smaller Rivals," *Wall Street Journal*, 6 November 1997, p. 1.

44. Peck, Theodore, and Ward, "Constructing Markets for Temporary Labour," 10.

45. Peck, Theodore, and Ward, "Constructing Markets for Temporary Labour"; Ward, "Going Global"; and Neugart and Storrie, "The Emergence of Temporary Work Agencies."

46. Manpower, Inc., "Manpower Historical Timeline."

47. Theodore and Peck, "The Temporary Staffing Industry."

48. Timothy Brogan, *Scaling New Heights: ASA's Annual Analysis of the Staffing Industry* (Alexandria, VA: American Staffing Association, 2001); and Theodore and Peck, "The Temporary Staffing Industry."

49. Staffing Industry Analysts, *Staffing Industry Resource Guide* (Los Altos, CA: Staffing Industry Analysts, 1993); and Ward, "Going Global."

50. Theodore and Peck, "The Temporary Staffing Industry."

51. Ward, "Going Global"; and Peck, Theodore, and Ward, "Constructing Markets for Temporary Labour."

52. Theodore and Peck, "The Temporary Staffing Industry."

53. Aaron Bernstein, "Now, Temp Workers Are a Full-Time Headache: A Ruling Could Make 'Permatemps' a Lot Pricier to Have Around," *Business Week*, 31 May 1999, p. 46.

54. For more on the "contest over 'employer' status," see Gonos, "The Interaction between Market Incentives and Government Actions"; Gonos, "The Contest over 'Employer' Status"; and George Gonos, "A Sociology of the Temporary Employment Relationship" (Ph.D. diss., Rutgers University, 1994). For an example of the temp industry's campaign to be considered the de jure employer of temps, see Edward Lenz, "The Status of Temporary Help Companies as Employers: A Legal Update," *Contemporary Times* (Summer 1985): 8–10.

55. *Vizcaino v. Microsoft*, No. 98-71388, 1999 D.C. No. CV-93-00178-CRD (9th Cir. 1999).

56. Quoted in Kirstin Downey Grimsley, "Revenge of the Temps: Independent Contractors' Victory in Microsoft Case May Have Wide Impact," *Washington Post*, 16 January 2000, p. H01.

57. *Vizcaino v. Microsoft* (9th Cir. 1999); also see Grimsley, "Revenge of the Temps."

58. *Vizcaino v. Microsoft* (9th Cir. 1999).

59. Although data on the tenure of Microsoft temps are not readily available, newspaper reports indicated that some of Microsoft's temps worked for seven years or more (Grimsley, "Revenge of the Temps").

60. Grimsley, "Revenge of the Temps"; also see Aaron Bernstein, "Programmers of the World Unite: An Effort by Microsoft Temps to Unionize Faces Big Odds," *Business Week*, 7 December 1998, available at http://www.businessweek.com/1998/49/b3607118.htm (accessed 17 April 2007).

61. Grimsley, "Revenge of the Temps"; and Ron Lieber, "The Permatemps Contretemps," *FastCompany.com* 37 (2000): 198, available at http://www.fastcompany.com/online/37/permatemps.html (accessed 17 April 2007).

62. Quoted in Grimsley, "Revenge of the Temps"; also see *Vizcaino v. Microsoft* (9th Cir. 1999).

63. Amicus Brief of the ITAA in Support of Motion for En Banc Review. Re: *Vizcaino v. Microsoft*, No. 98-71388 (9th Cir. 1999).

64. *Vizcaino v. Microsoft* (9th Cir. 1999). When it became clear that the company's growing number of temporary workers would be included in the lawsuit, Microsoft executives asked the temps to sign new contracts that required them to give up any money they might win from the lawsuit or stop working for the company. The courts found this action "outrageously arrogant" and strongly advised the company to amend the contract. See Grimsley, "Revenge of the Temps"; and Jay Greene, "Angry Judge Tells Microsoft to Redo 'Temp' Contracts," *Seattle Times*, 14 January 1999, available at http://community.seattletimes.nwsource.com/archive/?date=19990114&slug=2938611 (accessed 14 December 2009).

65. Quoted in Aaron Bernstein, "When Is a Temp Not a Temp? New Rulings May Up Companies' Hiring Costs," *Business Week*, 7 December 1998, p. 90.

66. *Vizcaino v. Microsoft* (9th Cir. 1999).

67. Quoted in Lieber, "The Permatemps Contretemps."

68. *Clark v. King County*, No. 95-2-29890-7 SEA (King County Superior Court 2000); also see Center for a Changing Workforce, "Permatemp Legal Developments: King County, WA Permatemp Case Settles," available at http://www.cfcw.org/legal.html (accessed 17 April 2007).

69. *Thomas v. SmithKline Beecham Corp.*, 297 F. Supp. 2d 773 (Ed. PA 2003); also see American Staffing Association, "Staffing Law" (January 2005): 7, available at http://www.americanstaffing.net/memberDocuments/products/s_law/pdf/0105law.pdf (accessed 17 April 2007); and Center for a Changing Workforce, "Permatemp Legal Developments: SmithKline Permatemps Win Settlement," available at http://www.cfcw.org/legal.html (accessed 17 April 2007).

70. Grimsley, "Revenge of the Temps"; Daniel Eisenberg, "Rise of the Permatemp," *Time*, 12 July 1999, p. 48; Ed Frauenheim, "Battles Wax and Wane in the 'Permatemp' Wars," *Workforce Management*, 24 October 2005, pp. 53–55; also see Lieber, "The Permatemps Contretemps"; and Bernstein, "When Is a Temp Not a Temp."

71. *Vizcaino v. Microsoft* (9th Cir. 1999); also see Grimsley, "Revenge of the Temps"; and Bernstein, "When Is a Temp Not a Temp."

72. *Vizcaino v. Microsoft* (9th Cir. 1999).

73. Grimsley, "Revenge of the Temps."

74. That is, minus a considerable chunk (nearly 30 percent) in lawyers' fees. For more details on the settlement, see the Web site of the law firm that represented Microsoft's permatemps: Bendich, Stobaugh, and Strong, "Microsoft Case," available at http://www.bs-s.com/cases/c-microsoft-vizcaino.html (accessed 17 June 2010).

75. Edward Lenz and Dawn Greco, *Co-employment: Employer Liability Issues in Third-Party Staffing Arrangements*, 4th ed. (Alexandria, VA: American Staffing Association, 2000); American Staffing Association, "Staffing Law" (September 2006); and Edward Lenz, senior vice president of the American Staffing Association, e-mail communication with the author, 18 December 2006.

76. As described by Edward Lenz, general counsel for the American Staffing Association, "The staffing industry responded to the [Microsoft] ruling with an intensive education campaign" (Edward Lenz, e-mail communication with the author, 18 December 2006). Also see American Staffing Association, "Staffing Law" (September 2006).

77. Lenz and Greco, *Co-employment*, 49–50.

78. Lenz and Greco, *Co-employment*, 51–52; also see American Staffing Association, "Staffing Law" (May 2006).

79. American Staffing Association, "Staffing Law" (September 2006); also see Edward Lenz, "Assignment Limits and Customer Concerns about Benefits Liability: Issues and Answers," *Issue Paper for the American Staffing Association* (7 July 2006); and Edward Lenz, "Assignment Limits and Customer Concerns about Benefits Liability," *Staffing Smarts* (January 2007).

80. U.S. Government Accountability Office, "Employment Arrangements: Improved Outreach Could Help Ensure Proper Worker Classification," GAO-06-656 (Washington, DC: U.S. Government Printing Office, 2006); also see American Staffing Association, "Staffing Law" (January 2006). For examples of cases in which "common law" employees lost because they were specifically excluded from the company's benefits plans, see *Edes v. Verizon Communications*, 288 F. Supp. 2d 55 (U.S. Dist. MA 2003); also see *Edes v. Verizon Communications*, 417 F.3d 133 (1st Cir. 2005); *Wolf v. Coca-Cola*, 200 F.3d 1337, 1340 (11th Cir. 2000); *Bronk v. Mountain States Tel. & Tel., Inc.*, 140 F.3d 1335 (10th Cir. 1998); *Abraham v. Exxon Corp.*, 85 F.3d 1126 (5th Cir. 1996); and *Curry v. CTB McGraw-Hill*, No. C 05-04003 JW, 2006 WL 228951 (N.D. CA 2006).

81. In this case, there was overwhelming evidence that the temps were "common-law" employees. The temps were recruited and hired by Verizon; they received all training and evaluations from the company's managers; they participated in peer review programs with Verizon's full-time employees; they had the authority to compose and sign letters on company letterhead; they had office keys, company e-mail addresses, and telephone numbers; they were invited to company functions, including Christmas parties; and, tellingly, they were told to identify themselves as Verizon employees and not as "temporary employees" (*Edes v. Verizon Communications* [U.S. Dist. MA 2003]). Also see *Edes v. Verizon Communications* (1st Cir. 2005); and American Staffing Association, "Staffing Law" (January 2006).

82. *Curry v. CTB McGraw-Hill* (N.D. CA 2006).

83. *Employee Benefits Protection Act of 2005*, HR 1058, 109th Cong., 1st Sess., 2005.

84. Employers would be required to pay at least $1.65 an hour in health care benefits in 2007, $2.50 an hour in 2008, and $3.30 an hour in 2009 (adjusted annually each year thereafter) to every employee that worked at least thirteen hours a week. In order to meet the requirement, employers could offer health insurance to their employees or contribute to a health care fund (*Responsible Employer Act*, NJ S 477/1320 [2006]).

85. Nikolas Theodore and Chirag Mehta, *Contingent Work and the Staffing Industry: A Review of Worker-Centered Policy and Practice* (Chicago: Center for Urban Economic Development, University of Illinois at Chicago, 1999).

86. *Equity for Temporary Workers Act of 1999*, HR 2298, 106th Cong., 1st Sess., 1999.

87. Rhode Island SB 2442 (2004); New Mexico HB 653 (2005) and SB 657; also see American Staffing Association, "Staffing Law" (May 2004).

88. *Staffing Firm Worker Benefits Act of 1997*, HR 1891, 105th Cong., 1st Sess., 1997. Also see the testimony of representatives of the National Association of Staffing Services at a congressional hearing on pension issues: House Ways and Means Committee, *Oversight of Pension Issues*, 105th Cong., 2nd Sess., 1998, pp. 135–146.

89. For example, see industry leaders' sharp repudiation of the 2006 New Jersey bill discussed earlier: "The New Jersey Staffing Alliance Response to the Proposed 'Responsible Employer Act' (S.477)," available at www.njsa.com/docs/The_Response.doc (accessed 18 April 2007).

90. Courts developed three "tests" to establish an employment relationship between a potential employer and employee: the "common-law" test; the "economic realities" test; and the "hybrid" test, which incorporated elements of the first two. In addition, the IRS developed its own test, called the "20 Factor Test," which was based on the "common-law" definition of employment. For an in-depth examination of these tests, see Charles Muhl, "What Is an Employee? The Answer Depends on the Federal Law," *Monthly Labor Review* (January 2002): 3–11. It must be noted, however, that because these tests and their definitions of "employer" and "employee" were developed in a piecemeal fashion, and different tests were used by different arms of the government, the end result was a complex and sometimes contradictory assortment of legislation governing the employment relationship (U.S. Government Accountability Office, "Employment Arrangements: Improved Outreach Could Help Ensure Proper Worker Classification," GAO-06-656 [Washington, DC: U.S. Government Printing Office, 2006]).

91. U.S. Equal Employment Opportunity Commission, "Enforcement Guidance: Application of EEO Laws to Contingent Workers Placed by Temporary Employment Agencies and Other Staffing Firms," EEOC Notice Number 915.002 (1997).

92. *Nationwide Mutual Insurance Co. v. Darden*, 503 U.S. 318, 323-4 (1992). Also see U.S. Equal Employment Opportunity Commission, "Enforcement Guidance"; National Labor Relations Board, *Riverdale Nursing Home*, 2-CA-27202 (1995); and Occupational Safety and Health Administration, "Employer's Responsibilities towards Temporary Employees," Standard Interpretation No. 1910.1200 (3 February 1994), available at http://www.osha.gov/pls/osha web/owadisp.show_document?p_table=INTERPRETATIONS&p_id=21393 (accessed 18 April 2007).

93. U.S. Equal Employment Opportunity Commission, "Enforcement Guidance."

94. Occupational Safety and Health Administration, "Employer's Responsibilities towards Temporary Employees."

95. Lenz and Greco, *Co-employment*, 18 (emphasis in original).

96. Edward Lenz, *Co-employment: Employer Liability Issues in Third-Party Staffing Arrangements*, 5th ed. (Alexandria, VA: American Staffing Association, 2003).

97. U.S. Equal Employment Opportunity Commission, "Enforcement Guidance."

98. Illinois HB 2298; Massachusetts HB 2385, HB 2849, HB 2849, and SB 60; New Jersey SB 477; Rhode Island SB 2442, SB 628, and SB 617; and Tennessee HB 17, HB 296, and SB 357.

99. Theodore and Mehta, *Contingent Work and the Staffing Industry*, 57.

100. Chris Benner and Amy Dean, "Labor in the New Economy: Lessons from Labor Organizing in Silicon Valley," in *Nonstandard Work: The Nature and Challenges of Changing Employer Arrangements*, ed. Françoise Carré, Marianne Ferber, Lonnie Golden, and Stephen Herzenberg (Champaign-Urbana: University of Illinois, Champaign-Urbana, Industrial Relations Research Association Series, 2000), 331–375; also see Esther Neuwirth, "Challenges Facing New Workforce Institutions: A Close-Up Analysis of an Alternative Staffing Service," in *Worker Participation: Current Research and Future Trends*, ed. Vicki Smith (Oxford: JAI Press, 2006), 319–342.

101. Virginia duRivage, "CWA's Organizing Strategies: Transforming Contract Work into Union Jobs," in *Nonstandard Work: The Nature and Challenges of Changing Employer Arrangements*, ed. Françoise Carré, Marianne Ferber, Lonnie Golden, and Stephen Herzenberg (Champaign-Urbana: University of Illinois, Champaign-Urbana, Industrial Relations Research Association Series, 2000), 377–392; Rosemary Batt, Harry Katz, and Jeffrey Keefe, "The Strategic Initiatives of the CWA: Organizing, Politics, and Collective Bargaining," Task Force Working Paper #WP15, presented at the Symposium on Changing Employment Relations and New Institutions of Representation (25–26 May 1999); and Chris Benner, *Shock Absorbers in the Flexible Economy: The Rise of Contingent Employment in Silicon Valley* (San Jose, CA: Working Partnerships USA, 1996).

102. Primavera Foundation, "Primavera Annual Report FY 2004–2005," available at http://www.primavera.org/about_us_annualreport.php (accessed 18 April 2007); and Primavera Foundation, "Employment Programs," available at http://www.primavera.org/employment_programs.php (accessed 18 April 2007); also see Theodore and Mehta, *Contingent Work and the Staffing Industry*.

103. *Angello v. Labor Ready Inc.*, NY Slip Op 08282 (NY Ct. App. 2006); also see *Angello v. Labor Ready, Inc.*, 22 AD3d 932; 802 NY S.2d 766 (NY App. Div. 3rd Dept., 2005).

104. U.S. General Accounting Office, "Worker Protection: Labor's Efforts to Enforce Protections for Day Laborers Could Benefit from Better Data and Guidance," GAO-02-925 (Washington, DC: U.S. Government Printing Office, 2002), 23.

105. Southwest Center for Economic Integrity, "Day Laborers Awarded $150, 000," *Taking Stock* 2, no. 1 (Spring 2004): 1.

106. *Angello v. Labor Ready Inc.* (NY Ct. App. 2006).

107. California AB 2402 (2004) and SB 1499 (2004); Florida HB 525 (2005); Illinois HB 3471 (2005); Rhode Island HB 7811 (2004), HB 7863 (2004), and SB 2879 (2004); and Wisconsin SB 396 (2004) and SB 106 (2005).

108. Illinois HB 3471 (2005); also see Illinois Department of Labor, "Governor Blagojevich Signs Legislation to Help Protect over 300,000 Day Laborers," available at http://www.state.il.us/agency/idol/news/dlspress.htm (accessed 18 April 2007).

109. Florida HB 525 (2005); and Rhode Island HB 7863 (2004).

110. There are many examples of cases in which temp agencies disputed liability for workers' injuries. For example, see *McGrady v. Olsten et al.*, No. COA02-1035, 159 N.C. App. 643, 583 S.E. 2d 371 (N.C. App. 2003); *Massey and Massey v. Shake et al. v. Olsten Staffing Services*, No. 47854-1-I (Wash. App. 2002); *Bogus v. Manpower et al.*, S/C No. 325, 823 S.W.2d 544 (Tenn. S/C 1992); *Dunnam v. Olsten Quality Care et al.*, No. 95-1739, 667 So. 2d 948 (Fla. App. 1996); *Henderson v. Manpower et al.*, No. 8310IC941, 70 N.C. App. 408, 319 S.E.2d 690 (N.C. App. 1984); *Colwell et al. v. Oatman and Labor Pool of Colorado*, No. 71-454, 32 Colo. App. 171, 510 P.2d 464 (Colo. App. 1973); and *Green v. Manpower et al.*, No. 474, 81 N.M. 788, 474 P.2d 80 (N.M. App. 1970).

111. *The Temporary Employee Protection Act*, 28-6.10 (1999), available at http://www.rilin.state.ri.us/Statutes/TITLE28/28-6.10/INDEX.HTM (accessed 18 April 2007).

112. California AB 2402 (2004); Massachusetts SB 46 (2004); and New York AB 8219 (2003).

113. American Staffing Association, "Staffing Law" (September 2004): 4.

114. David Reynolds, *Taking the High Road: Communities Organize for Economic Change* (Armonk, NY: M. E. Sharpe, 2002); and Theodore and Mehta, *Contingent Work and the Staffing Industry.*

115. Theodore and Mehta, *Contingent Work and the Staffing Industry.*

116. Unionizing temps did not guarantee them higher wages, better benefits, and safer working conditions, of course. Historically, however, unions have been some of the most reliable protectors of labor, providing workers with decent wages, better working conditions, health care, job security, and a host of other benefits.

117. The long-standing practice of hiring temps as strikebreakers was ongoing as of this writing. For example, U.S. Nursing Corp., the temp agency discussed in Chapter 3 that specialized in providing medical workers to hospitals involved in labor disputes, was still thriving. Also see an NLRB case in which a company illegally fired union organizers and replaced them with temps: National Labor Relations Board, *Engineered Plastic Components, Inc.*, 18-CA-17003, -17008, -17013, -17027, -17033, -17055, -17060, -17139, -17140, -17160, and -17164 (2004).

118. Long-standing precedent ruled that a bargaining unit consisting of both regular and temporary workers was a "multi-employer" unit and, as such, could not be legally recognized without the consent of all employers involved (National Labor Relations Board, *Lee Hospital*, 300 NLRB 947, 948 [1990]).

119. Quoted in Yochi Dreazen, "Regulators Probe U.S. Reliance on Temporary Workers—Expected Lifting of Restrictions on Organizing Temps Would Be a Coup for Unions," *Wall Street Journal*, 7 August 2000, p. A2; also see AFSCME, "Resolution No. 126: The Contingent Workforce," 31st International Convention, San Diego, CA (1994); AFL-CIO, "Statement by John J.

Sweeney, AFL-CIO President on the New GAO Report Shows Contingent Worker Incomes and Benefits Lag" (26 July 2000), available at http://www.aflcio.org/mediacenter/prsptm/pr07262000.cfm (accessed 18 April 2007); and Peter Kilborn, "Why Labor Wants the Tired and Poor," *New York Times*, 29 October 1995, p. E3.

120. Françoise Carré and Pamela Joshi, "Looking for Leverage in a Fluid World: Innovative Responses to Temporary and Contracted Work," in *Nonstandard Work: The Nature and Challenges of Changing Employer Arrangements*, ed. Françoise Carré, Marianne Ferber, Lonnie Golden, and Stephen Herzenberg (Champaign-Urbana: University of Illinois, Champaign-Urbana, Industrial Relations Research Association Series, 2000), 313–339; and Christopher Cook, "Temps Demand a New Deal," *The Nation*, 27 March 2000, available at http://www.thenation.com/article/temps-demand-new-deal (accessed 17 June 2010).

121. Quoted in Cook, "Temps Demand a New Deal."

122. For more on WashTech, see duRivage, "CWA's Organizing Strategies."

123. "Bothell Cingular Workers Joining Union," *Seattle Times*, 18 November 2005.

124. National Labor Relations Board, *Lee Hospital* (1990).

125. For more examples, see National Labor Relations Board, *Lee Hospital* (1990); National Labor Relations Board, *Continental Winding Company*, 7-CA-22770 and 7-CA-23067 (1991); National Labor Relations Board, *Brookdale Hospital*, 313 NLRB 592 (1993); and National Labor Relations Board, *JSP International*, 6-RC-11613 (1999).

126. National Labor Relations Board, *Flatbush Manor Care Center*, 313 NLRB No. 73, 29-RC-7764 (1993).

127. National Labor Relations Board, *Hexacomb Corp.*, 7-RC-20044 (1994).

128. National Labor Relations Board, *M.B. Sturgis/Jeffboat Div.*, 331 NLRB No. 173 (2000).

129. National Labor Relations Board, *M.B. Sturgis/Jeffboat Div.* (2000); National Labor Relations Board, *JSP International*, 6-RC-11853 (2000); National Labor Relations Board, *Lee Hospital* (1990); National Labor Relations Board, *TLI, Inc.*, 271 NLRB 789 (1984); and National Labor Relations Board, *Laerco Transportation*, 269 NLRB 324 (1984).

130. American Staffing Association, "Staffing Law" (January 2005): 2; also see Lenz, *Co-employment*.

131. Quoted in Nicholas Kulish and Carlos Tejada, "Labor Board Allows Organizing of Temps—Ruling Is Seen as Victory for Unions, but Some Say It Is Bad for Workers," *Wall Street Journal*, 31 August 2000, p. A2; also see Dreazen, "Regulators Probe U.S. Reliance on Temporary Workers."

132. "Bargaining Units for Temporary Workers," *New York Law Journal* (10 October 2000); also see Kulish and Tejada, "Labor Board Allows Organizing of

Temps"; and "Will NLRB's Recent Sturgis Ruling Help or Hurt Organizing, Bargaining?" *Daily Labor Report* 173 (6 September 2000): AA-1.

133. National Labor Relations Board, *Oakwood Care Center*, 343 NLRB No. 76 (2004).

134. American Staffing Association, "Staffing Law" (January 2005): 3.

135. Like its predecessor, this ruling involved direct-hire temps—short-term workers hired directly by federal agencies—rather than temps from private agencies such as Manpower and Kelly.

136. U.S. Office of Personnel Management, "OPM News Release: OPM to Limit Temporary Hiring Authority," 24 January 1994, available at http://www.opm.gov/pressrel/1994/PR940124.htm (accessed 18 April 2007).

137. U.S. General Accounting Office, "Federal Employees: OPM Data Do Not Identify if Temporary Employees Work for Extended Periods," GAO-02-296 (Washington, DC: U.S. Government Printing Office, 2002): 8.

138. U.S. Office of Personnel Management, "Temporary Employment within Land Management Agencies of the Federal Government" (Washington, DC: U.S. Government Printing Office, 1992); also see U.S. General Accounting Office, "Federal Employees: OPM Data Do Not Identify if Temporary Employees Work for Extended Periods," 20.

139. U.S. Office of Personnel Management, "Temporary Employment within Land Management Agencies," 2; also see U.S. Merit Systems Protection Board, "Temporary Federal Employment: In Search of Flexibility and Fairness" (Washington, DC: U.S. Office of Policy and Evaluation, 1994).

140. House Post Office and Civil Service Committee, *The Use of Temporary Employees in the Federal Government*, 103rd Cong., 1st Sess., 1993; also see U.S. Merit Systems Protection Board, "Temporary Federal Employment."

141. U.S. General Accounting Office, "Federal Employees: OPM Data Do Not Identify if Temporary Employees Work for Extended Periods."

142. U.S. General Accounting Office, "Federal Employees: OPM Data Do Not Identify if Temporary Employees Work for Extended Periods"; and U.S. Office of Personnel Management, "Temporary Employment within Land Management Agencies."

143. U.S. Office of Personnel Management, "Final Regulation: Use of Private Sector Temporaries," 61 Federal Register 19509 (1996).

144. U.S. Office of Personnel Management, "Final Rule: Government Use of Private Sector Temporaries," 54 Federal Register 3762 (1989).

145. U.S. Office of Personnel Management, "Final Regulation: Use of Private Sector Temporaries."

146. Françoise Carré and Pamela Joshi, "Building Stability for Transient Workforces: Exploring the Possibilities of Intermediary Institutions Helping Workers Cope with Labor Market Instability," Working Paper No. 1, Radcliffe Public Policy Institute (Cambridge, MA: Radcliffe Public Policy Institute, 1997); and AFL-CIO, "Statement by John J. Sweeney."

147. AFSCME, "The Union and the Contingent Workforce" (1996), available at http://www.afscme.org/publications/9811.cfm (accessed 18 April 2007); and Theodore and Mehta, *Contingent Work and the Staffing Industry*.
148. Theodore and Mehta, *Contingent Work and the Staffing Industry*.

CONCLUSION

1. Elmer Winter, "Money and Part-Time Jobs for Women," *McCall's* 88 (April 1961): 68–69.
2. *Personnel Journal* (October 1968): 693.
3. *The Office* (January 1971): 19.
4. Rebecca Blank, "Contingent Work in a Changing Labor Market," in *Generating Jobs*, ed. Richard Freeman and Peter Gottschalk (New York: Russell Sage Foundation, 1998), 258–294; Susan Houseman, "Flexible Staffing Arrangements in the U.S.," *The Worklife Report* 10, no. 4 (1997): 6; and Arne Kalleberg, Barbara Reskin, and Ken Hudson, "Bad Jobs in America: Standard and Nonstandard Employment Relations and Job Quality in the United States," *American Sociological Review* 65, no. 2 (2000): 256–279.
5. Sharon Cohany, "Workers in Alternative Employment Arrangements: A Second Look," *Monthly Labor Review* 121, no. 11 (1998): 3–22; also see Robert Parker, *Flesh Peddlers and Warm Bodies: The Temporary Help Industry and Its Workers* (New Brunswick, NJ: Rutgers University Press, 1994); Arne Kalleberg, Edith Rasell, Naomi Cassirer, Barbara Reskin, Ken Hudson, David Webster, Eileen Appelbaum, and Roberta Spalter-Roth, *Nonstandard Work, Substandard Jobs: Flexible Work Arrangements in the United States* (Washington, DC: Economic Policy Institute, 1997); Blank, "Contingent Work in a Changing Labor Market"; and Kalleberg, Reskin, and Hudson, "Bad Jobs in America."
6. For instance, see Françoise Carré and Chris Tilly, "Part-Time and Temporary Work: Flexibility for Whom?" *Dollars and Sense* 215 (January/February 1998): 22–26.
7. Yinon Cohen and Yitchak Haberfeld, "Temporary Help Service Workers: Employment Characteristics and Wage Determination," *Industrial Relations* 32, no. 2 (1993): 272–287; Lewis Segal and Daniel Sullivan, "The Temporary Labor Force," *Economic Perspectives* 19, no. 2 (1995): 2–19; Stanley Nollen, "Negative Aspects of Temporary Employment," *Journal of Labor Research* 17, no. 4 (1996): 567–581; Donna Rothstein, "Entry Into and Consequences of Nonstandard Work Arrangements," *Monthly Labor Review* 119, no. 10 (1996): 75; Kalleberg et al., *Nonstandard Work, Substandard Jobs*; Lewis Segal and Daniel Sullivan, "The Growth of Temporary Services Work," *Journal of Economic Perspectives* 11, no. 2 (1997): 117–136; Blank, "Contingent Work in a Changing Labor Market"; Cohany, "Workers in Alternative Employment Arrangements"; Kalleberg, Reskin, and Hudson, "Bad Jobs in America"; U.S. General Accounting Office, "Contingent Workers: Incomes and Benefits Lag behind Those of Rest of Workforce," GAO/

HEHS-00-76 (Washington, DC: U.S. Government Printing Office, 2000); and Michael Morris and Alexander Vekker, "An Alternative Look at Temporary Workers, Their Choices, and the Growth in Temporary Employment," *Journal of Labor Research* 22, no. 2 (2001): 373–391.

8. Parker, *Flesh Peddlers and Warm Bodies*; Blank, "Contingent Work in a Changing Labor Market"; Cohany, "Workers in Alternative Employment Arrangements"; Marisa DiNatale, "Characteristics of and Preference for Alternative Work Arrangements, 1999," *Monthly Labor Review* (March 2001): 28–49; and Morris and Vekker, "An Alternative Look at Temporary Workers."

9. Jamie Peck and Nikolas Theodore, "The Business of Contingent Work: Growth and Restructuring in Chicago's Temporary Employment Industry," *Work, Employment and Society* 12, no. 4 (1998): 655–674; George Gonos, "The Interaction between Market Incentives and Government Actions," in *Contingent Work: American Employment Relations in Transition*, ed. Kathleen Barker and Kathleen Christensen (Ithaca, NY: Cornell University Press, 1998), 170–191; Jamie Peck and Nikolas Theodore, "Contingent Chicago: Restructuring the Spaces of Temporary Labor," *International Journal of Urban and Regional Research* 25, no. 3 (2001): 471–496; Jamie Peck and Nikolas Theodore, "Temped Out? Industry Rhetoric, Labor Regulation, and Economic Restructuring in the Temporary Staffing Business," *Economic and Industrial Democracy* 23, no. 2 (2002): 143–175; Susan Houseman, Arne Kalleberg, and George Erickcek, "The Role of Temporary Agency Employment in Tight Labor Markets," *Industrial and Labor Relations Review* 57, no. 1 (2003); Jamie Peck and Nik Theodore, "Flexible Recession: The Temporary Staffing Industry and Mediated Work in the United States," presented at the Annual Meeting of the Society for the Study of Social Problems (24 November 2004); and Jamie Peck and Nik Theodore, "Temporary Downturn? Temporary Staffing in the Recession and the Jobless Recovery," *Focus* 23, no. 3 (2005): 35.

10. Katherine Newman, *No Shame in My Game: The Working Poor in the Inner City* (New York: Vintage Books, 1999); Gregory Acs, Katherine Ross Phillips, and Daniel McKenzie, "Playing by the Rules, but Losing the Game: Americans in Low-Income Working Families," in *Low-Wage Workers in the New Economy*, ed. Richard Kazis and Marc Miller (Washington, DC: Urban Institute, 2001); Annette Bernhardt, Martina Morris, Mark Handcock, and Marc Scott, *Divergent Paths: Economic Mobility in the New American Labor Market* (New York: Russell Sage Foundation, 2001); Vicky Lovell and Heidi Hartmann, "Increasing Economic Security for Low-Wage Women Workers," in Kazis and Miller, *Low-Wage Workers in the New Economy*; and Paul Osterman, "Employers in the Low-Wage/Low-Skill Labor Market," in Kazis and Miller, *Low-Wage Workers in the New Economy*, 67–87.

11. For instance, see National Labor Relations Board, *Allina Health System*, Cases 18-CA-16051-1, 18-CA-16051-2, 18-CA-16051-9, 18-CA-16051-10, 18-CA-16051-11, 18-CA-16051-12, and 18-CA-16051-13 (29 October 2004); and

National Labor Relations Board, *Engineered Plastic Components, Inc.*, Cases 18-CA-17003, 18-CA-17008, 18-CA-17013, 18-CA-17027, 18-CA-17033, 18-CA-17055, 18-CA-17060, 18-CA-17139, 18-CA-17140, 18-CA-17160, and 18-CA-17164 (10 August 2004).

APPENDIX

1. Howard Becker, "How to Find Out How to Do Qualitative Research," unpublished comment on National Science Foundation report, available at http://home.earthlink.net/~hsbecker/articles/NSF.html (accessed 28 September 2009).

INDEX

Able Body Labor, 115

Accountemps, 87–88. *See also* Half, Robert; Robert Half International

Adderley, Terrence, 33

Adecco, 116, 117, 184n20

Adia, 116, 184n20

Administrative management, 61, 63–64. *See also* Fayol, Henri

AFL-CIO, 136

AGS, 55, 57, 66, 68, 178n67. *See also* American Girl Service

American Federation of State, County, and Municipal Employees (AFSCME), 134, 140

American Girl Service, 32, 33, 36, 55, 57, 166n4. *See also* AGS

American Motors Corporation, 74

American Staffing Association (ASA), 123, 127, 133, 137, 168n29. *See also* Institute for Temporary Services (ITS); National Association of Temporary Services (NATS); National Association of Temporary and Staffing Services (NATSS)

Apple Computer, 89, 93–94

Asset model, 4, 159n17; post–World War II, 4–5; in the 1970s, 50, 53, 62, 63, 78; in the 1980s, 82, 84, 92–93, 95–103; in the 1990s, 140; for the twenty-first century, 10, 16, 107, 108, 130, 131, 134, 137, 141, 144–151; and the temp industry, 7, 8, 16, 23, 63, 64, 78, 92

Atlantic Nuclear Services, 90

AT&T, 96, 140

B and A Temps, 91

Babbage, Charles, 174n12. *See also* Babbage Principle

Babbage Principle, 17, 53. *See also* Babbage, Charles

Bank of America, 91

Belgium, 117. *See also* Temp industry, abroad

Blue Shield, 96, 97

Call centers, 111–112, 135

Canada, 45, 74, 88, 112. *See also* Office Overload

Career Blazers, 88

Erin Hatton is an Assistant Professor in the Sociology Department at SUNY Buffalo.